TOPICS IN TRANSLATION 14
Series Editors: Susan Bassnett (*University of Warwick*)
Edwin Gentzler (*University of Massachusetts, Amherst*)

Written in the Language of the Scottish Nation

A History of Literary Translation into Scots

John Corbett

Si c'est pas clair … inventes-en.
Si le passé te fait trop mal, construis-toi z'en un neuf.
(*Albertine, en cinq temps,* by Michel Tremblay)

If ye cannae remember it … invent it.
If the past isnae nice, make up a new wan.
(*Albertine, in Five Times,* trans. Bill Findlay & Martin Boardman)

MULTILINGUAL MATTERS LTD
Clevedon • Philadelphia • Toronto • Sydney • Johannesburg

For Chrystine Ray

Library of Congress Cataloging in Publication Data

Corbett, John
Written in the Language of the Scottish Nation: A History of Literary Translation into Scots/John Corbett
Topics in Translation: 14
Includes bibliographical references and index
1. Scots language–Translating. 2. Translating and interpreting–Scotland–History.
3. Literature–Translations into Scots–History and criticism. I. Title. II. Series.
PE2103.C67 1999
491.6'3802'09–dc21 98-37721

British Library Cataloguing in Publication Data

A CIP catalogue record for this book is available from the British Library.

ISBN 1-85359-431-8 (hbk)

Multilingual Matters Ltd

UK: Frankfurt Lodge, Clevedon Hall, Victoria Road, Clevedon BS21 7HH.
USA: 325 Chestnut Street, Philadelphia, PA 19106, USA.
Canada: 5201 Dufferin Street, North York, Ontario M3H 5T8, Canada.
Australia: P.O. Box 586, Artamon, NSW, Australia.
South Africa: PO Box 1080, Northcliffe 2115, Johannesburg, South Africa.

Typeset by Solidus, Bristol.
Printed and bound in Great Britain by WBC Book Manufacturers Ltd.

Contents

Preface

This book owes its existence to a wide number of friends and colleagues, but mainly to Susan Bassnett. Susan suggested the topic to me, and she has been an exemplary editor and guide as I have journeyed from initial curiosity to increasing fascination. At different stages, she and others have been kind enough to read and comment on drafts of the work in progress. Jeremy Smith, Theo van Heijnsbergen and Chrys Ray in particular deserve thanks for their valiant attempts to diminish my ignorance, enforce clarity, and steer me from error. My colleagues and students in the Departments of English Language and Scottish Literature at Glasgow University have prompted insights which have been useful along the road. I have benefited, too, from the observations of participants at seminars on British Cultural Studies in Argentina and Poland, and at a conference on 'Translation and Power' at the University of Warwick. I am grateful to the British Council and to the University of Glasgow for enabling my attendance at these events. It goes without saying that those flaws which remain are due to my own thrawn character.

A survey as broad as this one attempts to be relies heavily on the scholarship of others. My debt to more illustrious labourers in the field of Scottish translation will be obvious at a glance, but special mention should be made of Priscilla Bawcutt, R.J. Craik, Ronald Jack, Derrick McClure, and Graham Tulloch, whose work I have read with profit and pleasure. Among those who have nudged me in useful directions are Graham Caie, Christian Kay, Margery Palmer McCulloch, Jim McGonigal, Stuart Gillespie, George Philp, Larry Syndergaard and Jean Wilson. Bill Findlay has been immensely generous in sharing his articles and translations (published and unpublished); and I am grateful to Dr Kenneth Farrow for sending me his yet unpublished manuscript of *The Scots Iliad.*

Chrys Ray has been unstintingly supportive during the writing of this book. I hope it is a small measure of recompense if I dedicate it to her.

Acknowledgements

Every endeavour has been made to trace the copyright holders of literary material quoted. The author thanks Martin Bowman and Bill Findlay, John Calder, Kenneth Farrow, John Gray, Alexander Hutchison, Tom Leonard, Catherine MacLean, Edwin Morgan, William Neill, Catherine Scott, Heather Scott, Brian C. Tait, Hella Young, Carcanet Publishers, Agenda and Chapman Publishers, The Saltire Society, the Trustees of the National Library of Scotland, and the Scottish National Dictionary Association for granting permission to quote from copyright material, and apologises for any omissions made.

Works quoted from include J.K. Annand, 'O come all ye boozers' from *Songs from Carmina Burana,* MacDonald, and 'Elegy on the Depairture o Mary Queen o Scots on her Retour til her Kinrick o Scotland' from *European Poetry in Scotland: An Anthology of Translations,* Edinburgh University Press; Paul Blackburn, 'Bem platz lo gais temps de pascor', from *Poensa: An Anthology of Troubador Poetry,* University of California Press; Martin Bowman and Bill Findlay, *The House among the Stars* and *Albertine in Five Times;* Kenneth Farrow, *The Scots Iliad;* Robert Fitzgerald, *The Aeneid,* Random House; Sir Alexander Gray, 'Im Rhein, im heligen Ströme' from *Songs from Heine,* Porpoise Press; Alexander Hutchison, 'Deef the Mirk' from *European Poetry in Scotland: An Anthology of Translations,* Edinburgh University Press; Tom Leonard, 'Jist ti Let Yi No', from *Intimate Voices,* Galloping Dog Press; Hugh MacDiarmid, *A Drunk Man Looks at the Thistle* from *Complete Poems 1920–1976,* Martin Brian and O'Keefe; Sorley MacLean, 'Camhanaich/Dawn' from *Spring Tide and Neap Tide,* Canongate; Edwin Morgan, 'Eupatoria', and 'The Seafarer', from *Collected Translations,* Carcanet Press, and *Cyrano de Bergerac,* Carcanet Press; William Neill, *Tales Frae the Odyssey o Homer,* Saltire Society; Ezra Pound, 'Bem platz lo gais temps de pascor', from *The Translations of Ezra Pound,* Faber; William Soutar, 'Recognition', from *The Poems of William Soutar, a New Selection,* Scottish Academic

Press; Robert Garioch, 'The Wee Thief's Mither' from *European Poetry in Scotland: An Anthology of Translations,* Edinburgh University Press; Alexander Scott, 'Seaman's Sang' and 'Supermakar' from *The Collected Poems of Alexander Scott,* Mercat Press; Tom Scott, 'Ballat o the Hingit' and 'The Seavaiger' from *The Collected Shorter Poems of Tom Scott,* Agenda/Chapman; Sidney Goodsir Smith, 'The Twal' from *European Poetry in Scotland: An Anthology of Translations,* Edinburgh University Press; William Tair, 'La Mauvaise Reputation' from *European Poetry in Scotland: An Anthology of Translations,* Edinburgh University Press; Douglas Young 'Ye were the dawn' from *A Clear Voice,* Macdonald, and *The Puddocks,* Makarsbield; Louis and Celia Zukofsky, *Catullus,* Cape Goliard Press.

Chapter 1
Scotland in Translation

The Functions of Translation into Scots

To survey the history of translation into Scots is to explore in microcosm the history of Scottish literature and language, and their relationship to Scottish politics, history and social identity. Arguably the ideological implications of choosing Scots as a medium of translation are greater than those involved in choosing English. McClure (1991: 195) goes so far as to argue that:

> The English language belongs to no community in particular; or at any rate, to a community so vast and heterogeneous as to have no common features except common humanity and the English tongue. Scots, by contrast, is a language intensely territorial: one unique to a small and well-defined geographical area. Moreover, Scots is the language (or one of the languages) of a people in whom a strong and determined sense of national distinctiveness has persisted for almost three centuries after the loss of independent political status: a people whose nationality has been, because it must be, self-consciously asserted to a degree which at times seems perverse or incomprehensible to outsiders. And if this is not true of the entire Scots-speaking community, it is certainly true in general of *writers* of Scots, and most especially in the twentieth century, that the language is used overtly as a badge of national identity: that any piece of writing in Scots is an ideological statement, a proclamation that the writer is refusing to be identified with the politically and culturally dominant English-speaking community.

It is not necessary to agree with the sweeping generalisation about the homogeneity of English to grant that the choice of Scots is explicity an ideological assertion, particularly in the last three hundred years. This book is a historical survey of the development of this ideology as it is constructed in and through the Scots language as used in translations. As in any historical survey – indeed, any translation – this brief narrative is prone to the more or less conscious distortions brought about by selectivity and exaggeration, and also, no doubt, unintended errors of omission. Certainly, a history of Scottish translation which neglects even to mention anglophone translators such as Willa and Edwin Muir can only ever give a partial picture of the Scottish scene. Also among the more significant absences, are extended discussions of Scots translations in relation to their English and Gaelic counterparts. It would be fascinating to compare the histories of Gaelic and Scots translation, to explore highland and lowland conceptions of Scottish nationality through their respective recasting of source materials for an indigenous readership, but that must await a more expert hand than mine. Similarly, comparative critics can continue to mine the rich seam of Anglo-Scots literary relations. Kratzmann (1980), for example, considers the effect of Douglas's *Aeneid* (or *Eneados*) on later English translators; similar comparisons could be made, say, of English and Scots Horatian translations and imitations in the seventeenth to nineteenth centuries. Even so, my purpose here is deliberately narrow: to offer a history of literary translation into lowland Scots that is coherent, and which shows the changing functions of translation into Scots over a five-hundred year period. As Scotland has changed and the Scots language has changed, so have Scots literary translations and their uses evolved.

Translation and Scottish Literature

It is a reasonable argument that Scottish literature was founded on translation and adaptation. As the status of Older Scots rose to the stage where there was an audience for vernacular literature, anonymous Scots translations from French romances provided a form and an acceptable genre for Scottish versifiers. Even an original work like John Barbour's *Brus* (*c.* 1375) owes much to French models. Later, Gavin Douglas's *Eneados* (1513) provided Scots with the authority of the classics, and the sixteenth-century court poets of James VI used translation as a conscious strategy in building a literature that was overtly national.

In the gap between the Union of the Crowns in 1603 and the Act of Union of 1707, Scottish writers turned to an anglicised tongue, though the translations of William Drummond and Thomas Urquhart show that there is always something 'other' about written English for seventeenth-century literati whose speech, as we glimpse in both cases, was still strongly Scots. In the wave of Jacobite resentment following the Act of Union, and the revival of literature in the Scots tongue, most attention turned inwards towards Scottish folk traditions, but classical imitation and translation continued to lend prestige to, and afford the possibility of extending the range of, Scottish literature. In time, too, translators' attention turned to those European songs and ballads which corresponded to the native Scots forms.

Whether they were derived from classical or from European vernacular sources, the odes, songs and ballads translated in the eighteenth and nineteenth centuries were backward-looking, and tame patriotic nostalgia eventually replaced the rebellious edge of early Jacobite writings. Backward-looking, too, were the Victorian Bible translations, which initially were inspired by increasing philological interest in endangered minority European languages. The early twentieth century saw translation of near-contemporary poetry used by Hugh MacDiarmid to bring Scotland kicking and screaming into the modern age. Thereafter, the Lallans writers who took up MacDiarmid's baton either stuck to his modernist agenda, or extended their translations to key historical works in order to compensate for Scottish history's missed opportunities, and thereby to reconstitute a fractured tradition. Lallans writing was paralleled by developments in more localised vernacular writing. Meanwhile, regional Scots translations had their origins in the eighteenth-century literary revival, but in the twentieth century they too assumed the ambition of the Lallans writers while rejecting the synthesis of varieties intended to construct a new 'national' language. The rural translators were joined by translators into the newer varieties of urban Scots, the stigmatised speech of the working-classes. Translation from a wide range of prestigious literatures into these localised rural and urban varieties could do for a specific region and social class what earlier translators had done for Scots as a whole, namely, raise its status and establish its validity as a literary medium.

This thumbnail summary is, in short, the argument of the book, and the following chapters fill out the details. Chapter 2 considers the place of translation in the earliest developments of Scots and Scottish literature. Chapter 3 focuses on the 'father' of Scottish translation, Gavin Douglas, and assesses his contribution to Scottish translation practice. Chapter 4 surveys the court poets of James VI of Scotland; while Chapter 5 considers the relative status of Scots and English as vehicles for translation after the Union of Crowns. In Chapter 6, the role of translation in the Scots literary revival of the eighteenth century is discussed, as is the nineteenth-century vogue for ballad and Bible translation. The final two chapters focus on the twentieth century: Chapter 7 considers those translators who choose a reconstructed and extended Scots, or Lallans, as a medium of translation; and the last chapter discusses the work of those who opt for a medium closer to the spoken language of specific communities in Scotland. Overall, the book puts current practice in a historical and cultural context which should enrich our understanding of past and future translations into Scots.

Translation and Language Planning

Literary translation has long been perceived as one way in which to raise the status of a language – and, as noted above, translation still fulfils that vital role for Scots. Furthermore, the process of translation has always helped to define, redefine and push the boundaries of Scots. Ever since the observations of Gavin Douglas in the first Prologue to the *Eneados* in 1513, writers of 'Scots' (rather than 'Inglis', or English) have used the strategies necessary for literary translation to extend the registers and vocabulary available to Scottish writers. In expressing alien concepts in the indigenous tongue, translators are often compelled to borrow vocabulary items, or to invent new words and phrases. This activity is most pronounced in the sixteenth century, when the vernacular is still being adapted to a variety of genres hitherto articulated in Latin or French, and in the twentieth century, when there is a conscious effort to reverse the decline in Scots. Some of today's translators, such as Edwin Morgan and Liz Lochhead, have revelled in the experimental licence afforded Scots by the need to extend its registers and vocabulary; others, such as Sir Alexander Gray earlier this century, have viewed the modern synthesisers with a critical eye, and kept to a variety of Scots that is more consistently related to the speech of a particular community at a particular period.

In one sense it might be argued that the Lallans project to reconstitute a national language for Scotland has failed: the continuing correspondence in the Scottish broadsheet newspapers, the *Herald* and the *Scotsman* – noted by Gray in 1950, and still vigorously pursued in the late 1990s – would suggest little progress. Furthermore, in the history of language standardisation, it is fair to say that a poem in a given variety counts for much less than the adoption of that variety as the medium of education, or as the medium of communication by the governing bodies. The Lallans promoters will not have succeeded when the world's great literatures are translated into Scots, but when the Scottish Parliament debates its business in Scots and when its proceedings are minuted in Scots and reported in Scots by the country's media. Even so, cultural activity in Scots – even literary activity – keeps the use of Scots in the public eye, and in the eyes of the opinion-formers in Scottish society.

The relationship between the varieties of Scots used by translators today, and those varieties used in the past, is a problematic issue. The sixteenth century is sometimes seen as a golden age when peasant and courtier spoke a single Scottish tongue, and a common written language would be shared by the literate. This is only true to a limited degree. It is in fact difficult to reconstruct older Scottish speech from the written records which survive, and these records demonstrate that there was never a single standard variety of Scots common to all low-landers. Indeed, the concept of a 'standard' language is a relatively recent one, which is in many respects inapplicable to the conditions of the sixteenth century. When Gavin Douglas wrote, he had no rigidly codified language norms to conform to, although like most other writers of his time, he was relatively consistent, and avoided those spellings and expressions that he recognised were outlandish and highly localised. In the words of Smith (1996) his language variety was 'focused' but not 'fixed'. Two centuries later, Allan Ramsay was writing Scots in the context of a powerful impulse in favour of anglicisation. At times his verse is only lightly scotticised English. He was also reviving a dormant tradition of writing in Scots, and his models were primarily spoken, though he appealed to his rich knowledge of older Scottish literature. Ramsay's language was not standardised either, and from this period there evolve the two distinct general categories of synthetic Scots and vernacular Scots we know today: the former a language that nobody ever spoke, the latter eschewing nationalist aspirations in favour of highly specified local authenticity.

Translation continues to redefine the boundaries of each of the modern strains of Scots: the calques, borrowings and neologisms of Douglas Young's translations contributing to a much maligned but gloriously exotic 'high register' of Lallans; while in a lower key similar strategies are used to extend the registers of Edwin Morgan's Glaswegian translations. From a historical point of view, the standard-isation process in Scots can be said to have failed; even so, its 'failure' allows its users a range of connotations and effects that a standard language simply would not allow.

Translation and Nation

The title of this book, *Written in the Language of the Scottish Nation,* is an echo of Gavin Douglas, but the easy allusion – one of the first to make the link between Scotland and Scots – obscures the difficult question of what kind of nation Scotland is and was. Hobsbawm (1990) argues that the current concept of the 'nation state', as a political and economic entity, consisting of people of differing ethnic, religious, linguistic and racial affiliations, is relatively modern, dating back to the end of the eighteenth century. By this time, of course, Scotland was no longer an autonomous political entity, but had been subsumed into the larger 'nation', Great Britain. Earlier meanings of 'nation' across Europe imply ethnic homogeneity, a common language, shared cultural practices, or (as in Scotland, where, as noted in Chapter 2, most of these ties were absent) simply loyalty to a single monarch.

Douglas's *Eneados* is as crucial here as it is elsewere in this survey. In arguing for the 'Scottis natioun' he is compelled to argue for the 'langage of the Scottis natioun' and to emphasise its difference from English, for language difference is one of the markers of national difference. His translation is the patriotic expression of loyalty to a Scottish ruling aristocracy, the guarantee of Scottish nationhood. The fact that it was the Scottish king, James VI, who united the kingdoms of Scotland and England must have made it easier for the Scots to accept the constitutional changes of 1603; and when the Scottish dynasty was finally deposed in 1688, this insult still had the power to inflame the Jacobite sentiments of young Edinburgh merchants like Allan Ramsay who were thriving economically after the Act of Union.

With the king gone, who or what could guarantee the Scottish nation? Up to a point, those Scottish institutions which were guaranteed autonomy by the Union – the law, the church and the education system – served as substitutes for a Scottish court and parliament, but in time all three were subject to internal strife, in the case of the church, or increasing anglicisation, in the cases of the legal and educational professions. Even so, in the twentieth century, with the fragmentation of the British Empire, and the rise of small nation-states in Europe, a movement appeared in Scotland in favour of a modern, democratic nation-state along the lines of Norway or, in latter decades, Catalonia.

The concept of the Scottish nation, then, shifts and develops. Significantly, through all these changes, translation into Scots has consistently served to mark some degree of cultural independence, usually in implicit or explicit opposition to England and English. Gavin Douglas and King James VI explicitly distance themselves from English writers like Caxton and Gascoigne; Allan Ramsay and Robert Fergusson implicitly fashion themselves as Horatian figures, simultaneously of the Empire and distanced from it by choice; the ballad translators sought ethnic kinship with a wider Germanic and Scandinavian folk tradition; MacDiarmid and his heirs demanded intellectual identification with a wider European revolutionary modernism. In short, the translations from other languages helped fashion and refashion the self-image of Scotland – its ethnic roots and its intellectual affiliations, as these were perceived at different periods. It is significant that the two great periods of translation into Scots – the sixteenth and twentieth centuries – have been times when the process of national refashioning was at its most urgent.

Translation into Scots, then, serves as an index of national aspirations: it is at its most active at times of radical reassessment, and the choice of sources indicates something of the way that reassessment is being conducted.

Marking the Territory

In *Wittgenstein's Web,* quoted in Chapter 8, Sheena Blackhall observes that as dogs mark their territory with 'dug-pish', so she marks hers with words. The territories to be marked, however, keep changing. As I write this, Scotland is moving further towards a greater political autonomy than it has enjoyed for several centuries. Scottish literature and language are gaining a greater hold on school and university curricula than ever before. Beyond these shores, Europe, especially eastern Europe, has changed astonishingly in the past decade. The European Community continues to develop as a consequence of these changes – its development, too, directly and indirectly affects Scotland and the Scottish people. As these internal and external changes work through to individuals in their communities, future translators who choose Scots to chart the state of their nation will inevitably remake and reject the materials covered in this book as they see fit.

Scots, English and Translation Studies

This book offers a history of translation into Scots from the perspective of the relatively new field of 'Translation Studies'. Translation into Scots is a much older activity than Translation Studies, stretching back half a millennium, and it is a full two centuries since a Scot, Alexander Fraser Tytler, Lord Woodhouselee, provided one of the earliest codifications of the translator's craft to be published in English – his *Essay on the Principles of Translation* (1790). But Translation Studies has only in recent decades directed scholarly attention away from an abstract discussion of linguistic equivalences. The focus of Translation Studies is a consideration of the ideologies and power assymetries which govern the choice of texts to translate, the methods used in translation, and why some translations are published rather than others.

The use of Scots in translation has a diverse range of ideological implications, and they provide a remarkably sensitive index to our attitudes to national identity. Scots, after all, has sometimes been used in translations which are otherwise predominantly English, in order to communicate culturally stereotypical attitudes about national characteristics. Lefevere (1992: 48–9) refers to different translations of Aristophanes' *Lysistrata,* in which dialectal shifts between Dorian (Spartan) and Athenian in the source text are conveyed by dialectal shifts in the English texts. Jack Lindsay's translation is one in which

> the translator has put the speech of the Spartan characters in Scotch dialect, which is related to English about as much as was the Spartan dialect to the speech of Athens. The Spartans, in their character, anticipated the shrewd, canny, uncouth Scotch highlander of modern times. (Lindsay; quoted in Lefevere, 1992: 49)

Sommerstein likewise renders the Spartan/Athenian contrast as a Scots/English switch in his translation of the same play:

> Why, you rascal, you've got prickitis!
> – No, I hanna. Dinna be stupid.
> Well, what's that then?
> – It's a standard Spartan cipher-rod.
>
> (Sommerstein; quoted in Lefevere, 1992: 57)

Some superficial support for the choice of Scots might be found in the fact that it is sometimes labelled 'the Doric', although this term now largely applies to the Scots of the north-east. However, as Lefevere notes, Lindsay shows no sign of thinking deeply about the validity or the anachronistic effects of the cultural stereotypes he raises, a criticism made more pointed by Lindsay's conflation of the 'Scotch highlander' (who would have been a Gaelic speaker) with the lowlander (who would have spoken 'Scotch dialect'). Significantly, other translators use Pidgin or an exaggerated Southern American dialect to convey the marked – and low status – speech of the 'uncouth' Spartans. Lindsay and Sommerstein, however, are not alone in using Scots to represent the equivalent of Shakespeare's 'rude mechanicals' in English translations. Hatim and Mason (1990: 40) note the offence that can be given to a community by its speech variety being stigmatised in an English translation:

> We recall the controversy in Scotland a few years ago over the use of Scottish accents in representing the speech of Russian peasants in the TV dramatisation of a foreign play. The inference was allowed that a Scottish accent might somehow be associated with low status, something which, no doubt, was not intended. Like producers and directors, translators have to be constantly alert to the social implications of their actions.

Questions of status and the perception of speech communities, as refracted through the medium of their communication, are determined largely by one's perspective: an accent or dialect stigmatised in England or America might not be stigmatised in Scotland – and vice versa. The value-systems accorded to language varieties are culturally relative. The fact that this book looks at language and translation from a Scottish rather than an anglocentric perspective does not mean that its judgements are necessarily better than those arising elsewhere, but it suggests that they will be different. Further evidence of this difference can be found in the question of the translator's 'invisibility', that is, in Venuti's terms, the translator's use of a bland standard English to conceal the foreigness of translated texts (cf. Venuti, 1995a and 1995b).

Venuti (1995a) traces the history of translation into English as the victory of domesticating translation strategies over 'foreignising' strategies. According to Venuti, domesticating translators absorb the source text into the target culture as smoothly as possible, avoiding marked linguistic idiosyncrasies, to the extent that the source text becomes part of the target culture's canonical literature. The function of translation in forming national canons, and in influencing perceptions of cultural otherness has been crucial to Translation Studies. Domestication is effectively the strategy advocated by Tytler in the eighteenth century:

> I would therefore describe a good translation to be, *That, in which the merit of the original work is so completely transfused into another language, as to be as distinctly apprehended, and as strongly felt, by a native of the country to which that language belongs, as it is by those who speak the language of the original work.*
>
> (Tytler, 1790; quoted in Venuti, 1995a: 68)

Venuti argues that the strategy of 'transfusing' the source text into the target language has been dominant in English language translation ever since: reviews of translations, for example, consistently fuse the source text with the translation, and praise or condemn the translation in terms of how well the source text is naturalised into an English idiom. However, as Venuti indicates, the consequence of the Anglo-American preference for domesticating translations is that awkward sites of cultural difference are elided, and the reader is invited to see in the translated text only those aspects of the source culture that correspond to his or her own: domesticating translation is a form of cultural narcissism. Venuti therefore advocates 'foreignising' translations which employ non-standard, marked language in order to communicate the cultural difference articulated by the source text. Foreignising translations are few in English, and they tend to be held in low esteem. Ezra Pound is the most celebrated; his disciple, Paul Blackburn, found difficulty in being published in his own lifetime, although his translations of Provençal poetry have achieved posthumous recognition. Both Blackburn and his master, Pound, deviate from standard English in their respective versions of Bertran de Born's 'Bem platz lo gais temps de pascor':

> E altresim platz de senhor
> Quant es primiers a l'envazir
> En chaval armatz, sens temor,
> Qu'aissi fai los seus enardir
>   Ab valen vassalatge,
> E puois que *l'estorns* es mesclatz
> Chascus deu esser acesmatz
>   E segrel d'agradatge ...
>
> (De Born, quoted in Venuti, 1995a: 234–5; emphasis added)

> Thus that the lord pleaseth me when he is first to attack, fearless, on his armed charger; and this he emboldens his folk with valiant vassalage; and then when *stour* is mingled, each wight should be yare, and follow him exulting ...
>
> (Pound, 1952; quoted in Venuti, 1995a: 235; emphasis added)

>   And I love beyond all pleasure, that
> lord who horsed, armed and beyond fear is
> forehead and spearhead in the attack, and there
>   emboldens his men with exploits. When
>   *stour* proches and comes to quarters
>   may each man pay his quit-rent firmly,

follow his lord with joy . . .
(Blackburn, 1958; quoted in Venuti, 1995a: 236, emphasis added)

Pound and Blackburn share the strategies of the foreignising translator: archaisms, neologisms, convoluted syntax, deliberate obscurity – and forays into what Venuti calls 'dialect'. The obvious example in the above extracts is the translation of Provençal 'estorn' as 'stour'. Venuti (1995a: 234–5) observes:

> Pound's choice is virtually a homophonic equivalent, a calque, but it is also an English language archaism, meaning 'armed combat', initially in Anglo-Saxon, but retained in Middle and Early Modern English as well. It appears in Gavin Douglas's *Aeneid*, among many other literary texts, prose and poetry, 'pre-Elizabethan' and Elizabethan.

Although it no longer remains in standard English, 'stour' is a current Scots term, defined by the *Concise Scots Dictionary* as a fine dust or powder, presumably such as was raised by a storm or battle. As a term which is not available to standard English, 'stour' is available to 'foreignising' English translations, as are other Scots terms. Venuti's most extreme example of a foreignising strategy is Celia and Louis Zukofsky's translations of Catullus into an English which retains the sound (and only residually the sense) of the Latin sources:

> Gellius est tenuis: quid ni? cui tam bona mater
> tamque valens uiuat tamque venusta soror . . .
> (Catullus; quoted in Venuti, 1995a: 221)

> Coldham is rather run down, and who wouldn't be!
> With so kindly and sexy a mother,
> With a sister so sweet and lovable . . .
> (Moore, 1971; quoted in Venuti, 1995a: 221–2)

> Gellius is thin why yes: kiddin? quite a bonny mater
> tom queued veil lanced, *viva,* tom queued Venus his sister
> (Zukofsky, 1991; quoted in Venuti, 1995a: 222)

Amidst the slang, the neologisms and the borrowings here there is the word 'bonny' [handsome], which Venuti labels an archaism, but which could be equally well labelled a scotticism.

Venuti's claims about the dominant ideology in English translation favouring an 'invisible' translator going about domesticating his or her source texts have become part of the accepted currency of Translation Studies (cf. Bassnett, 1997: 9). Venuti, as I have noted, favours resistance to the dominant ideology, and this involves using 'deviant' language. However, Venuti's dichotomy implies that standard English is the norm against which 'visible' translators can kick. Significantly, Venuti's history of translation begins in the seventeenth century, when standards of written English are on the brink of a final codification and dissemination through an increasingly wide education system. Standard, colloquial, present-day English *is* the cloak which renders modern translators invisible. A history of translation from this perspective ignores a tradition of translation – of which Gavin Douglas's *Eneados* is a major work – in which standard English is not necessarily the given norm, and in which 'deviation' from standard English is a nativising rather than foreignising strategy. It ignores, namely, translation into Scots.

A history of translation from a Scottish perspective complicates Venuti's categories of 'fluent' and 'foreign'. Venuti (1995a: 311) argues:

> Contemporary translators need to develop a more sophisticated literary practice, wherein the 'literary' encompasses the various traditions of British and American literature and the various dialects of English.

In Scotland, translators have been putting Venuti's recommendations into practice for five hundred years, but not necessarily with the intention of rendering the translator visible, by foreignising the translated texts. Even so, as we shall see particularly in the discussion of twentieth-century translation, issues of language choice and the translator's visibility can help make sense of the issues in the debate over whether to use Lallans or 'vernacular' Scots in translation. In a linguistic context where norms and standards are themselves a site of contention, the relative visibility of the translator becomes even more problematical than in the modern Anglo-American tradition.

Chapter 2
'The Romanys now Begynnys'

'Lordingis, quha likis for till her
The romanys now begynnis her'

[Lords, who choose to hear,/The romance now begins here] (John Barbour, *Brus* I. 445–6)

Multilingualism in Early Scotland

Scotland has been a multilingual country from the earliest times, and it remains one today. The people from whom the modern nation takes its name, the Scoti, crossed the sea from Ireland around the fifth century AD, and they spoke a Celtic language which is the ancestor of today's Scottish Gaelic. At the time of their arrival, Brythonic Celtic, a cognate language related to modern Welsh, was already established in the south of the country, and, in addition, Pictish was spoken in the north. Two centuries later, the linguistic mixture was further complicated by the arrival in the south-east of settlers who spoke a northern descendant of Anglian, a variety of Old English. Later still, speakers of Old Norse, French and Dutch were to arrive in Scotland, while Latin was generally used as the European lingua franca of law, religion and scholarship. Given the various speech communities which contribute to the linguistic diversity of Scotland, then, translation would have been essential for interaction between them from the very beginning of Scottish history.

The beginnings of Scotland are conventionally traced to the unification of the Scots and the Picts by Kenneth MacAlpin in 843. The original area of Kenneth's kingdom, which was known as 'Alba' or 'Scotia' did not stretch south of the Firths of Forth and Clyde; however, by the eleventh century, the Scottish kingdom had extended to incorporate the Brythonic Celts of the south-west and the small group of Anglian speakers in the south-east. The extent to which the people of this area regarded themselves as 'one nation' is difficult to say: Duncan (1991) articulates the common view that a sense of Scottish community followed an effective period of monarchic rule in the twelfth and thirteenth centuries; while Broun (1994) argues that a sense of a nation which unifies Gaels and Picts can be traced in chronicles and legends as far back as the tenth century and the rulc of Kenneth MacAlpin's immediate successors. Both views argue that a sense of nationhood followed periods of effective kingship (e.g. Duncan, 1991: 13ff.), although Broun notes that 'to claim that Scottish identity emerged as an expression of a new political order is perhaps only to view the surface-stirrings of deeper social and economic developments' (1994: 54). Certainly the kingdom as envisaged by Broun would have had to deal with the changes involved in the extension of its territory south to Strathclyde and the Lothians, and the threat of Viking invasions and settlements in the ninth and tenth centuries. During this period, one of the languages of Scotland, Pictish, died out, and Brythonic Celtic was replaced by Gaelic in the south-west.

By the time of the Norman Conquest in England, Scotland was governed by Malcolm III, a Gaelic speaker. After the Norman Conquest, the community in the Lothians which spoke northern Old English was boosted by the arrival of refugees from Norman rule. Indeed, Malcolm gave sanctuary to the deposed English royal family, and in time married the Princess Margaret. Their sons, including the future king, David, spent time at the Norman court in their youth, and when David returned north, he set about establishing in lowland Scotland the feudal principles of Norman society he found in the south – in particular, he granted land to Norman barons, and he established monasteries and burghs. These social changes again had a linguistic impact: the new Norman aristocracy spoke and wrote Norman French, the merchants who were attracted to the new burghs spoke fast-evolving varieties of northern English, and the churchmen who ran the religious foundations used Latin as the language of administration and learning. As Grant (1994: 76) writes:

> The result [of the political changes of the tenth and eleventh centuries] was that in the twelfth century there were three main languages in Scotland, Gaelic, English and French – plus Latin for the Church and for administration, and Norse on the fringes – while behind the languages was an even greater variety of ethnic groups. Scotland was very much a hybrid kingdom – in stark

contrast to Wales and Ireland, where concepts of racial purity were more strongly maintained.

In early Scotland, then, multilingualism was the norm, and it would be wrong to speak of a single 'national language' which unified the various speech communities. In such a society, translation would also be common, and it is important to remember that some of the modern connotations of the word 'translation' would not necessarily adhere to medieval uses of the word. As Burnley (1989: 41) observes:

> Although Latin literacy was somewhat distinct from that in the vernaculars, it is quite apparent that the division between English and foreign languages was not comparable with that existing today. Indeed, Anglo-French was hardly a foreign language; rather a special style used for certain technical purposes, and those who for practical purposes were competent in Anglo-French would not have found it an impossibly difficult task to extend their competence to reading works of leisure composed in French, often in the recent past. The contents of many libraries in the fifteenth century consisted of works in French as often as in English. Any writer, therefore, until at least the middle of the fifteenth century, was likely to be able to turn in his search for *materia* to French sources. There was no reason why he should think of his action as translation in the narrow sense we now use the word: that is, as a process by which a text existing in one language and culture is transferred into linguistic items with a corresponding function in a second language and culture.

Although Burnley is writing about English, the situation in medieval Scotland is similar, up to a point. Certainly, in the lowlands, French, Latin, and the evolving northern variety of English, called 'Inglis' by its speakers, would have functioned as appropriate styles for different domains: for example, Inglis would be appropriate for trade and other everyday transactions, French would for a while continue to be used among the Norman aristocracy for polite conversation and the reading of literature, and Latin would be used for ecclesiastical and administrative purposes. Only Gaelic failed to occupy a linguistic niche in the lowland burghs, castles and monasteries – and the everyday use of Gaelic receded west and then north, to the highland domains where the clan system still exerted a powerful influence.

The linguistic balance of power, however, was to change along with social change in Scotland between the eleventh and fifteenth centuries. The weakening of the ties of the Scottish nobility to their

Norman French origins, and the economic and political gains made by the merchant classes in the lowland burghs saw the encroachment of Inglis into those domains earlier associated with Latin and French: administration, scholarship and literature. Although Scotland has remained a multicultural and multilingual country, in the period between the fourteenth and the seventeenth centuries one of its languages became predominant in the south, and for a spell it was raised to the point at which it could serve as a national language. This was the distinctive variety of northern English which was originally termed 'Inglis' and later became known simply as 'Scots'.

Latin into Inglis

Few written works predate David I's reign as king – Adamnan's Latin *Life of St Columba* is one of the few surviving works. During and immediately after his reign there are a few feudal charters and writs, again in Latin. One of the earliest charters, granted around 1124 by David I to Robert de Brus (a Norman ancestor of the later Scottish king), makes reference to the ethnic mix and cross-border relations of Norman Scotland:

> David dei gratia rex Scottorum omnibus baronibus suis et hominibus et amicis Francis et Anglis salutem. Sciatis me dedisse et concessisse Roberto de Brus Estrahanent et totam terram a divisa Dunegal de Stranit usque ad divisam Randulfi Meschin . . .

In this charter, reprinted in Croft Dickinson *et al.* (1952: 57–8), the King of Scots addresses his French and English friends (amicis Francis et Anglis), and grants land in the Scottish borders (Estrahanent, that is, Annandale) to the Norman, de Brus, an act witnessed mainly by English barons.

Over time, in the lowlands of Scotland, the Inglis of the barons and the burghers began to edge into some, at least, of the domains of Latin and French. By the end of the fourteenth century, the Acts of Parliament of Scotland were being written not in Latin but in Inglis. Some statutory genres show a mixture of languages being used: the Charters of the Friars Preachers of Ayr, for example, includes attestations, tacks and indentures in Inglis dating from the early fifteenth century. In accordance with this trend towards the use of Inglis in the fifteenth century, the Burgh Laws, which date back to the twelfth century and David I's reign, were translated from Latin into Scots. The example below illustrates this early technical translation of twelfth-century Latin into Inglis of the mid-fifteenth century:

LXVII

De vendentibus generaliter in burgo

> Omnes generaliter vendentes videlicet brasiatores pistores carnifices ac piscarii vendent omnibus tam transeuntibus quam aliis intraneis et extraneis quibuscunque et non plus retineant in domibus suis ad opus suum et familie sue nisi ad valorem quatuor denariorum quia totum residuum est commune omnibus ementibus Et qui aliter faciendo convictus fuerit dabit octo solidos ad forisfactum

Of sellaris of met and drynk

> All broustaris the whilkis sellis ale and thai that sellis brede or flesche or fysche and all hukstaris the whilkis byis and sellis communly, sal sell til al men als well gangand as cummand what somevir, and thai sall halde na mare in thair house to the oyse of thair hushalde gif that ony man wil by it bot to the valur of iiii d. oure nycht, and al the layff sal be common til al maner of man passand and cummand for thair payment. And wha dois the contrare of this and tharof be convyct he sal pay to his forfalt viii s.

> [All brewers who sell ale, and they who sell bread or flesh or fish, and all hucksters who buy and sell commonly, shall sell to all men who come and go, and they shall keep no more in their house over night, for the use of their household, if any man would buy it, but to the value of threepence, and all the rest shall be common to all manner of men coming and going, for their payment. And whoever does the contrary of this and is convicted thereof, he shall pay to his forfeit eight shillings.]

The problems and strategies of translating from an administrative lingua franca into a developing vernacular are suggested here. The syntactical patterns of the Latin sentences are reasonably closely followed by the Inglis version, and some of the lexical items are evidently loanwords: 'brasiatores/broustaris', 'valorem/valur', 'commune/common', and 'ad forisfactum/to his forfalt'. The title and introductory sentence of the Inglis version do, however, specify the type of vendor ('sellaris of met and drynk'), and the general-to-specific sequencing of the Latin version is reversed in the vernacular. It is not clear why this should have been done, unless 'sellaris' or 'hukstaris' were not considered to be as general as the Latin phrase 'omnes generaliter vendentes' – it is perhaps significant that both 'sellaris' and 'hukstaris' are postmodified in order to clarify their meaning. The range of reference, or perhaps the register of the vernacular terms, might have vexed the Inglis translator, prompting him to focus on the specific vendors to clarify or dignify his text. On the other hand, many of the Latin terms find easy equivalence in Inglis; for example, 'in domibus suis ad opus' becomes 'to the oyse of thair hushalde', and 'totum residuum' becomes 'al the layff'. The text reveals a language medium, which was once associated largely with everyday speech, employing translation to extend its range of registers, here into the written mode and the administrative domain. The syntax is based on the source language, from which certain words and phrases are also borrowed, when new concepts are introduced, or preferred, when a more elevated tone is desired.

The general trend towards using Inglis, then, gradually increased as the fifteenth century continued, particularly in communication which was directed towards the lowland burghers; however, Latin retained its prestige and was still used for many charters and indentures during this period. The continuing use of Latin in scholarship is evident in the fourteenth-century histories and chronicles of John of Fordun and Hector Boece, and as Jack (1972: 27–8) argues, Scottish links with Italy in the medieval period promoted interest in the humanist writers, and Latin literature, at the expense of Italian vernacular works:

> Until the seventeenth century a vast proportion of Scottish verse was itself written in Latin, the acme being reached by George Buchanan. This early preference for Latin sources delayed the first signs of Italian influence till the 1480s.

More recently, in a passionate plea for a reappraisal of what is meant by Scottish literature, Jack returns to his theme of 'a variety of voices' with renewed vigour, pointing out that a court poet like Sir Robert Ayton (1569–1638) inherited a polyglot tradition and took for granted that his literary activity should naturally move between languages:

> Ayton's assumption that any Scottish author may move easily from Scots-English to Anglo-Scots and to Latin constitutes another attack on the idea of the homogeneous language, but it does so with specific reference to their understanding of literature's position among the branches of knowledge. All early writers defined their position rhetorically – that is, as a branch of persuasive oratory. Within this scheme, linguistic variety rather than homogeneity was the key to success. (Jack, 1997: xv)

Latin, indeed, remained the main medium of Scottish academia up to the end of the seventeenth century, and its authority, as we shall see, lasted well beyond. Despite the longstanding prestige of Latin across a range of genres, legal, scholarly and literary, the encroachment of Inglis into its domains is seen, for example, in Andrew of Wynton's Inglis chronicle in the fourteenth century, and in John Bellenden's translation of Boece's chronicles in the sixteenth century (see Chapter 3). The encroachment of Inglis into the genres associated with Latin was no doubt facilitated by the presence of translations: a legal text might be composed in Latin, and so have the authority granted by the prestige language, but, in order to be more widely understood the text might be translated into Inglis. Through time, the host language (Inglis) would be associated with the authority of the law, and its status would rise accordingly. The language originally accorded prestige – Latin – would then slowly decline in use, if not authority. It was a long, slow process, slower in some genres (such as scholarly texts) than others, but in the translations of Latin legal texts into Inglis we can see its beginnings.

French into Inglis

Inglis also expanded into the domains of literature and of treatises on chivalry, where, after the Norman period, French held sway. The earliest extant Scottish literary epic, John Barbour's *Brus* or *The Bruce* (1375), while owing a debt to the historical events of sixty years before its composition, owes an equal debt to the structure and organisation of French romances. Indeed, this nationalist romance is followed in the next century, not only by Blin Hary's *Wallace*, but by translations into Inglis of the French romances *Lancelot of the Laik* and *The Buik of Alexander*. Both translated romances share with the *Brus* and the *Wallace* the themes of chivalric heroism and nationalist aspiration. Indeed, the similarity of *The Buik of Alexander* to Barbour's *Brus* tempted earlier scholars to claim Barbour's authorship of both works, despite the existence of a colophon dating *The Buik of Alexander* as completed in 1438. Ritchie (1925: lxiii–xcviii) lists various parallels in phraseology between the *Brus* and *The Buik of Alexander* in support of Barbour's authorship, and he argues that the translation is in fact an earlier work which strongly influenced the style of the *Brus*. The explicit date of *The Buik of Alexander*'s manuscript is explained away by scribal error, or 'improvement' (Ritchie, 1925: clix, n.) The two works are certainly similar, as a brief quotation will show. The episode in which the lone Scottish hero confronts and defeats an English posse at a ford has verbal echoes, according to Ritchie, of an early episode in *The Buik of Alexander* when Emynedus confronts some herdsmen who are stoutly protecting their cattle from his men. It is illuminating to compare the two Scots texts with a French version:

> Ferrant qui molt tost vait, broche des esperons,
> Et fiert le premerain qu'en vuide les archons
> Et l'auberc li fausa con ce fust auquetons
> (*Li Fuerres de Gadres*, 5, 3–5; in Ritchie, 1925: 4a)

> Ferrand he straik with spurris in hy,
> And straik the first sa rigorusly
> That throw the bodie he him bair;
> His Haubrik helpit him nocht ane hair.

> [Going, he struck with spurs speedily/And struck the first so rigorously/So that he bore him through the body/His coat of mail did not help him a whit.] (*The Foray of Gadderis* I, 117–20, in Ritchie, 1925: 4b)

> He smat the furst sa rygorusly
> With his spere, that richt scharply schare,
> Till he doun to the erd him bare.

> [He smote the first so rigorously/With his spear, that cut so sharply,/Till he bore him down to the ground.] (*Brus* VI, 137–9; in Kinghorn (ed.), 1960: 45–6)

The excerpt from *The Buik of Alexander* is obviously a rendition of the French text, but there is also a parallel between *The Buik of Alexander*'s 'And straik the first sa rigorusly' and the *Brus*'s 'He smat the furst sa rygorusly' – one token of more numerous correspondences. Given a single echo, one might argue for coincidence, but it is the multiplication of such coincidences that led scholars such as Ritchie to argue that the authors of *The Buik of Alexander* and the *Brus* were one and the same.

However, this view of the authorship of *The Buik of Alexander* has been generally dismissed; for example, McDiarmid (1988: 31–2) is particularly scathing:

> The comic obsession of Scots scholars with discovering yet more achievements by Barbour has made them dismiss the worded date, ignore the different rhyming practice, and stress the many phrases, even lines, lifted from the *Bruce*. The direction of the borrowing has not been considered; thus the Alexander poet speaks of the sweet-smelling flowers of the Ephesoun carpets because he has Barbour's description of the Irish fields in mind, and describes

> Porrus's fierce swordsmanship as producing a 'lardner' of bodies, a term obviously deriving from what Barbour tells us was the country tale of 'The Douglas Lardner'.

McDiarmid presents the view, now generally accepted, that Sir Gilbert Hay (*c.* 1400–60), a translator of French prose treatises such as *The Buke of Knychthede, The Buke of the Law of Armys, Secreta Secretorum* and *The Buke of the Governaunce of Princes* – all completed around the middle of the fifteenth century (see below) – is a likelier author of *The Buik of Alexander*, and he points out that the epilogue of a later version of the romance, the 1499 *Buke of Alexander the Conqueroure*, goes so far as to name him so. Scholarly disputes aside, it is clear that in its earliest period, original literature in Inglis is very similar in themes, and even in phrasing, to translated versions of French romances.

Effectively, lowland literature in Scots was born as a largely aristocratic readership of French romances began to switch to Inglis as a literary medium. As the language, still called 'Inglis' by its speakers and writers, expanded into the domains of government administration and literature, it naturally changed. As we saw in the previous section, the vocabulary of Inglis borrowed from Latin in order that novel concepts of law and trade could be expressed in the vernacular. Inglis further borrowed from French to augment its lexical resources in the domains of chivalry and administration. Moreover, those words which were borrowed in order to express new concepts also came with a set of associations – latinate and French vocabulary was associated with social and aesthetic prestige, and in purple patches the borrowed terms 'gilded' the vernacular, and elevated its tone. The general strategy of borrowing can even be seen in the brief excerpt from *The Buik of Alexander* quoted above. Even when terminology does not parallel that of the French source, the translator's vocabulary still has a substantial romance flavour. Words of French and Latin etymology include 'rigorusly' (L 'rigor'), and 'Haubrik' (OF 'hauberc', coat of chain-mail). By the fifteenth century, neither of these terms would have seemed exotic, although in combination with others of similar etymology they would have lent the verse a certain degree of dignity. Such terms would have become part and parcel of Inglis vocabulary as it added to its domestic functions by absorbing from other languages vocabulary to express the registers of chivalry, law and administration.

It is not a superficial conceit to link the early Scottish translations of French romances to these expanding domains of administration, chivalry and the law. The romances were in essence chivalric – they told of the exploits of knights, real or mythical – and they had an overt educational value: they aimed to provide a mirror for princes, and a model of good government. The incomplete romance, *Lancelot of the Laik,* is a good example of this tradition. It is a moot point whether *Lancelot of the Laik* should be properly considered a translation – like many other renditions from French sources, it edits and adapts its material. Lupack (1994: 4) writes:

> *Lancelot of the Laik* has its source in the French Vulgate *Lancelot.* It would, however, be a mistake to call it a translation of the French romance or even 'a paraphrase of the first part of the Vulgate *Lancelot*', as the *Manual of Writings in Middle English* calls it (I, p. 51). In the process of creating a verse romance from the prose of the French, the Scottish poet has translated some passages fairly closely, changed details in others, sometimes expanded on the text, sometimes abbreviated it. But the most obvious change he makes is to select a portion of the much longer source and focus on that.

The strategy is detailed in the original prologue to the verse romance – the Scottish poet spends some time listing the parts of the source material omitted in the Inglis version, and those parts retained. The justification for inclusion and exclusion are given in a passage which presents the stimulus for the translation: the poet is in love and the power of his love prompts him to translate a great love poem – or part of one:

> Thane in my thocht rolling to and fro
> Quhare that I mycht sum wncouth mater fynde
> Quhill at the last it fell into my mynd
> Of o story, that I before had sene,
> That boith of love and armys can contenn,
> Was of o knycht clepit Lancelot of the Laik,
> The sone of Bane was, King of Albanak,
> Of quhois fame and worschipful dedis
> Clerkis into diverss bukis rediss,
> Of quhome I thynk her sumthing for to writ
> At Lovis charge, and as I cane endit,
> Set men tharin sal by experiens
> Know my consait and al my negligens.
> Bot for that story is so pasing larg,
> Oneto my wit it war so gret o charg
> For to translait the romans of that knycht.

> It passith fare my cunyng and my mycht;
> My ignorans may it not comprehende.
>
> [Then in my thought rolling to and fro/Where I might find some strange matter/Until at last there fell into my mind/A story that I had seen before/That contained both love and arms;/It was of a knight called Lancelot of the Lake/Who was the son of Bane, the King of Albanak,/Of whose fame and admirable deeds/Learned men read in diverse books,/Of whom I intend to write something here/At Love's command, and as I am able to write,/Determined men shall therein by experience/Know my conceit and all my negligence./But because that story is so passing large/It would be so great a burden to my ingenuity/To translate the romance of that knight./It goes far beyond my cunning and my strength,/My ignorance may not comprehend it.] (I, pro. 196–213)

The originality of the prologue notwithstanding, the sentiments expressed therein are entirely conventional: the lovestruck poet pleads a becoming if insincere modesty and then launches into a preview of the structure of the romance. Lancelot's early years and adventures will be omitted and the story will focus on his friendship with Arthur and the way in which his military exploits in Arthur's service win him the love of his lady. Love might be the original stimulus for the poem, but 'weris' still figure prominently. The incomplete poem also contains a substantial passage in which an aged sage, Amytans, delivers political advice to Arthur before revealing to him the meaning of a troubling dream. *Lancelot of the Laik*, then, shares with *The Buik of Alexander* the themes of chivalric responsibilities and good government.

The language of *Lancelot of the Laik* is an interesting mixture of northern and southern varieties of English. The passage quoted above shows Inglis forms (e.g. 'quh-' spellings in 'quhare', 'quhill' and 'quhois') intermingled with English forms (e.g. 'know' rather than 'knaw'; 'so' rather than 'swa'). Various reasons have been suggested for the anglicised language of the romance (cf. Kratzmann, 1980: 231; Lupack, 1994: 2; Smith, 1996: 77): an English scribe might have introduced English variants; however, it is evident that Scottish poets in this period were influenced by the prestige of the southern literary vernacular established by poets such as Chaucer and Gower. In the love poem *The Kingis Quair*, probably written by James I of Scotland, and based in part on his period of imprisonment in England, the *Lancelot* poet would have had a prestigious Scottish model for an anglicised literary language. Although England and Scotland would have been perceived as separate kingdoms, the distinctiveness of the vernacular language of lowland Scotland clearly was not yet seen as a marker of national difference. *Lancelot of the Laik* suggests that the linguistic variation between Inglis and English was perceived as a distinction in register rather than as an expression of national identity: the southern variants in the Scottish translation would simply have been considered appropriate to the written literary register. The fact that early sixteenth-century poets, like William Dunbar, could cite Chaucer as sharing 'oure tong ... oure Inglisch' (*The Goldyn Targe*, ll. 254, 259) suggests that Inglis was still considered a common language between the two nations. If a Scottish writer favoured southern forms, it was because those forms were associated with an established post-Chaucerian literary tradition. Only much later would English forms be considered problematic to the expression of Scottish identity (cf. Jack, 1997).

Lancelot of the Laik demonstrates that Scots adhered to the mediaeval literary translators' typical practice of excerption, embellishment and transformation. As we have seen, the *Lancelot* poet focuses on the relationship between Arthur and Lancelot, and omits the sections on Lancelot's earlier life. The major embellishment in the surviving fragment is the advice given to Arthur by Amytans. This section has exercised many of the critics who have dealt with the romance – some arguing that the advice is directed implicitly to James III and relates to the problems of his reign. However, Lyall (1976: 25) cautions that the political advice is generalised and conventional, and Lupack (1994) argues that while the Amytans section is important it is not central to the poem as originally conceived. Amytans counsels Arthur to be virtuous, to remember that his fate is bound to God's providence, and that he should confess his sins against King Bane, Lancelot's father. Amytans' counsel may be unremarkable in itself, but it is significant insofar as it fits into a continuous strand of advice that dominates Scottish literature between the mid-fifteenth and mid-sixteenth centuries. Another Arthurian romance, *Golagros and Gawane,* a late fifteenth-century metrical romance in Scots, based on sequences in the French prose text, *Continuation Perceval,* has in Spynagros a similar character to Amytans. As Jack (1989) argues, Spynagros's spiritual counselling is more of a feature of the Scottish text than its French source, and as a whole *Golagros and Gawane* focuses much more intensely on Arthur's initial failure and subsequent success in achieving the high standards of chivalric virtue. Spynagros and Amytans are predecessors of later characters such as Gude Counsel in David Lindsay's *Ane Satyre of the Thrie Estaitis* (see Chapter 4).

Advice literature also figures in prose translations into Inglis in the fifteenth century, particularly in Sir Gilbert Hay, the poet of *The Buik of Alexander's*, renditions of French chivalric and administrative treatises such as *The Buke of the Law of Armys, The Buke of Knychthede*, and *The Government of Princes*. These translations are the earliest examples of literary prose in Inglis. *The Buke of the Law of Armys* will serve as an illustration of this genre of translation: it was translated from Honoré Bonet's *Arbre des Batailles* (c. 1387), so Hay informs us:

> at the request of ane hye and mychty Prince and worthy lord. William erle of Orknay – and of Cathnes / lord Synclere and chancelare of Scotland. in his castell of Rosselyn. The ȝere of oure Lord a thowsand four hundreth fyfty and sex/
>
> [at the request of a high and mighty Prince and worthy lord, William, Earl of Orkney, and of Caithness, Lord Sinclair, and chancellor of Scotland, in his castle at Rosslyn. The year of our Lord 1456]

Like Hay's other translations, then, *The Buke of the Law of Armys* was originally commissioned by an aristocratic patron who, presumably, preferred an Inglis text to a French one, or wished for a vernacular gloss to his French book. Hay's translation does have the appearance of a gloss: the content is presented in the form of reported speech, most sections beginning 'Here speris [asks] the doctour ...' or 'Now spekis he here ...'. The book traces the nature and history of war and battles, religious and secular, for example, 'Item, how grete Cartage was destroyit' (II, chap. xi), and it gives detailed advice about proper conduct in a vast range of situations, such as whether it is proper for a monk to defend himself against an abbot (it is), and 'Gif a man gais to were for vayn glore, quhethir he may be law of armes ask wagis or nocht' (IV, chap. xxxiii). Bonet, the Prior of Sellonet, wrote the 'Arbre des Batailles' between 1382 and 1387, during a period of civil war in his native Provence. The theme of the book – that war is proper and sanctioned by God, but that it must be conducted in accordance with God's laws – was as relevant to Scotland in the mid-fifteenth century. In 1452, only seven years before Hay began his translation, James II had invited the Earl of Douglas to dinner at Stirling Castle, and there stabbed him to death. James subsequently defeated Douglas's supporters in battle, and, as Hay began his translation, James was about to intervene in the English civil war between York and Lancaster. At the siege of Roxburgh in the summer of 1460, James was the victim of a fatal accident, and for nine years Scotland was ruled by regents.

Good government was a topic of urgent relevance, and, as in the Amytans section of *Lancelot of the Laik*, Hay follows Bonet in stressing the need for virtue in government, for example, in the concluding advice given to Emperors:

> And as in his governaunce and dedis touchand his awin persone, he suld efter the lawis civiles that ar his lawis, maid of him and his predecessouris. For he that makis lawis, and syne is transgressour himself of his awin propre lawis that he makis, he schawis him self to be a fule, or ellis his lawis to be littil worth. And thareto sayis the lawis canoun, Kepe the lawis that thou hast ordanyt to be kepit. For, nocht gaynstandand that his lawis may nocht bynd him self that is Emperour, nevertheles he suld lyve efter his lawis, sen lawis ar bot reuglis of vertues, maid for the governaunce of the brukle mankynde that ever is redy till excede in vycis.
>
> [And as in government and deeds touching his own person, he should [act] according to the civil laws that are his laws, made by him and his predecessors. For he who makes laws, and then is a transgressor himself of his own proper laws that he makes, he shows himself to be a fool, or else his laws to be of little worth. And thereto the body of laws says, Keep the laws that you have ordained to be kept. For notwithstanding that his laws might bind him self that is the Emperor, nevertheless he should live according to his laws, since laws are but rules of virtues, made for the government of weak mankind that is ever ready to exceed in vices.] (*The Buke of the Law of Armys*, IV, chap. cliiii; STS edn, p. 291)

Sir Gilbert Hay's prose translations of French chivalric treatises are further evidence of the linguistic shift in the reading practices of the Scottish aristocracy, and there is evidence that Hay's noble patron did read the translation, with some care. In the third chapter of Book IV, Hay follows Bonet in partially exempting the princes of France, Spain and England from subservience to the Emperor's command (cf. Stevenson 1901: lxxxv): 'And ȝit is thare sindry othir realmes that obeyis nocht to the Emperour, as France, Spaigneȝe and Ingland, the quhilkis has be writt thair jurisdiccioun imperiale' [i.e. 'And yet there are sundry other realms that do not obey the Emperor, such as France, Spain and England, which have by writ their imperial jurisdiction']. To the list of these nations, in a marginal note, William Sinclair has added 'Scotland' and 'Irland'. In the fifteenth century, then, the Scottish nobility had developed a taste for reading literature of different kinds in Inglis as well as – or even instead of – French. Moreover, at this time the readership was widening to incorporate a 'middling class' of merchants and burgesses, literate in Inglis, who were also eager for morally uplifting tales of chivalric nationalism. As a result, as Wormald (1981: 59) points out, Inglis, or Scots, was gaining in social value as it moved from a language of everyday interaction in the lowland burghs, to the accepted language of government and literature:

> [The] corpus of prose and poetry for a knightly and aristocratic audience used the same language that its audience employed in government. Much earlier than in England, vernacular became the language of government in Scotland. From the reign of James I almost all parliamentary legislation was in Scots, and the council records and treasurer's accounts are in Scots as far back as they survive, to the 1470s; only the register of the great seal and the exchequer rolls continued to use Latin.

By the end of the fifteenth century, then, Inglis was used in every sphere of domestic and public life in lowland Scotland, and, despite the continuing presence of Gaelic in the north and west, and the continuing prestige of Latin and French, it was coming to be seen as a national language. The Inglis which was taking on this role in Scotland, was, of course, closely related to the variety of English which was performing a similar function south of the border, and, in their expansion of domains and adoption of romance vocabulary, both varieties were undergoing similar processes, albeit at different rates. Most speakers, and the readers and writers of Inglis, still regarded the northern and southern varieties as part of the same overarching language. But although cognate, and – perhaps with some effort – mutually intelligible, they were becoming increasingly different in their vocabulary, spelling, pronunciation, and in grammatical features such as the use of the '-it' inflexion, rather than '-ed', in the regular past participle. As we shall see in Chapter 3, by the end of the fifteenth century these differences were beginning to be used, for the first time, as markers of a distinctively Scottish national identity. In making this distinction, translators were to lead the way.

Chapter 3
'Writtin in the Langage of Scottis Natioun'

The Context of Douglas's *Eneados*

Despite the existence of earlier Scottish renderings of works such as *The Buik of Alexander* and *Lancelot of the Laik*, the first major literary translation into Scots is, for good reason, held to be *Eneados*, Gavin Douglas's translation of Virgil's *Aeneid*. Douglas moves beyond the mediaeval tradition of literary translation, which allowed significant departure from and reworking of source texts – a tradition which is also evident in, for example, Robert Henryson's very Scottish versions of *The Morall Fabillis of Esope the Phrygian*, which are obviously indebted to continental models, but substantially refashion them to serve the Scottish poet's moral, political and aesthetic ends. Douglas's translation is the earliest Scottish translation to claim fidelity to the source text, and indeed to argue that this fidelity is a virtue. In doing this, Douglas's translation can also be regarded as the first attempt to render Virgil's text comprehensively into any variety of 'English' – the Prologue to the First Book reveals that the *Eneados* was partly prompted by Douglas's distaste of an earlier rendering of the *Aeneid* by William Caxton, one which was not based on the Latin text but on a French version. Douglas's translation, then, signifies a break with the mediaeval tradition as practised in Scotland – although it is possible to debate the extent to which he conforms to the ideals he proposes.

What were the conditions which allowed this new voice to be heard? The conclusion of the *Eneados* indicates that it was completed in 1513, the year of James IV's disastrous campaign against England, a campaign which resulted in the death of the king and many of his courtiers on Flodden field. Ironically, the war against England had come at the end of a period of fragile stability, during which James III and James IV had, sporadically, built bridges with their southern neighbours. Wormald (1981: 6–7) charts the series of marriage alliances and treaties by which the Scottish kings attempted to come to a new accommodation with the 'auld ally', France, and their mutual 'auld enemy', England. Although the attempts were doomed to failure, they did produce a period of relative peace, during which the arts received a measure of patronage from the Scottish court. The liveliness of Scottish letters in this period is testified to in William Dunbar's poem, popularly known as the 'Lament for the Makaris', which commemorates several generations of poets, many of whose poems are lost to us today. There had also been a gradual increase in literacy among the general populace beyond the narrow circles of the aristocracy and clergy (Lyall, 1989). Robert Henryson, for example, seems not to have been directly connected with the court – he is associated more with the town of Dunfermline, where he might have been a notary public, and perhaps a schoolteacher – certainly his poetry abounds with legal references and has a strongly didactic tone. Douglas's suggestion that 'masteris of grammar sculys' thank him for his efforts show that he also expects a readership for his translation well beyond the narrower confines of the court.

That literature served moral and national ends is a truism of Scottish literature from its earliest days. The earliest surviving work of any length, John Barbour's *Brus* (1375) stresses the truthfulness of the story alongside its pleasure: the implication is that a true story is not just pleasurable; part of the pleasure is in learning from actual events:

> Storyss to rede ar delitabill,
> Supposs that thai be nocht bot fabill;
> Than suld storyss that suthfast wer,
> And thai war said in gud maner,
> Have doubill plesance in heryng.
>
> [Stories are delightful to read/Even though they are nothing but fable;/And so stories that were true/If they were told well,/Would have double pleasure in the hearing.] (John Barbour, *Brus* I. 1–5)

The romance which follows, while sometimes based on historical incidents, is a mythologising of the mediaeval Scottish kingdom and its monarchy. This mythologising continues in the later epic, Blin Hary's *Wallace*, written in the 1470s under the patronage of Scotland's southern landowners (Wormald, 1981: 64; cf. Goldstein, 1993). Both tales celebrate Scottish heroes who defy English oppression, and offer tales of chivalry with the added spice of claimed authenticity.

However, even outright fables could claim a different kind of truth, a moral truth which justified the telling of tales. In his introduction to *The Morall Fabillis of Esope the Phrygian*, Robert Henryson famously lays claim to this kind of 'truth':

> The nuttes schell, thocht it be hard and teuch,
> Haldis the kirnill, and is delectabill.
> Sa lyis thair ane doctryne wyse aneuch,
> And full of fruit, under ane fenyeit Fabill.

> [The nut's shell, although it is hard and tough/Holds the kernel, and is delightful./So lies there a doctrine sufficiently wise/And fruitful, under a fictional Fable.] (Robert Henryson, *Prologue*, 15–18)

Douglas explicitly integrates his *Eneados* into this tradition of national mythologising and moral allegory. He stresses the Scottishness of his translation, principally by setting up a contrast between his Scots language and the 'suddroun' of the English nation – a contrast which was quite novel for a writer of his time. And, partly through the Prologues which he adds to each Book, partly through textual additions which pepper the narrative, and partly through the annotations which survive, in Douglas's hand, in one of the manuscripts, he elucidates the moral purpose of Virgil's epic. Douglas, in the Prologue to the First Book, yokes together, as did Barbour and Henryson before him, the twin pleasures of morality and artifice. In a criticism of Caxton, who omitted parts of the Sixth Book on the grounds that it was untrue, Douglas reasonably points out that the whole work is a fable, arguing thus:

> Virgill tharin ane hie philosophour hym schew,
> And vnder the clowdis of dyrk poecy
> Hyd lyis thar mony notabill history –
> For so the poetis be the crafty curys
> In similitudes and vndir quent figuris
> The suythfast materis to hyde and to constreyn;
> All is nocht fals, traste weill, in cace thai feyn.

> [Virgil thereby showed that he was a high philosopher/And that under the clouds of dark poetry/There lies hidden much notable history –/For so the poets by skillful crafts/In similitudes and under quaint figures/Hide and constrain truthful matter;/All is not false, trust well, wherever they feign.] (Douglas, *Eneados* I, Prologue, 192–8)

The argument is both clear and, by 1513, conventional: the false fable nevertheless holds a kernel of truth, 'in similitudes and vndir quent figuris'. Virgil is not only a weaver of tales, but a philosopher from whom moral virtues can be learnt. In particular, as Coldwell (1964: 19–38) argues, Virgil's *Aeneas* is seen as a mirror for princes and knights, and the epic is lauded as an infinite source of enjoyment:

> For every vertu belangand a nobill man
> This ornate poet bettir than ony can
> Payntand discryvis in person of Eneas –
> . . .
> Reid quha hym knawys, I dar this vndertak,
> Als oft as ȝe him reid, full weill I wait,
> ȝhe fynd ilke tyme sum mery new consait.

> [For every virtue pertaining to a nobleman/This ornate poet better than anyone/Described by depicting the person of Aeneas –/. . ./ Read, whoever knows him, I dare undertake this,/That as often as you read him, I know full well,/You find in him each time some merry new conceit.] (I, Pro. 325–7; 336–8)

Douglas's epic translation, therefore, is made to conform to the aesthetics and to the political and religious ideology of his time – much of the Prologue to Book Six, possibly as a further riposte to Caxton, is devoted to interpreting Aeneas's visit to the Underworld as Christian allegory. However, putting a Christian gloss on classical myth was commonplace in the mediaeval period – Henryson, for example, provides an explicit Christian 'moralitas' to his version of 'Orpheus and Eurydice', a poem we know Douglas was familiar with. It is possible to make too much of Douglas's interest in the political and religious themes of the *Aeneid* – in response to an argument that Douglas consistently and deliberately reconstructs Virgil's conception of fate as Christian destiny, Priscilla Bawcutt claims that the Scottish poet is largely concerned with elucidating elements that are already there in the source text:

> But Douglas does not impose upon Virgil a specifically Christian conception of destiny and its relation to the divine purpose; rather he tends to stress and expand those ideas that he could reconcile with his own religion. (Bawcutt, 1976: 126–7)

We do not need to argue that Douglas departed from the ethos of his source text in order to claim that the value of the *Eneados* lay in its contribution to Scottish culture of a set of ideals and behavioural models from which its noblemen could profit – and profit with pleasure. Virgil's *Aeneid* comes complete with elements which would appeal to a Scottish poet of the early sixteenth century – it has a strong, virtuous leader whose heroism helps found a nation. The fact that this hero belongs to pre-Christian legend would not be a significant problem in an age which had learnt to think allegorically, and to discern the moral wisdom in 'fenyeit fabill'.

Douglas was himself a nobleman, and there is a strong sense in the Prologues that he was writing for his own class: occasionally he addresses his 'gentill redaris' as 'ȝhe worthy noblys' (e.g. I Pro. 267). There is little suggestion here of the natural democracy sometimes associated with the tales of Bruce and, especially, of Wallace. Indeed, a theme of the Prologue to the First Book is his contempt for the unlearned:

> Greyn gentill ingynys and breistis curageus,
> Sik ar the pepill at ganys best for ws;
> Our werk desiris na lewyt rebalddaill,
> Full of nobilite is thistory all haill.

> [Young, gentle intellects and courageous breasts,/Such are the people that go best for us;/Our work is not intended for the unlearned common people,/Full of nobility is the whole history.] (I Pro., 321–4)

Douglas was neither 'lewyt' (unlearned) nor one of the 'rebalddaill' (common people). Coldwell (1964) and Bawcutt (1976) give more detailed accounts of the life of this poet, statesman and cleric than is possible here. Briefly, he was born around 1474, the third son of Archibald Bell-the-Cat, fifth Earl of Angus. The two elder sons were killed at the Battle of Flodden in 1513, and the family title passed to Douglas's nephew, also named Archibald, who later married Margaret Tudor, the widow of James IV.

In 1494, there are records of Douglas graduating from the University of St Andrews, where he would have studied grammar, logic, rhetoric, philosophy, arithmetic, geometry, music and astronomy. It is possible that Douglas went from St Andrews to the University of Paris, where he might have studied law, and theology with the Scottish theologian John Major (Coldwell, 1964: 7). Certainly, by 1497, Douglas was back in Scotland, embarking on a career in the Church. He was Provost of St Giles Cathedral by 1503, and there is some evidence that he left Scotland briefly thereafter, possibly living in England and Rome. The early part of the sixteenth century marks the period of Douglas's creative activity, his own poem, *The Palice of Honour* probably being completed by 1501, and the *Eneados* being finished in 1513, the same year as Flodden. The political upheaval caused by the aftermath of Flodden accelerated his ecclesiastical and political career, and effectively ended his career as a poet.

Evidently an ambitious man, Douglas became involved in intrigues to gain the Abbey of Arbroath and the Bishopric of St Andrews, intrigues in which he was aided by his alliance with Margaret Tudor, James IV's English widow. He was denied these prizes, but in 1515 the Bishopric of Dunkeld became vacant, and Margaret sought her brother Henry VIII's support on behalf of Douglas in an appeal to the Pope. Douglas duly became Bishop of Dunkeld, despite opposition from other Scottish factions, particularly the regent Albany. Some of the opposition centred on Douglas's exploitation of his English contacts to curry favour, and Douglas was actually imprisoned in 1515–16 in Edinburgh Castle, then St Andrews Castle, on the charge of treason. However, Albany softened his opposition to Douglas, and released him – even so, Douglas had to take the Cathedral of Dunkeld by force, since it had been occupied and was being held by a rival, Andrew Stewart, son of the Earl of Atholl, who had been elected Bishop by the Chapter of Dunkeld.

In 1516 Albany signed the Treaty of Rouen, which reaffirmed the alliance of France and Scotland against England. Douglas was present at the signing, but, significantly, returned to Scotland through England, under a promise of safe-conduct signed by Cardinal Wolsey. The rest of Douglas's life was lived under the shadow of conflict between the factions ruling Scotland – Margaret Tudor, whose marriage to Douglas's nephew soured; and Albany, who spent much of his time in France. Douglas's English associations were often the cause of public accusation, and probably contributed to his second failure to secure the Bishopric of St Andrews when it fell vacant in 1522. By September of that year Dunkeld too was vacant, Douglas having died, possibly of the plague.

I have dwelt on the career of Scotland's first great literary translator in order to review some familiar truths and ironies. First of all, the *Eneados* is a work of moral and political idealism, written by a man who was personally ambitious, and whose noble birth gave him opportunities to exercise political power and indulge in complex intrigues. It is a work of Scottish nationalism written in a climate of hostility against England – yet it is written by a man whose family ties and personal loyalties linked him to the English royal family and English ecclesiastical influence. It is possible to be cynical about the divergence of Douglas's literary idealism and his pragmatic career; for example, Coldwell (1964: 37–8) judges him harshly:

> His life as a poet ended in 1513, not so much perhaps because his time was filled with activities and occupations, or because he chose to resign poetry to younger emotions, as because his poetic philosophy was deliberately repressed in favour of a career he could not intellectually defend. His *Aeneid* is an affirmation of the political convictions of the Renaissance; the latter half of his life proclaimed the aristocratic right to be selfish and was acquiescent to the advantages of the hour.

We need not necessarily be as judgemental as Coldwell to recognise that Douglas's *Eneados* is a complex work, whose self-proclamation as a mirror for nobles stands awkwardly in relation to the facts of the translator's life. This seeming mismatch between professed ideals and pragmatic action should serve as a salutary caution as we consider in more detail Douglas's comments on translation and the way he put his words into practice.

Douglas's Theory of Translation

It is fair to comment that Douglas's reputation as a translator is greatly enhanced by the simple fact that he added to Virgil's books original prologues, the first of which deals in some detail with the subject of translation, and the difficulty of rendering the 'scharp sugarate sang Virgiliane' into a 'bad harsk spech and lewit barbour tong'. Much of the translator's modesty about his own poor talents and inadequate mother tongue, in comparison with Virgil's genius and the beauty of Latin, is conventional, as is one of the reasons Douglas gives for daring, despite his inadequacies, to embark upon the translation – he had a patron:

> My speciall gud Lord Henry, Lord Sanct Clair
> Quhilk with gret instance diuerss tymys seir
> Prayt me translait Virgill or Homeir
> Quhais plesour suythly as I vndirstude
> As neir coniunct to hys lordschip in blude
> So that me thocht hys request ane command . . .
>
> (I, Pro; 86–91)

> [My special good Lord Henry, Lord Sinclair/Who with great insistence on diverse occasions/Asked me to translate Virgil or Homer/

Whose pleasure truly so I understood,/As nearly conjoined to his lordship in blood,/That I took his request to be a command . . .]

Bawcutt (1976: 92–3) notes that the only departure from the convention of dedicating a literary work to a distinguished patron is in Douglas's presentation of Sinclair as a close kinsman, almost an equal in rank. She argues plausibly that the translation may have originated in a mutual love of books, and a mutual desire to make the Latin classics available to a Scottish readership beyond the learned class of 'clerkis'. Bawcutt also observes that Douglas may have hoped for some reward from his rich kinsman, a hope that would have died with Sinclair on Flodden field.

The less conventional reason for translating Virgil was, however, the existence of an earlier prose translation by William Caxton of a French rendering of the epic. Much of the Prologue to the First Book is taken up with a 'flyting' – a form of poetic insult which is a long-established feature of Scottish poetry from the mediaeval period until the present day – against Caxton and his despised translation:

I red his wark with harmys at my hart,
That syk a buke but sentens or engyne
Suldbe intitillit eftir the poet dyvyne;
His ornate goldyn versis mair than gilt
I spittit for dispyte to se swa spilt
With sych a wyght, quhilk trewly be myne entent
Knew neuer thre wordis at al quhat Virgill ment –
Sa fer he chowpis I am constrenyt to flyte.

(Douglas, *Eneados* I, Prologue, 146–53)

[I read his work, hurt to the quick/That such a book, without meaning or skill/Should be named after the divine poet:/His ornate golden verses, more than gold –/I spat in contempt to see such spilled/By such a fellow, who truly to my mind/Never knew three words at all of what Virgil meant –/As far as he distorts them so I am constrained to flyte.]

Douglas's flyting goes beyond rhetorical convention and strikes a new note in the history of translation into Scots – the idea that a literary translation should be in some way faithful to the source text, that the poet should not alter the original author's text to suit his own ends. Some caution is required here, as Lefevere (1992: 33) notes:

'Fidelity' in translation can . . . be shown to be not just, or even not primarily a matter of matching on the linguistic level. Rather, it involves a complex network of decisions to be made by translators on the level of ideology, poetics, and the Universe of Discourse.

The Universe of Discourse (in other words, the whole system of knowledge, beliefs, expectations and values) evolves and alters over time, and what was considered faithful at one period might not be so considered at another. As noted in Chapter 1, Burnley (1989: 40ff.) argues that most mediaeval translators of literature – up until the end of the fifteenth century – had little interest in 'the textual and linguistic aspects of their work'. He comes to this conclusion through a consideration of the use of the term 'translation' by different mediaeval writers in England, alongside a consideration of the linguistic and cultural milieu of England in the Middle Ages – a milieu which is not dissimilar to that of southern Scotland of the time. Burnley argues that in the multilingual and multicultural environment of mediaeval Britain, writers would not necessarily consider renditions from one language to another as a 'translation' in the modern sense, particularly if the rendition was from French to English. For those involved in law and administration, cross-linguistic interactions involving Latin, French and English would have been an everyday occurrence, possibly something they thought about as monolinguals think about register shifts from formal to informal, or technical to general. This concept of translation and adaptation, then, would have influenced the Universe of Discourse in which Caxton published *Æneydos*, his prose version of Guillame le Roy's French romance. He may have considered himself as broadening the audience for the tale beyond the social sphere which was competent in French (and by the late fifteenth century competence in French had declined, even among the nobility), but he explicitly acknowledged that his version was based on a French adaptation, and would not have thought of his abridgement as an insult to the Latin original. In contrast, as Bawcutt (1976: 80–2) demonstrates, an index of Douglas's concern with his fidelity to Virgil is the frequency with which he returns to the question in his prologues:

The drery fait with terys lamentabill
Of Troys sege wydequhar our all is song,
But followand Virgil, gif my wit war abill
Ane other wys now salt that bell be rong
Than euer was tofor hard in our tong.

(Douglas, *Eneados* II, Prologue, 8–12)

[The dreary fate with lamenting tears/Of Troy's seige far and wide is sung,/Without following Virgil; if my wit is able/Another way now shall that bell be rung/Than ever before was heard in our tongue.]

Douglas, at the beginning of the sixteenth century, constructs his own translation practice in opposition to Caxton's and, by implication, in opposition to the tradition that Caxton represents – for Douglas the Latin text is a hallowed representative of a different and superior culture and it deserves respect. Douglas argues that if he has failed to give sufficient respect to Virgil's sense, then it is because his Scots vernacular is inadequate, not because he wishes, for his own ends, to emphasise one aspect of the story more than another:

Sum tyme I follow the text als neir I may,
Sum tyme I am constrenyt ane other way.
Besyde Latyn our langage is imperfite
Quhilk in sum part is the causs and the wyte
Quhy that of Virgillis verss the ornate bewte
Intill our tung may nocht observit be
For thar be Latyn wordis mony ane
That in our leyd ganand translatioun hass nane ...

[Sometimes I follow the text as closely as I can/Sometimes I am constrained another way./In comparison to Latin our language is imperfect/Which to some extent is the cause and the reason/Why the ornate beauty of Virgil's verse/May not be observed in our tongue/For there are many Latin words/That in our language have no translation ...] (Douglas, *Eneados* I, Prologue, 357–64)

Despite dwelling on the linguistic inadequacies of Scots compared to Latin – an insistence which may again derive as much from conventional modesty as any real anxiety – Douglas is nevertheless aware that a good translation does not follow the source text word for word. He cites 'Sanct Gregor' and Horace (I, pro., 395ff.), both of whose advice is to follow the 'sentence' of the original. Burnley (1989: 52) notes that

> the primary significance of *sentence* in Middle English is of course the 'meaning, import' of a linguistic utterance, whether that utterance be syntactically of word, phrase, text, or indeed of sentence length.

In appealing to classical authority, then, Douglas may be seen as claiming the licence to translate freely. But, as Bawcutt argues (1976: 110–27), a focus on 'sentence' need not conflict with Douglas's claim to follow Virgil rigorously. She demonstrates Douglas's desire to be faithful to Virgil's 'meaning' or 'import' by showing the extent of his reliance on Ascensius's commentary on the *Aeneid* – though it sometimes led him astray, Douglas is concerned, like Ascensius, to clarify the obscurities found in the original, to make it accessible to his wider audience. The translation is also at times a gloss on the source text – as Bawcutt shows in detail, Douglas explains geographical references, clarifies nomenclature, and uses commentaries to elucidate the culturally specific terminology of war and religious beliefs. Bawcutt sees this focus on 'sentence' as a contributor to one of the main features of Douglas's style (1976: 115):

> This explicitness is one of Douglas's most striking characteristics as a translator. Again and again, where Virgil is brief, succinct, or allusive, implying far more than is actually stated, Douglas turns hints or ambiguities into definite statements. This largely though not entirely derives from his concern with making the 'sentence' plain.

A flavour of Douglas's translation practice can be given by comparing a short passage from his version of Book Two with that of a modern translation, by Robert Fitzgerald (1983). The extracts below are from the speech of Synon, or Sinon, the Greek spy left by Ulysses' departing navy, with the task of convincing the Trojans to accept the wooden horse within their city walls. At first the Trojans abuse their Greek prisoner, but on hearing his cries they then take pity on him:

> All molestatioune cessit and lattyn be,
> We hym exort reherss and tobe bald,
> Of quhat lynnage he was and quhat he wald,
> And to remembir gude hope of ferm supple
> Happynnys oft to personeris in captiuite.
> He at the last this fenȝeit dreid dyd away
> And on this wyss onone begouth to say:
> 'Forsuyth, Schir Kyng, I sall quhat euer betyde
> Grant to the all the verite and nocht hyde,
> Nor be na ways, me lyst nocht to deny
> That of the Grekis menȝe ane am I.
>
> Thys principaly I wald thou vndyrstude:
> Thocht frawart fortoun miserabill and bayr of gude
> Hass maid Synon, sche sal nocht mak hym als,
> Quhat euer he says, nowder lear nor fals.'
>
> (Douglas, *Eneados* II, 28–42)

The whimpering speech brought us up short; we felt
A twinge for him. Let him speak up, we said,
Tell us where he was born, what news he brought,
What he could hope for as a prisoner.
Taking his time, slow to discard his fright,
He said:
'I'll tell you the whole truth, my lord,
No matter what may come of it. Argive
I am by birth, and will not say I'm not.
That first of all: Fortune has made a derelict
Of Sinon, but the bitch
Won't make an empty liar of him, too.'

(Fitzgerald, *Aeneid* II, 100–11)

These two translations are obviously different in several respects – a difference which only in part can be traced to Douglas's use of a different version of Virgil from Fitzgerald. As Coldwell wryly remarks (1964: 55), 'we assume, falsely, that sixteenth century translators used the Loeb Classics'. Bawcutt takes up this point, and notes that 'Douglas, when he diverges from the text of a modern edition of the *Aeneid*, is often translating readings that had scholarly acceptance in the sixteenth century' (1976: 96). Thus, Coldwell's notes to the extract given above (1964: 159) demonstrate Douglas's debt to his main commentators, Ascensius and Servius. For example, where Douglas exhorts Synon 'to be bald' (l. 29), he is following Ascensius's 'damus animum', which has no authority in Virgil. The form of address 'Schir Kyng' is consistent with the address 'O rex' found in Ascensius elswhere in his commentary. The main divergence between Douglas and Fitzgerald comes at the beginning of the extracts: in Douglas, the Trojans command Synon to *remember* that prisoners can often expect hope of succour ('ferm supple'); in Fitzgerald, they command him to *tell* what he could hope for as a prisoner. Again the divergence does not originate with Douglas; he is following Servius's 'memineret [remember] in captivo veriloquium fiduciam esse vitae' rather than Virgil's 'memoret [tell], quae sit fiducia capto'.

Given the state of sixteenth-century textual scholarship, then, Douglas does make a sincere attempt to be true to the 'sentens', or the intention, of Virgil, and to that extent, to make a faithful translation. Both Douglas's and Fitzgerald's versions however, are inevitably products of their own time and culture, and the target language of each rendition carries resonances that fix them to their own particular periods. The Fitzgerald translation carries associations of twentieth-century legal formulae in its 'I'll tell you the whole truth, my lord'. Douglas's phrase, 'I sal ... Grant to the all the verite', conveys a similar sense of moral outrage without necessarily conjuring a specific legal process. The cultural specificity of each translation is most interesting in the treatment of the idea of fortune. In the context of post-feminist America, Fitzgerald's politically incorrect description of fortune as a 'bitch' is possibly intended to cause his readers to lose any sympathy for Synon, who represents, after all, the epitome of Greek deceit. No such signal of Synon's untrustworthiness is necessary in Douglas's translation: the sinfulness of the very act of maligning 'frawart fortoun, miserabill and bayr of gude' is a clue to Synon's character. A recurring motif in Scottish poetry of the period is the often terrible punishments which befall those who bewail their fortune, and, by doing so, call into question divine providence. There are many vivid illustrations of this: in Robert Henryson's 'The Testament of Cresseid', the heroine is afflicted with leprosy, and forced outside society. She bewails her cruel fate until a chance encounter with the lover she previously abandoned forces her to accept responsibility for her own actions. In a more comic vein, in Dunbar's 'The Fenȝeit Freir Of Tungland', the alchemist John Damien takes to the air on home-made wings and is attacked by birds. Lamenting the fickleness of fate, he suffers a literal and spiritual fall. Under the circumstances, then, the narrator of 'The Kingis Quair' is lucky to escape with an upwards tug on the ear when he questions his temporary descent on fortune's wheel. One of the grand themes which presumably attracted Douglas to Virgil's *Aeneid* was that of the good king accepting the divine plans of the gods, even when they conflicted with his personal desires and ambitions – as Ogilvie (1980: 125) writes of Virgil's hero:

> He may still be a creature of emotion – indeed the epic ends with his succumbing to primitive passions of violence and killing his rival Turnus – but he accepts his role as the destined leader (*fatalis dux*) in a divinely-planned enterprise. As he had said earlier, 'it is not of my will that I make for Italy', but now, whatever his misgivings, he carries out his mission with resolution. In other words, he is a man conscious of a religious vocation.

Like all the other Scottish poets of his day, schooled by Boethius' *De Consolatione Philosophiae* to combine Roman stoicism with a Christian concept of providence, Douglas does not have to labour Synon's blasphemy when he denounces fortune as 'bayr of gude' (i.e. 'devoid of goodness'). His readers would have identified it straight away and drawn the appropriate conclusions. The point may be a small one, but it again illustrates the way in which certain key concepts – here the role of fate in our lives – evolve over periods of time and in different places, from Augustan Rome, to sixteenth-century Scotland, to present-day America, and how changes in attitude to such concepts – changes in the Universe of Discourse – affect our readings of texts and their translations. A truly faithful translation is, after all, impossible: one would not only have to render the source text accurately, one would also have to recreate the context of the source text, and convey the implicit assumptions and world-view of the original readers. Douglas knows his limitations and he pushes the notion of fidelity as far as he practically can:

> God wait in Virgill ar termys mony a hundir
> Fortill expone maid me a felloun blundir.
> To follow alanerly Virgillis wordis I weyn,
> Thair suld few vndirstand me quhat thai meyn.
>
> [God knows, in Virgil there are many hundreds of terms/Which to explain would make me a great fool./If I followed only Virgil's words, I know,/Only a few should understand what they mean.] (I, Pro., 389–92)

In the final account, Douglas's comments on the goals of translation might be too pragmatic to be graced with the term 'theory' – he aims to be faithful to his master's sense, clarify his obscurities, and render an epic from another culture comprehesible to his own in a manner that is both entertaining and educational. Even given the modesty of his aims, he achieves them with spectacular success, and in doing so becomes Virgil's first 'translator', in the modern sense, in either English or Scots.

The Language of the Scottish Nation

If Douglas's translation of the *Aeneid* is marked by a new self-consciousness about the responsibilities of the translator to the source text, then it is also remarkable for the translator's view of the medium of translation. It is often noted that Douglas was one of the earliest writers to name his mother tongue as 'Scottis' rather than the conventional term, 'Inglis'. This insistence on the Scottishness of the translation can only be partly explained by Douglas's antipathy to the 'buke of Inglys gros' published by 'William Caxton, of Inglish natioun', and his wish to distance his own translation from the earlier travesty. The desire to insist on the Scottishness of the work can be better explained as linguistic patriotism – *Eneados* is one of the first documents in which the medium of Scots is used as a symbol of nationhood:

> Quhat so it be, this buke I dedicait,
> Writtin in the langage of Scottis natioun.
>
> (I, Pro., 102–3)
>
> [Whatever it is, I dedicate this book,/Written in the language of the Scottish nation.]

Just how unusual this identification of Scots with Scotland was at the time can easily be illustrated by comparing Douglas's First Prologue with the *Flyting* of his two near contemporaries, William Dunbar and Gavin Kennedy. A 'flyting' in Scots is a poem which consists mainly in the exchange of vituperative insults between rivals – as Douglas flytes against Caxton in the First Prologue. In Dunbar and Kennedy's flyting, the mother tongue of each poet is taken as a cue for insult by the other: Dunbar derides Kennedy's native Gaelic as barbarous, while Kennedy responds by upholding his own 'Irish' (i.e. Scots Gaelic) as 'all trew Scottis mennis leid' (all true Scotsmen's language), and identifying Dunbar's 'treacherous' tongue with the English incomers who arrived at the invitation of King David in the twelfth century. As noted in Chapter 1, Dunbar himself seemed to make no distinction between his own language and the language of Chaucer, which he conventionally reveres as a model of vernacular poetry, 'oure Inglisch'. Douglas, too, pays ritual obeisance to 'venerabill Chauser, principal poet but peir' (venerable Chaucer, principal poet without peer) while nevertheless criticising the southern poet's translation practice (I, Pro., 339–46). The difference between Douglas and Dunbar is that while the former also positions himself within a Chaucerian tradition of vernacular poetry, he nevertheless recognises that the differences in the vernacular varieties employed in the north and south are capable of marking a national distinction. In this perception, Douglas does seem to depart from the consensus of his time, as McClure (1981) observes. McClure speculates that Douglas's perception of the difference between Scots and English was in part a result of his travels in England, where he would have been struck by the strong divergence in pronunciation that would have made the speech of the English and Scots much less similar than the written form would suggest.

Possibly another factor in Douglas's emphasis on his Scottish medium is the desire to reach as wide a Scottish audience as possible – to render Virgil in language 'braid and playne' (broad and plain) –

Kepand na sudroun bot our awyn language
And spekis as I lernyt quhen I was page.

(I, Pro., 111–12)

[Keeping no southern, but our own language/And speak as I learned when I was a page.]

This desire to translate prestigious literature into 'plain' language links into Renaissance debates in England on the relative merits of 'pure', native vocabulary versus 'inkhorn' or learned terms of foreign origin (cf. Hermans, 1985), and it also corresponds to the evolution of a plain prose style in Reformed Scotland to render the word of God in unadorned language (cf. Lyall, 1988). It also prefigures the much later wish to give voice to 'our awyn language', the language of the people.

Even so, before we become seduced by the concept of an essentially Scottish democratic intellect, it is well to remind ourselves that Douglas's primary audience was the Scottish aristocracy, and that the translator, personally and politically, had considerable sympathy with the English secular and ecclesiastical hierarchy. Douglas's motives for translating are laudable, but they should not be viewed simplistically as manifestations of a Scottish patriot's desire to make a Latin classic accessible to his countrymen, great and lowly. There may be a germ of truth in this, but the reality is more complex, as Douglas himself is quick to point out:

Nor ȝit sa cleyn all sudroun I refuss
Bot sum word I pronunce as nyghtbouris doys:
Lyke as in Latyn beyn Grew termys sum,
So me behufyt quhilum or than be dum
Sum bastard Latyn, French or Inglys oyss
Quhar scant was Scottis – I had nane other choys.

(I, pro., 113–18)

[Nor yet do I completely refuse all southern language,/But some words I pronounce as my neighbours do:/As there are in Latin some Greek terms,/So I was required, rather than be dumb,/To use some bastard Latin, French or English/Where Scots was scarce – I had no other choice.]

At face value, this passage is a recognition that the medium of Scots is by itself inadequate to the task of translating Virgil, and an admission that the translator will plunder the resources of Latin, French and – again, significantly viewed as a foreign language – English. The justification for borrowing rests on the claim that not even Latin is a 'pure' language. Underlying the passage, however, is the complex situation that Douglas, like his noble contemporaries, had some degree of access to two closely related language varieties: Scots and English. Owing to the historical influence of the Norman aristocracy and of the Catholic Church, both of these varieties were themselves strongly influenced by French and Latin. It would simply have been impossible for Douglas to restrict himself to 'Scottis' in a linguistic environment where there was not yet a fully developed standard language, either in England or Scotland. The concept of a 'standard' language is a relatively modern one – I use it here to mean a variety of language whose spelling, vocabulary and grammar has been codified by dictionaries and other reference books, which has been widely accepted by society as the 'natural' form of written discourse in formal and public situations, and which is disseminated as such through a mass education system. In these terms, English did not acquire a full standard variety until the eighteenth century, and while there have been various attempts to standardise Scots, no comparable written variety has been widely accepted and taught in schools. In an environment where a degree of linguistic variation was tolerated and indeed expected, Douglas recognised that those features which were unique to his own country's vernacular nevertheless enabled it to do service as the language of a nation, even while he realised that this northern variety could embrace elements of the cognate southern variety. While Scotland retained political sovereignty, there was no widespread sense that the Scots needed to mark their cultural individuality through their language behaviour – and neither for Douglas, who bucked this trend, was there a strong sense that he should spurn the use of anglicisms. For Scots translators, this situation, of course, was later to change (see Chapter 7).

What characteristics of Scots, then, might Douglas have noticed as distinguishing his own speech from that of his southern neighbours, and what features of 'bastard English' did he bring into his translation of Virgil? We have little direct evidence of what features of their written language Douglas and his contemporaries would have regarded as markedly Scots. However, the stylistic strategies of the Scots makars do provide indirect evidence of what they regarded as native speech and the literary uses for which it was regarded as appropriate. William Dunbar commanded the widest range of the Scots stylists, at one extreme writing poetry of religious and courtly celebration in a Scots impregnated with Latinisms and occasional anglicisms, and at the other extreme writing bawdy comic narratives in a language marked by northern features – namely, vocabulary with its roots in

Old Norse and in Gaelic. The narrative style of the *Eneados* shows little evidence of the marked shifts from courtly to bawdy styles that distinguish, for example, Dunbar's 'The Tretis of the Twa Mariit Wemen and the Wedo'. Prologues apart, the *Eneados* owes more to the tradition of Scots romances which goes back to the fourteenth century *Brus* by John Barbour: occasional latinisms raise the tone, a French flavouring links classical heroism to the chivalric code, and anglicisms are liberally employed to accommodate metre and rhyme. Take, for example, the description in the Fourth Book of Dido going hunting with her Carthaginian nobles:

> Nobillys of Cartage, hovand at the port
> The queyn awatys that lang in chawmyr dwellys;
> Hyr ferss steyd stude stampyng, reddy ellys,
> Rungeand the fomy goldyn byt gynglyng;
> Of gold and pal wrocht hys rych harnasyng.
> And scho at last of palyce yschit owt,
> With huge menȝe walking hir abowt,
> Lappyt in a brusyt mantill of Sydony
> With gold and perle the bordour al bewry,
> Hyngand by hir syde the cayss with arowis grund;
> Hir bricht tressis envolupyt war and wond
> Intil a quhayf of fyne gold wyrin threid;
> The goldyn button claspyt hir purpour weid –
> And furth scho passyt with all hir cumpany.
>
> (IV, chap. iiii, 8–21)

> [Nobles of Carthage, heaving at the gateway,/Await the queen who dwells long in her chamber,/Her fierce steed stood stamping at the ready,/Gnawing the foamy, jingling, golden bit;/His rich harnessing is wrought of gold and opal./And she at last emerged from the palace,/With a huge company walking around her,/ Wrapped in an embroidered cloak of Sidon/With the border all surrounded in gold and pearl,/The quiverfull of arrows hanging by her side;/Her bright tresses were enveloped and wound/Into a coif of fine gold wiry threads;/And golden buttons clasped her purple clothes –/And she passed forth with all her company.]

This is as close to a courtly style as Douglas gets in the narratives in the *Eneados,* although, as Bawcutt (1976: 193–4) notes, Douglas favours 'learned, semi-scientific language' in stretches of the Prologues, and also in his shorter poem, 'The Palice of Honour'. It is this decorative, aureate quality of poems which tends to be praised when one poet of the period praises another; for example, when Douglas or Dunbar praises Chaucer, 'rois of rhetoris all', or indeed when Sir David Lindsay praises Douglas for his use of 'Inglis rhetorick' (which for him is presumably synonymous with 'Scottis rhetorick'):

> Allace for one, quhilk lampe wes of this land,
> Off Eloquence the flowand balmy strand,
> And, in our Inglis rhetorick, the rose,
> As of Rubeis the Charbuncle bene chose:
> And as Phebus dois Synthia presell,
> So Gawane Dowglas, Byshope of Dunkell,
>
> Had, quhen he wes in to this land on lyue,
> Abufe vulgare Poetis prerogatyue
> Boith in pratick and speculatioun ...
> (David Lindsay, 'The Testament of the Papyngo', 22ff.; quoted in Bawcutt, 1976: 193–4)

> [Alas for one, who was the lamp of this land,/Of Eloquence the flowing, balmy stream,/And, in our Inglis rhetoric, the rose,/As the carbuncle is the choice of rubies:/And as Phebus outshines Cynthia,/So Gavin Douglas, Bishop of Dunkeld,//Had, when he was alive in this land,/Precedence over vernacular poets,/Both in practice and in theory ...]

There are elements of this prized eloquent, courtly style in the hunt scene in Book Four of the *Eneados*. The emphasis on precious stones and colours – gold, opal and purple – is complemented by a vocabulary that is substantially derived from romance sources: 'port', 'chawmyr', 'ferss', 'pal' ('opal'), 'rych', 'harnasyng', 'palyce', 'yschit', 'menȝe' ('company'), 'brusit' ('embroidered', from Medieval Latin 'brusdus'), 'mantill', 'perle', 'bordour', 'cayss', 'tressis', 'envolupyt', 'quayf' (coif), 'fyne', 'button', 'purpour', 'passyt' and 'cumpany'. Of course, many of these romance items would have been well-established both in Scots and Middle English – 'port', for example, entered the languages in their Old English phase – and most have their equivalents in present-day English. Here Douglas does not employ elaborate latinate neologisms to the extent that, say, he and Dunbar do in their more rhetorical passages; nevertheless, Douglas's romance terminology here functions to raise the tone of a passage that describes the riches of the queen as she pursues an archetypically aristocratic activity.

The romance terms are studded into a passage whose remaining terms are largely shared by both Scots and English – though the Scots pronunciations may diverge from the 'suddron': 'hovand', 'dwellys', 'steyd', rungeand', 'fomy', 'goldyn', 'byt', 'gynglyng', 'wrocht', 'lappyt', 'bewry' ('surrounded'), 'hyngand', 'arowis', 'grund', 'wond', 'threid', 'weid', and 'claspyt'. None of these terms is distinctively northern in itself. However, the morphology of some of the terms, and the grammatical items in the passage have more of a distinctively Scottish flavour.

From the Prologue to the First Book, we know that Douglas was sensitive to the differences between Scottish and southern English forms and pronunciations. Distinctively northern features in the passage quoted above are the participial inflexions '-and' in the verbs 'hovand' ('heaving'), 'rungeand' ('gnawing'), and 'hyngand' ('hanging'). In Scots these contrast with the nominal inflexion '-ing/-yng', here found in 'harnysyng' and the attributive 'gynglyng' ('jingling (bit)'). There is, however, evidence of the move towards the southern form in the inflexion of 'walking' – here used as a verb but with the nominal inflexion, '-ing'. Other northern features include the use of 'scho' rather than 'she', the '-it/-yt' inflexions which mark the past tense of the verb ('yschit', lappyt', 'envolupyt', 'claspyt' and 'passyt'), and the subject-verb concord that allows a 'singular' verb to follow a 'plural' subject: 'Nobillys of Cartage ... awatys ...'.

Even so, these features are probably most accurately described as 'northern' rather than 'Scottish' because they can usually be found in northern Middle English texts as well as in Scottish ones. Indeed, in present-day English, most people pronounce the past tense of many of the verbs listed ('enveloped', 'clasped', 'passed') with a /t/ inflexion, although the English spelling is '-ed'. Older Scots, however, also had an '-it' spelling (pronounced /ɪt/ or /t/) where, in present-day English, the pronunciation (either /ɪd/ or /d/) corresponds to the '-ed' spelling. For example, in the passage quoted above, we find 'forgaderit' ('foregathered'), and 'payntit' ('painted'). Both Scots and English, of course, share the basic principle that the regular past tense is realised by an inflexion which ends in a similar type of consonant, namely an alveolar or dental plosive, either voiced or unvoiced. That Douglas describes his language as 'Scots', then, is more a political or nationalistic assertion than a claim justified on purely linguistic grounds. Nevertheless, it is true that, given the rising influence of southern English in England, many of the features of the northern English variety, for example the distinction between the nominal and verbal forms of the present participle, were receding towards the Scotland-England border, a process which continues to the present day (cf. Glauser, 1974; Smith, 1996). Furthermore, the legitimacy given to the northern variety by its use in Scotland for public as well as domestic discourse, lends weight to Douglas's appropriation of it as a national language.

To summarise, then, Douglas's Scots was a language variety that shared many characteristics with southern English, and which was in many respects very closely related indeed to northern Middle English. Both northern and southern varieties had their roots in dialects of Old English, but the northern variety was more coloured by Norse borrowings. Both varieties looked to French and Latin for prestigious borrowings. For these reasons many of Douglas's contemporaries and successors continued to identify their 'vulgar tongue' with Chaucer's 'Inglis'. Certain features, nevertheless, made the northern variety distinctive, and the political autonomy of Scotland gave this distinctive variety an institutional status which it did not have in the north of England. Douglas was one of the first to recognise the power of Scots to mark political and national difference, and his translation, despite its self-deprecatory tone when it compares its 'corruppit cadens imperfyte' with Latin, 'the maste perfite langage fyne', is nevertheless a major attempt to establish a distinctive identity for Scots by demonstrating its ability to give a superior and more accurate rendering of Virgil than was done by Caxton's 'Inglis gros'. And despite his protestation that he lacks the 'fowth [abundance] of langage' to translate Virgil faithfully, the longstanding success of his translation pays tribute to the continuing power of the Middle Scots poets and their chosen medium.

The Influence of Douglas's *Eneados*

Although Douglas's *Eneados* continues to be read, and although it can be seen as a pioneering work, its immediate influence is, ironically, more evident in England than in Scotland. Perhaps the timing was wrong: the translation was completed just as Douglas's patron, Lord Sinclair, and his king marched off to military disaster at Flodden. The relatively peaceful climate that had led to the flowering of Scots poetry came to an abrupt end. Douglas himself became embroiled in the factional rivalry that accompanied rule by a minor, and in the background the turmoil of the reformation was brewing. Edwin Morgan (1976: 197) writes:

> He [Douglas] extends the range of Scots, and his translation ought to have been one more landmark in the development of a Scottish language. That it was not such a landmark, that it came at the end

> of a phase of Scottish cultural growth rather than the beginning was hardly Douglas's fault. The national or patriotic implications of what Douglas had achieved (despite his being in his own life a renegade from Scotland who died in exile – never trust the teller, trust the tale!) had to wait until the eighteenth century revival, and Thomas Ruddiman's edition of 1710.

Bawcutt, too, observes that the immediate influence of the *Eneados* was slight, despite the apparent popularity of the poem, judged by the number of extant manuscripts and publications in the sixteenth century:

> The *Eneados*, unlike the *Palice of Honour*, does not seem to have been imitated by the Scottish poets. Yet there are signs that it was read attentively by those who possessed copies, or by the scribes themselves. Marginal comments on some of the manuscripts ... indicate that the *Eneados* was a living work for a generation or two after Douglas wrote it, and that it sometimes evoked a response similar to that aroused by the *Aeneid* itself. (Bawcutt 1976: 196)

The marginal comments suggest that Douglas's translation was seen as a source of rhetorical figures, and that the work was indeed seen as giving moral guidance to princes. However, Douglas did not found a school of Scots translators in the sixteenth century – as we shall see, his influence is much more profound in the twentieth century. There is some evidence of indirect influence: Bawcutt (1976: 198ff.) discusses the debts that the English poets Surrey and Sackville owed to Douglas's *Eneados*, and she speculates that:

> It may perhaps have been used side by side with the text of Virgil, fulfilling a function similar to the Loeb editions of the classics today. For more than half a century Douglas's *Eneados* was the only complete translation available to English readers as well as to Scottish. (Bawcutt, 1976: 200)

This was the case until Thomas Phaer and Thomas Twyne translated the entire *Aeneid* between 1558 and 1573 – this version supplanted Douglas's in the seventeenth century, and the Scottish translation languished until Thomas Ruddiman's edition of 1710, printed in Edinburgh, and heralding a revival in writing in Scots.

There were further Scots translations in the sixteenth century. The most prominent in the reign of James V was John Bellenden (*c.* 1495–*c.* 1547), who translated into Scots prose the *Scotorum Historia*, compiled by Hector Boece, and published in Paris in 1527. Royan (1998) compares Boece's Latin text with Bellenden's 'creative translation', and concludes that the vernacular *Chronicles of Scotland* at times represents a deliberate refashioning of the source text. Bellenden's translation of the *Chronicles* was completed four years after Boece's Latin version, and this was followed two years later, in 1533, by a translation of the first five books of Livy's history of Rome. A poet as well as a prose translator, Bellenden might have been influenced, if indirectly, by recent Scots vernacular poetry and in particular by the success of Douglas's verse translation of Virgil. Certainly he created what Rod Lyall calls 'a new kind of courtly prose ... which is more self-consciously Latinate than anything [John] Ireland produced' (Lyall, 1988: 173). Bawcutt speculates that the young John Bellenden may have known Douglas personally, and his prologue to the translation of Boece's *Chronicles* is indebted to Douglas's 'Palice of Honour' (Bawcutt, 1976: 194–5).

Unlike Douglas, however, Bellenden does not use the prefaces to his translations as meditations upon the nature of translation, nor upon the nature of his linguistic medium. The preface to the *Chronicles* is directed personally to his patron, James V, and is largely taken up with a defence of the reading of history. Like Douglas's translation, Bellenden's has an educational value – the past is reconstructed to give the young king models of good and bad rule, and to warn him against 'auaricious pepill and vayn flattoraris' (avaricious people and vain flatterers). There is an element of entertainment, however, for 'Quhat is he that will nocht reioiss to heyre the marciall factis of thai forsy campionys, King Robert Bruys and Williame Wallais?' (What is he who will not rejoice to hear the martial facts of those doughty champions, King Robert the Bruce and William Wallace?). The primary motive for this volume is nevertheless to instil into the King a sense of his history, and through this a sense of nationhood. He who has no sense of history, according to the *Chronicles*, is dangerously innocent:

> Thairfor sayid Marcus Cicero, 'He that is ignorant of sik thingis as bene done afoir his tyme, for lak of experience, is bot ane barn.' For thir reassonis, maist nobill Prince, I, that bene þi native and humyll servitour sen thi first infance, be impulsioun of luff and vehement affeccioun quhilk I bere vnto the samyn has translatit 'The History of Scotland' sen þe first begynning þerof in wlgair langage; and þocht the charge was importabill throw tedious laboure and feire of this huge volume, quhilk has impeschitt my febill ingyne, havand na crafty witt nor pregnant eloquence to

decoir the samyn, ȝite I am constranit for schort tyme to bring this my translacioun to licht, nakit of perfeccioun and rethory, siklike as implvme birdis to flicht.

[Thus said Marcus Cicero, 'He who is ignorant of such things as were done before his time, for lack of experience, is but a child.' For these reasons, most noble Prince, I, who was your native and humble servant since your early childhood, by the impulse of love and vehement affection which I bear for the same, have translated 'The History of Scotland' since the first beginning thereof in vernacular language; and though the command was achievable through tedious labour and fear of this huge volume, which has hindered my feeble ingenuity, having no crafty wit nor pregnant eloquence to decorate the same, yet I am required for a short time to bring this my translation to light, naked of perfection and rhetoric, like unfeathered birds [are brought] to flight.]

The protestations of inadequacy echo Douglas's, and like Douglas they are conventional and not supported by the work itself, which still reads well. It is interesting to note that the protest still focuses on the question of 'rhetory' – concern for the narrative skills for which we value the *Eneados*, the *Chronicles* or even *The Canterbury Tales* is absent from the criticism of the Middle Scots writers. Yet it is the narrative skills which present readers most admire in the older writers, as in the passage below in which the Roman conquest of Albion is blamed on the Britons' arrogant refusal of help from the Scots:

The nixt ȝere following King Edere past to Inuernes, quhair he be merchandis of France was aduerteist that Iulius had pacifijt France to his impyre, and was providing ane new army to return in Britan, to revenge the inuiris done to him in the ȝere afoir. Edeir, hering thir tythingis, send his ambassiadouris to Cassibillane, to schew þe hye dangeris apperand to his realme, and promittit x^{m} chosin men to support him, as he did afoir. Thir ambassiadouris cumin to Lundoun, schew thir offeris to Cassilbane. Nochþeless, the Britonis, movit be vayn arrogance, that the gloir of victory suld nocht be takin fra þame, refusit to haif supple of Scottis or Pichtis, and ansuerit, þai war nocht brocht to sik febilnes, to haif support of nychtbouris all tymez quhen inimeis list invaid thame, and thairfor had the samyn pussance that ȝere as þai had afoir, quhen thai dantit the Romanis. Edeir and his nobillis had na litill admiracioun of the arrogance of Britonis refusing his support aganis the Romanis, dantaris of the warld,

> and iugit þerfor the nobill realme of Britan, be pryde of ane small victory, to sustene sum tyme grete displesour; quhilk was wele sene in þe end of thir weeris. For Iulius within schort tyme returnyt in thir landis; at quhais cuming the pepill quhilk war left to resist him, effrayit be infinit multitude of schippis, fled awaye. (Book Three, chap. iii)
>
> [The following year, King Edeir travelled to Inverness, where he was notified by French merchants that Julius had taken France into his empire and was providing a new army to return to Britain, to revenge the injuries done to him the year before. Edeir, hearing this news, sent his ambassadors to Castlebane, to show the great dangers appearing to his realm, and promised ten thousand chosen men to support him, as he did before. These ambassadors, having come to London, showed their offer to Castlebane. However, the Britons, moved by vain arrogance, so that the glory of victory should not be taken from them, refused to accept help from the Scots and Picts, and answered that they had not been brought to such weakness that they required support from their neighbours every time their enemies invaded them, and therefore, they had the same strength that they had previously, when they defeated the Romans. Edeir and his companions had little admiration for the arrogance of the Britons in refusing his support against the Romans, conquerors of the world, and judged therefore that the noble realm of Britain, by its pride in a small victory, would sometime suffer a great upset; which was well seen in the conclusion of these wars. For Julius within a short time returned to these lands; at whose arrival the people who were left to resist him, frightened by the infinite multitude of ships, fled away.]

The influence of Latin is evident in the romance vocabulary chosen here ('aduerteist', pacifijt', 'impyre', 'iniuris', 'arrogance', 'admiracioun', 'sustene', etc.), and echoes of Latin syntax can be heard in some of the constructions here: as Lyall (1988: 173) points out, Bellenden is fond of rendering a Latin ablative with a Scots past participle, as in 'Thir ambassiadouris *cumin to Lundoun* schew thir offeris to Cassibillane.' Still, the prose is clear and serviceable, and occasionally a felicitous Scots expression pleases the ear, as when the Romans are described as 'dantaris of the warld'.

Hector Boece, the Scots author of the Latin version of the *Chronicles* was an imitator of Cicero and Livy (Lyall, 1988: 173), and it is understandable therefore that Boece's translator was also attracted to Livy's history of Rome. Bellenden completed the first five books of Livy's history in 1533, and again the prologue and preface of the work are addressed to his patron, James V. The preface once more justifies the reading of history, even ancient history, for the moral lessons it offers. At the beginning of the preface there is a suggestion that Bellenden, like Douglas, is prompted to translate by the presence of inadequate renderings of the Latin authors:

> I wate nocht gif I war to do ane profitabill werk, gif I wrate þe dedis of romanis sen the first begynnyng of rome; peraventure I dar nocht write þe samyn þocht I could. And ȝit I se þare werkis of lang begynnyng and richt divulgate to þe pepill, sen new authoris belevis Ilk day owthir to write þe said history with mair faith and sikkernes, or ellis be þare crafty eloquence traistis to vincuss the rude langage of anciant authoris. (I, Pro.)
>
> [I do not know if I would do profitable work, if I wrote about the deeds of the Romans since the first beginnings of Rome; perhaps I dare not write the same, though I could. And yet I see their works of long beginning and right made known to the people, since new authors believe every day either to write the said history with more faith and certainty, or else by their skillful eloquence trust to vanquish the rude language of the ancient authors.]

Amidst the convoluted syntax here, we can again discern Bellenden's conventionally modest stance combined with what appears to be an ironic swipe at the 'new authors' who pop up each day, with exaggerated claims to translate the ancient works faithfully and to conquer the 'rude langage' in which they are couched. Either the reverence with which Douglas viewed Latin had been greatly diminished by Bellenden's time, or Bellenden is sarcastically belittling 'sic pluralite of writaris' by exposing their views of Latin. Perhaps, after all, the possibilities are not incompatible – Douglas was unusual in that his high esteem for Latin was made manifest in his attempt to be faithful to his source text; the translators mentioned by Bellenden might not have had such scruples. It is interesting that Bellenden does not attempt explicitly to correct the impression of Latin as a 'rude language'; his reasons for translating Livy lie in the prestige of the Roman authors and in the fact that their works have achieved lasting fame – a fame with which he wishes to be associated. Yet there is a definite note of irony in Bellenden's off-hand description of the ten-a-penny translators and the arrogance of their faith in their 'crafty eloquence', particularly when here and in his translation of Boece he stresses the 'tedious laboure' which he invests in his own renderings.

It is this scrupulousness which links Bellenden to Douglas, and which distinguishes them both from most other translators of the period.

Bellenden, then, was not primarily a literary translator, although his translations have some literary qualities; and in his prose he sought principally to achieve moral instruction rather than aesthetic gratification. In this he differs from Douglas before him, and the Scots literary translators who followed him. Even so, his translations do seem to owe a debt of inspiration to Gavin Douglas, and in his material debt to his patron, James V, Bellenden foreshadows the relationship between the courtly band of writers and translators, and James VI, their patron, guide and fellow practitioner. But before James VI and the court poets were to renew a nationalistic programme of literary translation, a social revolution was to sweep the nation: the Reformation. With the reformation of the kirk in Scotland, an urgent demand was created for the translation into Scots of religious works – mainly, of course, the Bible. That this demand was not wholly satisfied changed the course of the nation's language.

Chapter 4
'Of Translations and Chaunges'

> [God] made my tong a trumpet, to forewarne realmes and nations, yea, certaine great personages, of translations and chaunges, when no such thinges were feared, nor yet was appearing. (D. Laing (ed.) *The Works of John Knox*, Edinburgh, 1846–64; Vol. IV: 229)

Translation and Reformation

John Knox's self-proclaimed prophecy, quoted above, exaggerates the extent to which the demand for some form of religious reformation went unheeded in Scotland, in the period before his conversion from Catholicism to the Lutheran cause in 1544. The abuses to 'John Commonweal' at the hands of both the kirk and nobility had been dramatically detailed at length by Sir David Lindsay in *Ane Satyre of the Thrie Estaitis*, an early version of which was probably performed in 1540. In this play, one character, Gude Counsel, a spiritual heir to moral guides such as Amytans in *Lancelot of the Laik*, seeks to advise King Humanity, and to expose the false clergy as vices and flatterers. He fails, and the fall of the nation into moral decay is only halted by the arrival of the reformist Divine Correctioun. A performance in Linlithgow Palace before James V led directly to the king chastising his bishops and threatening to send them 'unto his uncle of england', Henry VIII, to learn first-hand of Reformation there (Carpenter, 1988: 205). In the reformist enthusiams of the age, the act of translation took on a new moral imperative: where before translation had enabled literate lowland Scots to gain access to the letter of the law and to continental and classical literature, now it gave them a direct route to the very word of God. Lindsay recognised this moral imperative in passing references to William Tyndale's English translation of the

New Testament, completed in Cologne in 1526, both in *Ane Satyre of the Thrie Estaitis*, and also in his later poem *The Monarchie* (1554):

> Bot lat us haif the Bukis necessare
> To Commoun weill and our Salvatioun
> Justlye translatit in our toung Vulgare.
>
> (ll. 678–80)

> [But let us have the books necessary/To our common good and our salvation,/Justly translated into our vernacular tongue.]

As Wright (1988) demonstrates, the demand for a Scots translation of scripture is evident from well before the Reformation settlement of 1560. As early as 1533 Alexander Alesius, an exiled Lutheran, wrote a letter of protest to James V, in Latin, protesting the right of the people to hear the word of God in their mother tongue; and, in 1543, the Scottish Parliament passed an Act briefly making it, in the words of John Knox, 'free to all man and woman to reid the Scriptures in thair awin toung, or in the Engliss toung' (Laing (ed.) Vol. 1: 100; quoted in Wright 1988: 167). However, Wright also observes that

> the Bible's role in the Reformation in Scotland is in some ways a paradoxical one. The most forceful Scottish champion of free access to the vernacular Bible [i.e. Alesius] himself wrote nothing in English, let alone Scots. The Scottish Reformers relied on English translations, and made no attempt to provide a Scots version. Nor did they succeed in having an English Bible (or New Testament) produced in Scotland until 1579, in a reprinting of the Geneva Bible with not the slightest attempt at adaptation in vocabulary or spelling for a Scottish readership. (Wright, 1988: 155)

Although no Scots translation of the Bible was produced in Scotland, there was one substantial scotticised version printed outwith the country but obviously intended for a readership within Scotland: Murdoch Nisbet's New Testament (*c.* 1520–34?).

Nisbet was what was termed at the time a 'lollard'. In Sir Gilbert Hay's translation of *The Buke of the Law of Armys*, he occasionally extends the term 'heresy' in the source text to include 'lollardy' – 'And rycht as evill bitter wateris gerris mony folk dee temporaly, sa dois the bitter heresy and lollardy the saule dee spiritualy' [And just as evil bitter waters make many folk die temporally, so does bitter heresy and lollardy make the soul die spiritually.] (Book I, chap. vii; Stevenson (ed.) 1901: 20, see also p. lxxviii, n.). The lollards, to whom Hay was so opposed, were early Protestants, and around the end of the fifteenth century they were joined by the Ayrshireman, Murdoch Nisbet (Tulloch, 1989: 3–4). During the reign of James V, Nisbet was driven into exile, and there he began his Scots version of the New Testament. Nisbet's sources were, in fact, not too far from home: most of his work is a scotticised version of John Purvey's English revision of the New Testament, ascribed to Wycliffe, and based on the Latin Vulgate version of the Bible used commonly throughout Catholic Europe. Later, Tyndale's English translation from the Greek must have come into his possession, for he used this as the basis of an appended prologue to the Epistle to the Romans. Finally, he used Luther's revised preface to the New Testament (1534) as the basis of his own prologue (Law, 1901: xv–xvi; Tulloch, 1989: 4).

The result was a scotticised version of an English translation. Nisbet's translation of Luther's preface can be compared with Tyndale's rendering of the same (Law (ed.), 1901: 1–2, 1–2n.):

> For Euangelion is a Greke word, and is alsmekill to say in Inglis as a gude message, gude newis, gude mery tithingis, or sic a confortabill word as makis a man to syng, to be glaid, and his hart to leape for joy; lyke as quhen Dauid had ourecum grete Goliath that come a gud swete message and confortable new tydingis amang the pepile of the Jewis. (Nisbet)

> Euangelion (that we cal the gospel) is a greke word, and signyfyeth good, mery, glad and ioyfull tydinges, that makyth a mannes hert glad, and makyth him synge, daunce, and leepe for ioye. As when Davyd had killed Golyath the geaunt, cam glad tydinges vnto the iewes ... (Tyndale)

It is abundantly clear that the Scots and English versions are not so far apart as to be mutually unintelligible. Like writers before Gavin Douglas (and many after), Nisbet refers to his mother tongue as 'Inglis', and most of the vocabulary in the extract above is shared between the northern and southern language varieties. The most obvious differences are in grammatical inflexions (e.g. the Scots '-is' plural, and the '-is' present tense, as opposed to English '-es' and '-yth'), and in distinctive spellings such as 'quhen' ('when').

The immediate influence of Nisbet's New Testament was negligible; indeed, the only surviving manuscript stayed in his family for several generations, before passing into the ownership of the Boswells of Auchinleck. Law (1901: xiii) notes that:

> It will be remarked that the family tradition nowhere describes Nisbet's 'new book' as in any way distinctively Scottish. Dr M'Crie

> (in his 'Life of Melville', vol. ii. p. 404), referring to the 'True Relation,' seemed to have no suspicion that the MS. was anything more than an ordinary copy of Wycliffe's version. But it is manifestly the work of a Scottish scribe, who, taking Purvey's revision of Wycliffe as a basis, altered the grammar and vocabulary wherever necessary to make his manuscript intelligible or easily readable to his own countrymen, and that scribe is clearly no other than Murdoch Nisbet himself.

As suggested above, the claim that Nisbet 'altered the grammar and vocabulary wherever necessary' is perhaps overstating the case. Wright (1988: 156) argues that 'Apart from adapting it to Scottish orthography, he changed little of its vocabulary, and then as often in the direction of the Wycliffite original as in favour of Scotticisms'. Tulloch (1989) is in agreement with this view, and he makes the further point that Nisbet uses vocabulary shared with English, where modern Scots writers would substitute a distinctively Scottish term:

> By comparison with modern texts, and starting with modern preconceptions about Scots, Nisbet's Scots may seem to share too much with English. Many words we have come to expect in modern Scots texts do not appear: Nisbet, for instance, regularly uses *ask, child* and *knaw* rather than *speir, bairn* and *ken* as a modern writer would do. (Tulloch, 1989: 8)

The most ambitious attempt by a 'modern writer' to produce a Scots Bible is William Lorimer's twentieth-century translation of the New Testament from the Greek, and this is considered in some detail in Chapter 7. Meanwhile, an illustration of Nisbet's style in the gospels is given below (Matthew ix: 1–8):

> Ande Jesus went vp into a boot, and passit ouir the watir, and com into his citee. And, lo, thai brocht to him a man seek in parlasie, liand in a bed: and Jesus saw the faithe of tham, and said to the man seek in the paralasie, Sonn, haue thou traist; thi synnis ar forgevin to thee. And, lo, sum of the scribis said within tham self, Thou blasphemys. And quhen Jesus had sene thar thouchtis, he said, Quharto think ye euile thingis in your hartis? Quhat is it lichtar to say, Thi synnis ar forgevin to thee; outhir to say, Ryse thou, and walk? Bot that ye wit that mannis sonn has power to forgeve synnis in erd, than he saide to the seekman in paralasie, Ryse vp, tak thi bed, and ga into thin hous. And he raase, and went into his hous. And the pepile seand, dred, and glorifiit God, that gaue sic power to men. (Law (ed.), 1901: 44)

The differences between Purvey and Nisbet's version are slight, consisting once more in grammatical inflexions, and spellings such as 'quharto' and 'quhat' where Purvey has 'wherto' and 'what'. The only significant change is Nisbet's 'seek in parlasie' (later 'paralasie') where Purvey has 'sike in palesie': in this case Nisbet is closer to the Vulgate's 'paralyticum', and his spelling of 'seek' is evidently a representation of a Scots pronunciation still heard today. Given that neither Purvey nor Tyndale's English versions would have been unintelligible to Scottish readers, Nisbet's rendering of them seems calculated only to make the text more Scottish in tone – to present a version of the scripture, in Lindsay's words, 'translatit in our toung Vulgare'. The reasons why its influence was minimal are probably varied: Tyndale's translation of the New Testament from the Greek was possibly considered a greater authority than Purvey's translation from the Latin Vulgate – it might be pertinent that Lindsay calls for a version 'justlye translatit'. Moreover, the Scottish printing industry was weak compared to the English and continental presses, and, at the time, Nisbet's rendering of Purvey into Scots was possibly considered too close to the source to merit publication in its own right. Indeed, the publication of Nisbet's text had to wait until 1901, when the historic absence of a Scots Bible, and the damage to the development of Scots caused by this absence, were more keenly felt. The editors of the Scottish Text Society had in fact been considering compiling a partial Scots Bible from excerpts translated by a variety of authors, before the Nisbet version came to their notice (Law, 1901: viii).

Nevertheless, Lindsay's complaint in *The Monarchie,* is evidence of some anxiety in sixteenth-century Scotland that the language of the Reformation was a southern variety, now increasingly associated with a different nation. Famously, John Knox's Catholic opponent, Ninian Winzet, attacks Knox on the grounds of his unpatriotically anglicised language:

> Gif ze, throw curiositie of nouationis, hes forzet our auld plane Scottish qhilk zour mother lerit zou, in tymes cuming I sall wryte to zou my mind in Latin, for I am nocht acquyntit with zour Southeroun. (J.K. Hewison (ed.), 1888: 138; quoted in Wright, 1988: 170)
>
> [If you, through curiosity about novelties, have forgotten our old plain Scots, which your mother taught you, in future I shall write my mind to you in Latin, for I am not acquainted with your 'Southern'.]

There are various different reasons why the Scottish reformers' writings appeared in anglicised form. It seems likely that the early reformers were 'weakly tied' to their native speech communities and so more open to linguistic change – they were often writing from exile, and it is probable that they saw themselves addressing audiences on both sides of the Scottish-English border. Given the stress they laid on the authority of scripture, it is not surprising that their written language would be influenced by English vernacular translations by people like Tyndale. On the other hand, as Lyall (1988: 177–9) argues, it is possible that the anglicisation of the reformers has been exaggerated by circumstances beyond their control: particularly the anglicising practices of printers, both contemporary and subsequent.

The Bible was not the only reformist text translated into Scots: one of the more significant was John Gau's translation from Danish of Christian Pedersen's *Den rette vey till Hiemmerigis Rige* – itself a translation from German of a Lutheran tract. Gau was another exile, living in a Scottish community in the city of Malmö, and his text was published by Danish compositors. Mitchell (1888: xxxiii) notes the affinity between Gau's Scots and Pedersen's Danish, although it is likely that Gau was acquainted with German versions of the tract too. This affinity is unsurprising given the strong Norse influence on Scots in general. Lyall (1988: 176) notes that Gau's *The richt vay to the Kingdome of Heuine* (1533) exhibits 'that terse, unadorned style which was to become characteristic of Protestant prose', and which prefigures the plain style later to characterise much Scots prose. The example of Gau's prose style below is taken from his discussion of the twelve articles of the Christian faith:

> Faith is noth ane thing quhilk ane man cane giff to hyme selff quhen he wil bot it is ane greit gyft of God the quhilk renwis the hart and makis ane nev mã quhair be for he wes of ald adame in ewil desiris and sinful lyff / to trow / that is to stãd fast at Godis vord quhat he promisis to wsz quhat euer it be that he wil fulfil his promis na mã cane haiff this faith of hime selff bot the spreit of God giffis this licht in the hart ãd renwis it inuertlie /(cf. Mitchell (ed.), 1888: 31)
>
> [Faith is not a thing that a man can give to himself when he wishes, but it is a great gift of God, which renews the heart and makes a new man, where before he was of old Adam in evil desires and sinful life – to trust – that is, to stand fast by God's word, what he promises to us, whatever it be, that he will fulfill

his promise – no man can have this faith himself, but the spirit of God gives this light in the heart, and renews it inwardly]

Although I have modernised the long <s> in the extract above, I have retained other features, principally the minim in <ã>, which indicates that a nasal, here <n>, has been omitted in the text: thus <mã> signifies 'man'. The text is instantly recognisable as Scots, given the 'quh-' spellings, and again the characteristic verb and noun inflexions, for example in 'makis' and 'desiris'. The spellings of words like 'greit' and 'ald' also suggest Scots pronunciations. The Danish influence is evident in other spellings, for example, 'renwis' ('renuis' = 'renews') and 'ewil' ('euil' = 'evil'). Mitchell (1888: xxiii) suggests that the substitution of <w> for Scots <u> is a direct imitation of Pedersen's orthography, and might reflect the influence on Gau's written style of his long residence in Denmark.

The influence of the reformers on Scottish culture was deep and long-lasting. The doctrine of salvation by faith, gifted by God, which gains early expression in the above passage from Gau, returns to haunt the Scottish imagination in later works, most notably James Hogg's *The Private Memoirs and Confessions of a Justified Sinner*. In the sixteenth century Scottish spiritual and political life underwent a revolution, a revolution sparked by changes in attitudes towards established religion throughout Europe, and fanned by the availability of translations, in Scots and in English. If English translations rather than Scots ones were to dominate in later years, this was only partly the fault of the Scottish reformers, some of whom were concerned to provide translations in the northern tongue, but whose aspirations were ultimately thwarted by printing conditions, and by changing attitudes towards the forms of language most proper for literary expression in the new United Kingdom. Early in the next century *the* Authorised Version of the Bible was, of course, compiled in English at the command of a Scottish-born king, James VI and I. This event itself was the culmination of fundamental translations and changes, taking place at the heart of the Scottish court as the sixteenth century drew to a close.

The Court Poets of James VI

As noted in the previous chapter, Gavin Douglas's *Eneados* was not immediately taken up as a model for further verse translations into Scots – only John Bellenden's prose translation of Livy can be seen as continuing the task of rendering large-scale works of classical literature into the vernacular. The seventy years between 1513 and 1584 in Scotland were marked by turmoil and social revolution: they were the years of Flodden, of the Reformation, and of the arrival and despatch of Mary, Queen of Scots. Kratzmann, in his study of the secular poetry of this period, makes a good case for its intrinsic interest, but he nevertheless observes :

> In England there was a vogue for translation of the classics, illustrated by the Ovidian works of Golding and Turberville (both in 1567). The great example of Gavin Douglas seems to have inspired no similar enterprise in Scotland, and the absence of large-scale verse translation constitutes the major difference in the state of secular poetry between the realms. (Kratzmann, 1988: 122)

This is not to say that Scotland was not open to broader continental influences between the reigns of James IV and James VI. The renaissance architecture of the royal palace in Stirling Castle pays homage to the culture of James V's French bride, and the carved oak medallions, dating from 1542, which decorated the Queen's Presence Chamber, have continental analogues and were apparently the work of two Scots and a Frenchman (McKean, 1985: 11–12). Later, John Knox himself bears witness to Mary, Queen of Scots' introduction of French masques as courtly entertainments in Scotland. The Auld Alliance was culturally alive in the mid-sixteenth century, as can be seen, for example, in Alexander Montgomerie's debt to the French poet, Marot (Lyall, 1993: 79–94). But it was the accession to the throne of the young James VI, and a new period of post-Reformation stability, that set the scene for a conscious attempt to instigate a Scottish renaissance, and central to that project was literary translation.

The principal force behind this project was James VI himself. As Jack (1988: 124) observes:

> Tutored by the great Latinist George Buchanan, he came to regret the classical bias in his learning, lamenting that 'They gar me speik Latin ar I could speik Scottis'. Feeling this way, he was ready to fall under the cultural influence of his father's cousin, Esmé Stuart with his knowledge of the French literary world. Another older man, Alexander Montgomerie also impressed the young king with his vernacular verses, which drew mainly from French and earlier Scottish sources.

One of Montgomerie's more celebrated sonnets is a rendering of Ronsard's 'Hier soir, Marie, en prenant maugré toy':

So swete a kis yistrene fra thee I reft
In bowing down thy body on the bed,
That evin my lyfe within thy lippis I left.
Sensyne from thee my spirits wald never shed;
To folow thee it from my body fled
And left my corps als cold as ony kie.
Bot when the danger of my death I dred,
To seik my spreit I sent my harte to thee;
Bot it wes so inamored with thyn ee,
With thee it myndit lykwyse to remane;
So thou hes keepit captive all the thrie,
More glaid to byde then to returne agane.
Except thy breath thare places had suppleit
Even in thyn armes thair doutles had I deit.

[So sweet a kiss last night from you I took/In bowing down your body on the bed,/That even my life within your lips I left./Since then my spirits would never part from you;/It fled from my body to follow you/And left my corpse as cold as any key./But when I feared the danger of my death,/I sent my heart to you to seek my spirit,/But it was so enamoured with your eye/It was likewise minded to remain with you:/So you have kept all three captive,/More glad to remain than to return again./If your breath had not taken ('suppleit') their places,/Doubtless I would have died, even in your arms.

The orthography in this poem suggests that, despite Douglas's affirmation of the distinctiveness of Scots, a quality which was to be reaffirmed by James VI, the evolution of a standard written English was impacting on secular written Scots as well as on the religious prose of the reformers even in the late sixteenth century. The impact is undeniable, although at times it is exaggerated by some later editions' use of anglicised printed sources, rather than more densely Scottish manuscript versions. Here we can see the incursion into Montgomerie's spelling of several anglicised forms; for example, 'cold' rather than 'cauld', the digraph <wh-> rather than <quh-> , and the suffix <-ed> in 'inamoured' (cf. 'myndit', 'keepit', 'suppleit' and 'deit'). However, it is unlikely that the presence of anglicised written forms necessarily signifies an anglicised pronunciation – the word 'spirits' only scans if it is pronounced as the monosyllable 'spreits' – which is in fact its form elsewhere in the poem.

The young James VI drew Montgomerie into a coterie of poets

whose work he encouraged, not only with his patronage but with his active participation and guidance. While in his late teens James published *Ane Schort Treatise Containing Some Reulis and Cautelis to be observit and eschewit in Scottis poesie,* an essay in which the 'rules and cautelis [i.e. 'cautions'] governing the writing of Scots poetry (again explicitly contrasted with English poetry) were made explicit. The treatise follows Du Bellay, Gascoigne and Puttenham in a project both literary and patriotic, as the Preface makes clear. James states two reasons why he has committed himself to print:

> The ane is, As for them that wrait of auld, lyke as the tyme is changeit sensyne, sa is the ordour of Poesie changeit.
>
> . . .
>
> The vther cause is, That as for thame that hes written in it of late, there hes neuer ane of thame written in our language. For albeit sindrie hes written of it in English, quhilk is lykest to our language, zit we differ from thame in sindrie reulis of Poesie, as ze will find be experience. (Arber (ed.), 1869: 54)
>
> [The one is, as for them that wrote in old times, just as the time has changed since then, so has the order of poetry changed ... The other cause is that, as for those who have written about it lately, not one of them has written in our language. For although several have written about it in English, which is most like our language, yet we differ from them in sundry rules of poetry, as you will find by experience.]

Of his sources, James makes special mention of Du Bellay, whose *The Defence and Illustration of the French Language* had been published in Paris in 1549. Du Bellay's *Defence* is a vigorous and patriotic argument in favour of treating vernacular languages as equals of the classical tongues, despite the acknowledged fact that the vernacular languages have not reached the 'perfection' attained by Greek and Latin. From Du Bellay, James may have inherited his ambivalence towards the act of translating: while praising translation as 'this most praiseworthy labour' (chap. 5), Du Bellay argues that it is itself insufficient to give perfection to the French language, and he castigates at length poor translators, calling them *traducteurs* ('traducers') rather than *traditeurs* ('translators') (chap. 6). Du Bellay seeks to inspire patriotic confidence in his mother tongue, not by despising the classical tongues, but by encouraging his compatriots to compose works that equal the ancients in expression and beauty.

Likewise, in the *Reulis and Cautelis,* James presents a view of translation that on the surface conflicts with his own practice of translating and his encouragement of others to do the same:

> But sen *Inuentioun*, is ane of the cheif vertewis in a Poete, it is best that ze inuent zour awin subiect, zour self, and not to compose of sene subiectis. Especially, translating any thing out of vther language, quhilk doing, ze not only essay not zour awin ingyne of *Inuentioun*, but be the same meanes, ze are bound, as to a staik, to follow that buikis phrasis, quhilk ze translate. (Chap. VII, Arber (ed.), 1869: 66)
>
> [But since Invention is one of the chief virtues in a poet, it is best that you invent your own subject yourself, and not compose with given subjects. In particular, translating anything out of another language, which doing, you not only fail to test your own ingenuity in Invention, but by the same means, you are bound, as if to a stake, to follow the phrases of that book which you translate.]

Here we can see James both recognising and straining against Douglas's directive in the Prologue to the First Book of the *Eneados* that a translator must respect and be faithful to his source. Such fidelity constrains the renaissance poet, one of whose 'chief vertewis' is 'inventioun'. But, like Du Bellay, James's practice suggests that he recognised the value of good translations, and that his comments are largely directed at poor translations. A good translation, in James's terms, would nevertheless combine originality with a respect for the source text and result in a free imitation rather than a literal translation. Du Bellay also saw good translations as imitations by inspired poets, transformations of the source texts, 'grafted and applied to their own tongue' (Du Bellay, Chap. VII, trans. Turquet, 1939: 37). Jack (1972: 56) presents James's position thus:

> Imitation and invention may be skilfully handled together by experienced artists, but minor poets, following in their footsteps, adopted a more literal approach, which produced verse sounding like the first awkward steps in French or Latin translation. This would explain why James, in his own poetic output, translated Du Bartas' *Uranie* and used as sources Desportes, Saint Gelais, Constable and Montgomerie.

James's own success in matching his actions to his words is debatable. His reputation as a poet has perhaps suffered unduly from the fact that his social status granted him influence, and a self-conceit, both of which ran well beyond his literary skill. While making out a case for considering James a worthy if unexceptional member of the court poets, McClure acknowledges that his translations can fall well below the standard he himself set forth. McClure is particularly critical of James's translation of *Uranie* by Du Bartas, a poet James esteemed so highly that he invited him to Scotland and entertained him at the Scottish court:

> Though the French poet has no longer the reputation, in his own country, or elsewhere, which he had among his contemporaries, it is easy to recognise the qualities in his work that appealed to James: the devoutly Protestant orientation of his thought, his erudition and firmly intellectual approach, his grandiose choice of subjects. As a fluent speaker and reader of French, too, James would no doubt have been intrigued by Du Bartas's neologisms and linguistic experimentation. But little can be said in praise of James's *Uranie*. The movement of his pentameters is inflexible and plodding compared to the alexandrines of his original, and his use of couplets instead of Du Bartas's *abba* quatrains has a dismally confining effect on the expression of his thought. The translation is close, at times almost literal. (McClure, 1990: 102)

Rather more successful are some James's sonnets, for example, his rendering of Desportes' *Diane* I, 5:

> Haill mirthfull May the moneth full of joye!
> Haill mother milde of hartsume herbes and flowres!
> Haill fostrer faire of everie sporte and toye
> And of Auroras dewis and summer showres!
> Haill freind to Phoebus and his glancing houres!
> Haill sister scheine to Nature breeding all,
> Who by the raine that cloudie skie out pouris
> And Titans heate, reformes the faided fall
> In woefull winter by the frostie gall
> Of sadd Saturnus tirrar of the trees!
> And now by Natures might and thine, they shall
> Be florish'd faire with colours that agrees;
> Then lett us all be gladd to honour the,
> As in olde tymes was ever wonte to be.

Jack (1972: 118–119) comments on the way in which James here weds invention and imitation:

> The process of conscious variation within a fixed frame is evident from the start. Desportes' spring is 'heureux' and James's

'mirthfull'; Desportes' 'fait que l'hyver morne à regret se retire', James' 'reformes the faided fall in wofull winter by the frostie gall'; in Desportes' 'le ciel rit' and 'les forests ont repris leur vert accoustrement'; in James's 'harstume herbes and floures' flourish, while people enjoy 'everie sport and toye'; Desportes introduces the figures of Zephyrus and Mars, James replaces them with Aurora and Saturn.

The king's practice in imitating and adapting continental models was therefore at least as influential as his cautions against translation. It might also be asked whether James's writings displayed the essential Scottishness which he had argued would be evident 'be experience' to anyone reading his compatriots' poetry. Certainly the *Reulis and Cautelis* display many features of Scots – the 'quh-' spellings, and various further reflections of Scots pronunciation (e.g. 'knawledge', 'chyldheid', 'langer'); the '-is/-it' inflexions' and several Scots grammatical items, for example, 'gif' ('if'), 'abone' ('above'); and a small number of distinctively Scots lexical items, for instance, 'kythis' ('appears'), and 'thrawin' ('forced violently'). The language of the sonnet may not seem, at first sight, particularly Scottish, but here appearances may be deceptive. Granted, there are only a few indications of the provenance of the translator, notably in the plural inflexion '-is' in 'dewis' (l.4) and in the singular verb concord of 'cloudie skies out pouris' (l.7) and 'colours that agrees' (l.12). Moreover, as in the *Reulis and Cautelis* only a very few of the words in the sonnet are peculiar to Scots: 'scheine' (l.6, 'bright'; cognate with 'sheen'), and 'tirrar' (l.10, 'stripper', from ME 'tirve' and cognate with 'turf'). Compared with the *Reulis and Cautelis,* the sonnet's spellings are anglicised yet these spellings conceal distinctively Scots pronunciations of those vocabulary items which are shared between Scots and English. Examples of anglicised spellings of terms common to Scots and English (i.e. 'common core' items) include the rhymes 'flowres/showres/houres/pouris'. In Middle Scots the first three of these would have been pronounced with an /u:/ phoneme, as /flu:rz, ʃu:rz, u:rz/ while 'pouris' would have been a half-rhyme /po:rz/. The digraph spelling of the vowel obscures the monophthongal articulation, as it does also in 'cloudie' /klu:di/ and 'now' /nu:/ . The vowel in 'olde' (l.14) would have been pronounced something like /a:ld/, a slightly longer phoneme than would have been found in 'all', /al/ in the previous line, and in the rhymes 'all/fall/gall/shall'. Consonantal markers of the Scots accent would have included the /x/ phoneme in 'might' (l.11) and the /s/ pronunciation in 'shall' (cf. Aitken, 1977, 1996).

In short, in this translation by James we see a continuation of the trend noticed above in Montgomerie's rendering; that is, we see a Scots sonnet in which anglicised spelling forms serve to obscure Scots patterns of rhyme and assonance. There were probably various reasons for this anglicisation: the gravitational pull of the increasingly standardised variety of spelling south of the border, which was disseminated by the ever-wider availability in Scotland of texts printed in England; and the longstanding tradition, going back to the fifteenth century, of marking high-style Scottish verse with slightly anglicised spellings, mainly in homage to Chaucer. Certainly the work of James VI embodies a paradoxical reaffirmation of the distinctive nature of Scots writing at a time when there was an increasing tendency to represent Scots pronunciations using an orthography which originated in England.

Given the circumstances of its adoption, it may indeed be anachronistic to think of sixteenth-century orthography as 'English' and 'Scots' as if these were absolutely distinct terms. Considerable variation in spellings was still possible in sixteenth-century Scotland, and the perception that linguistic forms can be related to national identity was still in an embryonic phase – it is unlikely that many Scots would have regarded, for example, the <ch/gh> alternatives in 'richt' and 'right' as markers of Scottishness and Englishness respectively. Such a perception would only gradually have evolved with the establishment of the <gh> grapheme in standard English. Even so, it is significant that John Stewart of Baldynneis's verse, largely composed before the Union, is still clearly identifiable today as Scots, in spelling, vocabulary and grammar. Stewart was very much James's creature, a man who, unlike the older Montgomerie, owed his position at court and his literary reputation to his royal mentor, and his poetry shows the influence of his patron's literary precepts. *Roland Furious,* his 'abbregement' of Ariosto's *Orlando Furioso,* which survives in a single manuscript, presented to the king, has been extensively discussed by R.D.S. Jack (e.g. Jack, 1972: 57–74). Jack offers convincing evidence that Stewart knew the Italian source text, although the Scotsman's version ultimately owes more to Desportes' *Roland Furieux* and *Angélique,* and to a French prose version by Jean Martin, published in 1543. In a way, Stewart in abridging Ariosto, and relying heavily on intermediate texts, is marking a return to medieval traditions of translating – that is, he takes the matter of the source text and adapts it to his own purposes. It is not a technique that Douglas would have approved of, but Ariosto, as an Italian vernacular poet, probably did not command quite the same respect as the hallowed Virgil. Certainly Stewart regarded some aspects of his source text as 'tedious and prolixt', and at the beginning of Canto V he sets out his stall:

> This work of myn behuifs me schers it so,
> Quhyls heir, quhyls thair, quhyls fordwart and behind,
> The historie all interlest I find
> With syndrie sayings of so great delyt
> That singlie most I from the rest out spind,
> As the unskilful prentes imperfyt,
> Quho fyns the gould frie from the laton qhyt.
>
> (Canto V; Jack and Rozendaal (eds), 1997: 331)

> [This work of mine requires me to cut it so:/Sometimes here, sometimes there, sometimes before and after,/I find the history all interlaced/With sundry sayings of such great delight/That I must spin out single strands from the rest,/Like the unskilful, imperfect apprentice,/Who refines the gold, free from the white lead.]

Stewart's practice, then, casts further light on the different ways in which the status of the source text influences the way that a literary translator defines his or her role. For Douglas, the *Aeneid* is a model of perfection, which he feels bound to respect and so translate as faithfully as possible. In contrast, Stewart uses the licence to invent, granted by his fellow 'apprentice', James VI, in the *Reulis and Cautelis,* in order to embroider those incidents in his source texts which capture his own imagination, and to omit those which he finds digressive and boring. The dominant image of the translator here is the alchemist, transforming the dull lead of his source text into the spun gold of his translation. Despite the modesty topos (which is itself a thinly veiled compliment to his patron) the translator here sees his goal as improving upon the raw material of his sources. The result is a narrative which is more tightly focused than the original source. Jack (1978: 22) sums up the poem's strengths thus:

> Numerous parallels between Orlando and Angelica implicitly present in the Italian are explicitly stressed in the Scottish 'abbregement'. Both fall through sins against God, one by deserting the Christian cause, the other through pride. One conquers love after a long period of subjugation, the other is entrapped by love after disdaining it. Yet by these different paths they find inner harmony, because one adds passion to her overpowering intellect, the other finds reason where earlier the madness of passion had reigned.

Stewart's trademark rhetoric is well-suited to expressing the heightened state of passion bordering on madness. In the extract below, from Canto XI, Roland's descent into madness begins with his reading of a letter from his rival Medor to Angelique, which celebrates the consummation of Medor and Angelique's passion:

His chin declyning on his brest did fall
And cloud of cair held doune his cumlie front,
Quhair left was no audacitie to brall
For boyling baile his boudin braine haid blont.
Great, egar grief so grivous did surmont,
That he onnawayis mycht relasche his wo
With wofull words, as umquhyle he was wont;
Nor yit no teiris from his eine could go,
His liquid humor suffocat was so
As quhan in veschell wyd with narrow throt
The wattir choks and may not flow thairfro
For great aboundance that dois in it flot.

(Canto XI; Jack and Rozendaal (eds), 1997: 338)

[His chin fell declining on his breast/And a cloud of care drew down his handsome brow,/Where there was no audacity left to soar,/For boiling sorrow had blunted his grief-swollen brain./ Great, keen grief so grievously did surmount/That he in no way could relieve his woe/With woeful words, as once he was wont;/ Nor yet could any tears go from his eyes/His liquid humour was so stifled,/As when in a broad vessel with a narrow throat/The water chokes and may not flow therefrom/For the great abundance that flows in it.]

This is clearly Scots, although there are a few indications of English influence, in the spelling of 'no' (e.g. l. 270, rather than Scots 'na'), and the variation between the Scots plural 'eine' (l. 270, 'eyes') and its English equivalent, 'eis' (i.e. 'eyes', found elsewhere in the poem, e.g. l. 261). Still, Stewart retains a largely Scots orthography (for example, the 'quh-' spellings), the Scots verb inflexions (e.g., the '-it' preterite), and a fair proportion of Scots lexical items: e.g. 'brall' ('soar'), and 'boudin' ('swollen with grief'). Moreover, the Scots spellings are suggestive of certain features of pronunciation, particularly the monophthong /o/ found in 'throt' and 'flot' and the /wa/ found in 'wattir'. Stewart's adaptation of Ariosto's poem is certainly a *tour de force*, which, as Jack suggests, deserves to rank alongside Douglas's *Eneados* as an example of Scots translation in the sixteenth century. It is of further interest as a conscious attempt to put into practice the precepts of a princely patron – one who laid great store by rhetorical flourishes. Lefevere (1992: 15) has observed that 'Patronage is usually more interested in the ideology of literature than in its poetics, and it could be said that the patron "delegates authority" to the professional where poetics is concerned.' James VI is an exception to this rule – he was a patron who was at least as interested in the poetics as in the ideology of writing and translating in Scots – and his influence on Stewart is therefore doubly powerful.

At the end of the sixteenth century, poetry was still the most prestigious form of literary endeavour in Scotland. Prose was, however, gaining ground as the medium used in histories, pamphlets, treatises and holy writ. As we have seen, James VI turned his hand to prose writing, in the *Reulis and Cautelis,* and later he was to compose essays on such diverse topics as tobacco and witchcraft, as well as politics. As James's grandfather, James V, had commissioned John Bellenden to translate the Latin prose of Livy into Scots, so in the 1590s, James VI encouraged William Fowler, the secretary to his wife, Queen Anne, to translate a major work of prose into his native tongue. But true to the taste of the times the treatise was not to be a work of classical antiquity, but the vernacular Italian of a writer whose very name had already become synonymous in Scotland with iconoclastic cynicism and political expediency: Machiavelli.

Fowler was another of the court poets whose literary career is marked by an interest in translation and imitation. He diverges from the earlier court poets, Montgomerie, Stewart and James VI himself, in being attracted directly to Italian more than to French sources. Rather than Ronsard, Desportes or Du Bartas, Fowler favoured Petrarch, whose *Trionfi* had been well known at the Scottish court since the time of Mary, Queen of Scots (Jack, 1972: 76–7). In the preface to his translation of the *Trionfi,* Fowler echoes the motivation that had spurred Douglas's translation of the *Aeneid,* as well as Du Bellay's complaint against 'traducers':

> I perceawed, bothe in French and Inglish traductionis, this work not onelie traduced, bot evin as It war magled, and in everie member miserablie maimed and dismembered, besydis the barbar grosnes of boyth thair translationis, whiche I culd sett doun by pruif (wer not for prolixitie) in twoe hundreth passages and moe. (I, 16; quoted in Jack, 1972: 77)
>
> [I perceived, both in French and English translations, this work not only traduced, but even, as it were, mangled, and in every

> member miserably maimed and dismembered, besides the barbarous grossness of both their translations, which I could set down by proof (if it were not for prolixity) in two hundred passages and more.]

However, Fowler's adaptation of Petrarch is not regarded as a great improvement on the versions he lambasts, although a later attempts at Petrarchan love cycle, the *Tarantula of Love*, has met with a more favourable critical response. *The Prince*, probably composed in the 1590s, remains unfinished, and, like Murdoch Nisbet's *New Testament*, it was not published until long after its composition. Machiavelli's work, however, had already achieved considerable notoriety in Scotland during the sixteenth century, Mary Queen of Scots' secretary, Robert Maitland of Lethington, being branded 'a scurvie scholar of Machiavellus' lair', and even given the nickname 'Mitchell Wylie' (Praz, 1928: 6). There were various versions of *Il Principe* in currency for Fowler to consult, and he supplemented his reading of the original with English and French translations, particularly that of D'Auvergne, as well as a Latin translation by Sylvester Telius (see Jack, 1972: 86–9). Jack speculates that James VI and Fowler might have collaborated on the manuscript of *The Prince*, and that the king's involvement explains the omission of certain passages – on princely conquests and the rise of citizen-princes – which might not have been to the monarch's taste. In other respects, the translation carries on the tradition of princely advice seen in the earlier translations of such as Gilbert Hay. The difference is that the façade of chivalric nobility has been stripped to reveal a secular pragmatism, evident in the discussion of whether it is better for a prince to be feared or beloved:

> I will an*n*suer to that: it wer expedient and a thing full of surtye and adwa*n*tage to be bothe; bot yet, seing it is a thing imposseble that they ca*n* fal togeather, it is mair suretye for a p*ren*ce to be feared then loved. For considdering that men un*iver*sallye ar for the maist p*ar*t ingrait, variable, dissemblers, flyers from hasards, and follouers of gaine and co*m*moditie, and whils as they do there aue*n* turnes they ar to be disposed be the, and will offer to shed there blood, spend there guds, hasard there lyfe and there children for thy saik, whils thow hes no occasi*oun* to try or employ thame, bot quhen thy affairs craveth there continue*n*ce, thou sal see thame turne there clok another way; so that the prence that leneth altogether to thair words & faith, finding him naked and destitut of all other preparations, exspecting there succours sal ruyne him self suddenly, be reason that these frendships that ar

> conqueshed and soudart wit*h* silver& not be the greatnes and sterknes of hart and curage ar bot deserved and bought, and so ca*n* not be keped nor contenued nor employed in thy necessetie. (Fowler, *The Prince*, chap. 17, in Meikle (ed.), 1936: 117–18)
>
> [I will answer that: it is expedient and a thing full of security and advantage to be both; yet seeing it is impossible that they can fall together, it is safer for a prince to be feared than loved. For considering that men universally are for the most part ungrateful, variable, dissemblers, flyers from risk, and followers of gain and commodity, and sometimes as they serve their own ends, they put themselves at your disposal, and will offer to shed their blood, spend their goods, risk their life and their children for your sake, when you have no occasion to test or employ them; but when your affairs crave their constancy, you shall see them turn their cloak another way; so that the prince who depends wholly on their words and faith, finding himself naked, and destitute of all other preparations, expecting their support, shall ruin himself suddenly, because these friendships that are acquired and soldered with silver, and not by the greatness and strength of heart and spirit, are only service due to a superior (= 'deserved'), and bought, and so cannot be kept or continued, nor employed in your need.]

The Scots of Fowler's prose, which survives in a much-corrected manuscript, shows the increasing tendency towards anglicised forms. Again the translation largely utilises those vocabulary items shared with southern English: the only lexical items in the passage quoted which might cause the non-Scot to pause for a moment are 'deserved', which derives from 'dew service', or 'service due from a tenant to a superior'; and 'soudart', which is cognate with the English 'soldered' but shows typical Scots 'l'-vocalisation and the reduced past-tense marker '-t'. Elsewhere, the Scots '-it' inflexion is replaced by '-ed'; the Scots present inflexion '-is' is replaced by '-eth; 'and the Scots '-is' plural inflexion is also cut to '-s'.

The passage also shows variability in the orthography. Again some Scots forms are evident ('mair' rather than 'more') but even the distinctive 'quh-' spellings are being interspersed with 'wh-' forms, resulting in the co-occurrence of forms like 'which' and 'quhome'. 'Whiles' is an interesting hybrid, showing an inflected Scots form with an English spelling. Again, the translation, which is thought to date from the 1590s, provides evidence that written Scots in the latter years of the reign of James VI is beginning to become less distinguishable from the written English south of the border, despite the avowed linguistic nationalism of the court poets and writers. Indeed it is one of the ironies of the late sixteenth century that acts of translation, which as Jack (1972: 87) affirms are 'also acts of faith in the Scottish nation, and particularly in its resurgence under the rule of the poet-monarch James VI' – and which were accompanied by a ringing endorsement of the distinctive identity of the host medium by that poet-monarch – should nevertheless be marked by a creeping tendency to erode the very forms which marked the linguistic difference of Scots.

Changes in Scots in the Sixteenth Century

It is sometimes argued that the national language of Scotland before the Union of the Crowns was lowland Scots, and that after the departure of the Scottish Crown south in 1603, the state language of the new United Kingdom became English. This view imposes more modern notions of an established standard written language upon a much more flexible linguistic situation north and south of the Scottish-English border in the sixteenth century. In both realms, we can see processes of evolution towards standard written forms, but while these changes continued in England, they were abruptly curtailed in Scotland. Since the changes in the nature and status of Scots in the sixteenth century profoundly affect later translations into Scots, it is worth reviewing here what these changes were.

A standard language imposes conformity and suppresses variety: a set of approved spellings, words and grammatical rules are disseminated through a mass education system, and social pressures enforce the use of these forms as the mark of an 'educated' writer. The final codification of standard written English as a medium for dissemination through an increasingly broad education system did not occur until the eighteenth century, although, of course, the processes of standardisation were evolving for four centuries before then (cf. Smith, 1996: 65–78). The presence of a standard, or even a standardising, language inevitably means that the written form of a language gradually moves away from a systematic representation of the corresponding spoken forms – witness the arbitrary nature of present-day English spelling. In earlier centuries, when the relationship between pronunciation and its written representation, or orthography, was less fixed, there was the possibility of written language representing local ways of pronouncing words, without the written representation being marked as abnormal or 'uneducated'. This flexibility partly accounts for the inconsistencies we find in Middle Scots spellings – another reason is of course individual idiosyncracies in determining the relationship between a particular sound and the sequence of written characters which represent it. Thus, for example, in Middle Scots texts we find alternations in <quh-/wh-> spellings representing /xw/, <ch/gh> spellings representing /x/, and in <ai/a-e> spellings representing Middle Scots /e:/ (cf. Aitken, 1977, 1996). As we saw in the passage from Fowler's *The Prince*, what would now be viewed as spelling inconsistencies are found within a few lines in the same manuscript. This state of affairs was not unusual in the sixteenth century, in Scotland and England.

Curiously, despite the potential for phonetic or near-phonetic spellings, sixteenth-century written Scots, like written English of the period, is *not* strongly regionally marked: in other words, although it is not a standard language, Scots of this period can be understood as a standardised language. It does not have the fixity of a modern written standard, but there is a set of norms which acts as a focus for writers, 'rather than a set of shibboleths from which any deviation is stigmatised' (Smith, 1996: 70). Effectively, then, the practices of Middle Scots writers were such that extremely idiosyncratic, local or regional manifestations were avoided, but there was greater variation in spelling, word-choice and grammatical structure than would be found acceptable today. A detailed analysis of trends in Scots prose writing between the fourteenth and seventeenth centuries suggests that variation in written Scots was slowly decreasing, and a Scots standard was being established (Meurman-Solin, 1993); but the Union of the Crowns diverted the establishment of a distinctive, public written language in Scotland.

This linguistic situation helps explain the complex characteristics we find in Middle Scots translations. On the one hand, from the time of Gavin Douglas onwards, there was a consciousness that the differences in the norms governing Scots and English could be used to mark a distinctive Scottish identity. As we have seen, James VI also insisted on the separateness of Scots and English – which would be known 'by experience'. On the other hand, these norms were uncodified and unspecified, they were not regulated by the education system, and divergence from the norms was not widely stigmatised. As we have seen, certain sounds still found in Scots but no longer in English – such as the consonant /x/ – could equally well be represented by the conservative English spelling <gh> as by the Scots spelling <ch>, and so adoptions of what we now consider the 'English' variable would not necessarily have smacked of linguistic betrayal in sixteenth-century Scotland. In such circumstances, given the political and economic rise of England relative to Scotland, and the Scottish court's ultimate translation to London, and given the close kinship between the linguistic systems of Scots and English, it is not entirely surprising that Scots translators – including James VI – began to move towards the norms governing English rather than Scots. This move began before the Union of the Crowns, but it accelerated considerably thereafter.

Chapter 5
'Wonders of the New Speech': Translation after the Union of the Crowns

William Drummond of Hawthornden: The End of an Auld Sang?

It could be argued that the work of William Drummond of Hawthornden (1585–1649) has no place in a study of translations into Scots. He was born near Edinburgh, and graduated from the capital city's university, and, after a period of travel in England and France between 1605 and 1610, returned to the family estate to succeed his father as laird. However, Drummond chose not to publish in a distinctively Scottish idiom, composing both his poetry and prose in a written variety that was almost indistinguishable from that of the literati of the English court. MacDonald (1976: 196) notes that Drummond's early manuscripts are composed in Scots and that they use the customary <quh-> and <y> spellings, as well as vocabulary items such as 'speir' ('ask'), and inflexions such as <-it> in words like 'kepit'. However, MacDonald (1976: 196–7) continues:

> In his published work Drummond attempted to erase Scotticisms, but occasionally examples survived his vigilance, some spellings and particularly some pronunciations.

A few elements of Drummond's native Scots can indeed be discerned in his poetry, and not only because they escaped 'his vigilance'. Drummond began publishing his poetry in 1616, more than a decade after the Scottish court's departure for London, and it is tempting to view him as representing the last flickering flame of Scottish court poetry, or even as the poet who finally betrayed the Scottish tongue. Kastner (1913: xliii) stresses the imitative nature of his muse, observing that 'a full third of Drummond's compositions are translations or close paraphrases' and speculating that most of the rest are 'adaptations from foreign models'. The implicit criticism is that Drummond carried Renaissance notions of imitation to extremes. However, in recent decades this assessment has been questioned – Jack (1972: 113–44) presents a detailed case for viewing Drummond as the climactic figure in the Scottish court poets' project of adaption and imitation of Italian sources. MacDonald (1976: ix) supports the argument that Drummond 'was the best poet Scotland produced between Douglas and Ramsay'; and Edwin Morgan, a modern poet and translator into both Scots and English, views Drummond as a key transitional figure in the Scottish literary tradition, someone who effectively 'showed that English could be used, and that others would use it after him' (Morgan, 1977: 200). It is as a transitional figure, at the end of one tradition and the beginning of a new accommodation with English, that we shall consider Drummond here.

Drummond is an interesting figure for reasons beyond the literary and linguistic: his life is remarkably well-documented, and much of his library catalogue has been reconstructed to show in fine detail the reading tastes and practices of a Scottish landowner, poet and pamphleteer of the early seventeenth century (MacDonald, 1971). MacDonald notes that Drummond seems to have started seriously compiling his own collection of books on his visit to London in 1606, and he continued purchasing books for the rest of his life. Drummond organised his library primarily according to language and then according to subject – the typical cataloguing system for a period when most scholarly literature would still be in Latin, and all European vernacular texts might be lumped together as recreational literature. Drummond systematically ordered his works into Latin, Greek, Hebrew, Italian, French, Spanish and English (including Scots). It is likely that Drummond had some reading knowledge of all these languages, and clearly the translations that he possessed helped him do this. MacDonald (1971: 139) refers to the abundance of translations and also to Drummond's record of his own reading in his reconstruction of Drummond's very active use of his books:

> Before Drummond ever began to learn Italian he had read *The courtier* in English, as well as Guazzo's *Civil conversation*, Ariosto's *Orlando furioso* and Tasso's *Gerusalemme liberata*. When he started to learn French in 1607 while he was at Paris and Bourges there were at once French translations in his reading list: Montemayor's *Diana* (from the Spanish), Tasso's *Aminta*, Sannazzaro's *Arcadia* and the *Circe* of Gelli. Although there are one or two works on grammar and several dictionaries in Drummond's catalogue (he

had, for instance, Florio's *Worlde of words*), the number of books in more than one language is evidence of learning a foreign tongue: he must have taught himself by comparing the Italian original with its English or French translation. Thus in 1610 – the year in which he seems to have begun his Italian studies seriously – he read Sannazzaro in both Italian and French, and did the same with the first part of Petrarch's *Rime*, Guarino's *Pastor Fido*, Tasso's *Aminta*, and Bembo's *Gli Asolani*. The *Gerusalemme liberata* he read in Italian and English.

MacDonald goes on to note that by 1614 Drummond had started reading in Spanish – and that through all this prodigious linguistic activity in the European vernaculars he never stopped reading the Latin works which form the bulk of his library. Indeed one of the atypical poems Drummond published – probably only in broadside in his own lifetime, although it was later printed in 1684 and reprinted several times thereafter – is a macaronic burlesque in a Latinised Scots, based on an actual dispute between two Fife families over a right-of-way. The *Polemo-Middinia inter Vitarvam et Bebernam* (*c.* 1645) is an astonishing work, partly because of its linguistic virtuosity, and partly because it reveals Drummond's willingness to combine mock-Latin with a Scots that rarely surfaces in his 'genteel' offerings. A brief quotation gives the flavour of the satire; the translation which follows is by a recent editor (Maclaine, 1996: 45):

Nec mora, marchavit foras longo ordine turma,
Ipsa prior *Neberna* suis stout facta ribauldis,
Roustaeam manibus gestans furibunda goulaeam,
Tandem muckcreilios vocat ad pellmellia fleidos.
Ite, ait, uglei felloes, si quis modo posthac
Muckifer has nostras tenet crossare fenestras,
Juro ego quod ejus longum extrahabo thrapellum,
Et totam rivabo faciem, luggasque gulaeo hoc
Ex capite cuttabo ferox, totumque videbo
Heart-blooddum fluere in terram. Sic verba finivit.

(95–104)

[Without delay, the throng marched forth in a long line,/The lady of Newbarns herself first, strengthened by her clowns,/Carrying furiously in her hands a rusty gully [large knife]/At last she calls to the dungbasketers who were frightened and in utter confusion,/ 'Go', she says, 'You ugly fellows. If in the future/Any dungcarrier even tries to cross past our windows,/I swear that I shall cut out

> his long throat/And tear up his whole face, and his ears with this gully/I shall cut ferociously from his head, and I shall see all/Of his heart's blood flow into the earth.' So she finished speaking.]

Although this poem is not itself a translation, and represents only a minor part of Drummond's literary activity, it is significant in that it fuses two languages, and that one of these is Scots – the terms, 'ribauldis', 'gullaeo', 'ad pellmellia', 'fleidos' 'thrapellum', 'rivabo', and 'luggasque' all derive from Scotticisms: 'rebald' (villain), 'gully' (knife), 'at pell mell' (headlong), 'fleyd' (frightened), 'thrapple' (throat), 'reive' (tear), and 'lugs' (ears). Obviously, Drummond associates Scots with a low register, and uses it to realise the 'mock' element in 'mock-heroic', but he uses Scots with confidence and energy, and he obviously expects his Latin-educated readership to understand and appreciate the linguistic farrago. The saturation of Latin into Scots can be read as a parodic invocation of the aureate Scots poetry of the late mediaeval period, and its glut of classically derived neologisms presages the work of that other great Scottish translator of the seventeenth century, Thomas Urquhart of Cromarty.

Given the extensive practical use that Drummond, as an extremely systematic reader, made of the translations in his possession, it is tempting to speculate that his own, imitative, literary output might have been partly conditioned by his desire simply to understand and master the subtleties of the works he was reading. But, as Jack (1972) has demonstrated in detail, there is much more to Drummond's translations and imitations than the desire to follow slavishly the sources offered by foreign masters. As Jack points out, Drummond followed his Scottish contemporaries in acknowledging Petrarch as the preeminent European love poet, yet his own adaptations favour other, more minor, poets, such as Sannazaro, Guarini and Marino. The comparative neglect of Petrarch as a direct source might be due to the growing consciousness of an established tradition of literary translation – the intertextuality of Scottish poetry at the time is so complex that an ostensibly 'Petrarchan' poem by Drummond might derive in fact from an earlier Scottish poet, such as Fowler or Alexander, which in turn may or may not have Petrarch as a direct source (see Jack 1968, 1972). In such circumstances, translation from better-known sources might be avoided, loose translation might be favoured, or translation from less popular sources might be privileged. These appear to be the strategies favoured by Drummond. As we have seen, much of the time he opts to translate minor European poets, while the poems in which he adapts a revered European master usually pay homage to their origins by departing from them in a systematic fashion – as Jack (1972: 118) argues, it is 'the very neatness of the divergences' which points to the sources. For Jack, a 'crucial piece of evidence' for this claim is a Petrarchan echo found in the opening quatrains of a sonnet in *Poems* II (9):

> Sweet *Spring*, thou turns't with all thy goodlie Traine,
> Thy Head with Flames, thy Mantle bright with Flowrs,
> The *Zephyres* curle the greene Lockes of the Plaine,
> The Cloudes for Joy in Pearles weepe downe their Showrs.
> Thou turn'st (sweet Youth) but *ah* my pleasant Howres
> And happie Dayes, with thee come not againe,
> The sad Memorialls only of my Paine
> Doe with thee turne, which turne by Sweets in Sowres.

Jack identifies as a possible source a sonnet by Petrarch, which begins:

> Zefiro torna e 'l bel tempo rimena
> E i fiori e l' erbe, sua dolce famiglia,
> E garrir Progne e pianger Filomena,
> E primavera candida e vermiglia;
> Ridono i prati e 'l ciel se rasserena;
> Giove s'allegra di mirar sua figlia,
> L'aria e l'acqua e la terra è d'amor piena,
> Ogni animal d'amar si riconsiglia.

The similarities are evident: in both versions the joyful return of spring is heralded by a personified nature. In Petrarch, the flowers and plants constitute Zephyr's 'sweet family', the meadows laugh, and the animals fall in love. Drummond picks up these themes, but varies them. The roles of Spring and Zephyr are reversed: Zephyr's 'dolce famiglia' becomes the 'goodlie–Traine' of Spring, although Zephyr's association with flowering meadows is retained – Drummond has him curling 'the greene Lockes of the Plaine'. Moreover, where Petrarch's sky clears, Drummond's weeps for joy, prefiguring the more melancholy turn that the Scottish poem will take in comparison with the Italian's unmitigated high spirits. In an age in which most European poets ransacked Petrarch for images and themes, Drummond and his contemporaries no doubt could rely on a well-established familiarity with the source texts, which became less a canon to be transmitted, and more a background against which their own subtle variations could be cast, recognised, and appreciated.

Drummond, then, like the earlier court poets, positioned himself within a common European tradition. However, as noted earlier, he did not generally use the Scots linguistic system available to him as a signal of his national affiliation. While remaining at home in Hawthornden, south of Edinburgh, he nevertheless strove to master the linguistic system centred in London and the court of the recently united kingdoms. The lines quoted above serve as an example of Drummond's anglicising tendency: the rhymes 'Flowrs/Showrs/Howrs/Sowres' probably do not retain the Scottish monophthong /u/ – the <ow> digraph suggests a southern diphthong. However, as the *Polemo-Viddinia* demonstrates, Drummond still had access to the Scots language system, and could avail himself of it in his serious poetry when he saw the need, as is evident in the following madrigal (*Poems* I, iii):

> Like the *Idalian* Queene
> Her Haire about her Eyne,
> With Necke and Brests ripe Apples to be seene,
> At first glance of the *Morne*
> In *Cyprus* Gardens gathering those faire Flowrs
> Which of her Bloud were borne
> I saw, but fainting saw, my Paramours.

The rhymes here do signal Drummond's Scottish provenance: the conservative <n>-plural in 'Eyne' survives in spoken Scots to this day, while in this poem 'Flowrs', despite its spelling, rhymes with 'Paramours', rather than with, say, 'Sowres' [sours]. Drummond is probably aware of the Scotticisms – he is making use of them to preserve rhyme. Yet the English influence is strong even in this poem: the periphrastic 'Idalian Queene' echoes 'the bright Idalian starre' mentioned in Jonson's *Hymenaei* and MacDonald (1976: xxi) observes that Drummond copied this phrase into his notebooks, alongside Jonson's gloss of the term as referring to Venus. Although his general preference is for English, then, Drummond moves between English and Scots as each serves his immediate purpose, and in his drifting from one linguistic system to the other, he prefigures the poetic code-switching that is found in the work of later Scots revivalists, such as Burns (cf. Smith, 1996).

Drummond as a translator is unlike most Scottish poets before and after him, in that he does not transmit works in another tongue so much as digest and then reconstitute them. As Spiller (1988: 150) says:

> Drummond is one of the most intertextual of our poets, constantly weaving into his verse echoes of others'; and his poetry is unreadable on the assumption that sweet verse must be the

> private expression of a unique soul. The ghosts of half the love poets of Renaissance Europe whisper among his lines: from foreign poets he will often translate and adapt directly, masking them in the change of tongues; from his own countrymen he will take suggestions and echoes, chiefly from Sidney but also from Shakespeare, whose sonnets he may have known, and whose preoccupation with time and change is melodiously like his own.

The inclusion of Sidney and Shakespeare among 'his own countrymen' is telling: in some ways Drummond typifies the post-Union court poets' ceasing to cultivate a distinctive idiom from that of their southern neighbours. In other ways, however, his verse marks a return to the earlier perspective of the Scottish poets of the fifteenth and early sixteenth century, who saw little substantial difference between Chaucer's English and their 'Inglis', and who drew on the southern literary tradition without feeling their own national identity was being compromised. What had changed in the intervening century, of course, was the political alignment of Scotland and England.

Unlike Gavin Douglas, the pre-eminent poetic translator of the previous century, William Drummond was not a public figure, although in the later years of his life he cultivated an interest in history. He was a supporter of the monarchy, and conservative in his political and religious opinions, and he must have been disturbed by the upheavals following James VI's death and the rising discontent north and south of the border caused by the inept reign of Charles I. In Scotland, popular discontent focused on the Episcopalian king's attempt to introduce a revised Prayer Book into Presbyterian worship. Resistance to this measure led in 1638 to the signing of the National Covenant in Edinburgh, a document condemning various Catholic practices and pledging to uphold 'the true religion'. Drummond, despite his natural monarchism, accepted the National Covenant too. Although the Covenant also pledged to maintain the king's authority, it was an implicit rejection of Charles I's doctrine of the Divine Right of Kings, and it symbolises Scotland's ambivalence about the reign of Charles I – the Scots supported him as heir to the Stuart dynasty, but resented his arrogance and his Anglicanism. The Scottish Covenanters' clashes with Charles's troops – the so-called Bishops' Wars – might be seen as precursors of the English Civil War of 1642. Such a perspective might be reinforced by the Solemn League and Covenant signed in 1643 by the Scottish Covenanters and the English Parliament, whereby the Covenanters pledged to support the Parliament against the Royalist troops. Not all Scotland was united against the

Royalist cause, however. The English Civil War resulted in dissent among the Scottish Covenanters – the Earl of Montrose sided with the king and raised a Highland army against his erstwhile allies, before being defeated by David Leslie in 1645. Even so, when the king was defeated in 1646, and executed two years later, the Scottish Covenanters found themselves in a dilemma. They had not wished to bring down the Stuart dynasty, only alter its direction towards presbyterianism. Accordingly, the very Scots who had fought against Charles I and his Royalist troops were instrumental in proclaiming as king his eighteen-year-old heir and then fighting to re-establish the Stuart dynasty in England.

In the midst of these political upheavals, in 1649, Drummond died. His last few years had been spent concentrating on domestic affairs at his estate in Hawthornden. The last and perhaps the greatest of the Stuart court poets had lived to see James VI's literary circle shift to London and become subsumed in English culture. The intertextual, multicultural collage that is Drummond's poetry, and his choice of an English idiom with only occasional Scottish colouring, can be seen as his attempt to both distil the vernacular European tradition and position himself as one of the first generation of *British* writers. In this, of course, he predates the birth of Great Britain as a political entity by half a century; nevertheless, his ambition was clearly to be recognised not as a Scottish or English writer and translator but as a fusion of the two. He died just after Charles I's execution, knowing that the dream of a United Kingdom under a Scottish king had also died. The melancholy nature of much of his poetry, his obsession with death and change, is certainly appropriate.

Sir Thomas Urquhart of Cromarty: The Road to Rabelais

As Drummond was slipping into his last years at Hawthornden, a young Scot from outside Inverness was among the Royalist troops led by the Earl of Montrose. Thomas Urquhart of Cromarty (1611–1660) was from an economically troubled Catholic family recently turned Protestant, and his sympathies were firmly Royalist and Episcopalian. When Aberdeen was retaken by the Covenanting forces, he escaped to England, where he was part of the court circle for three years, being knighted in 1641. At this time he began his literary career, composing two books of epigrams which received little attention, and an eccentric treatise on trigonometry, which received less. In 1642, Urquhart's father died, and his son took on responsibility for the family debts, combining spells at the estate in Cromarty with periods of travel abroad. Like many other Scots, Urquhart was appalled at the execution of Charles I, and in 1649 and 1650 he took part in different Royalist uprisings in Scotland and England, latterly under the leadership of Charles II. The Scottish Royalists were defeated at Worcester, and Urquhart was imprisoned, first in the Tower of London, and then in Windsor Castle. In a short story, 'Logopandocy', based on Urquhart's writings and life, Alasdair Gray imagines an encounter in the Tower of London between the Royalist Scot and Cromwell's Latin secretary, John Milton – in Gray's fictional narrative, they talk at hilarious cross-purposes about their different literary ambitions (Gray, 1984: 180). One result of Urquhart's incarceration was that the English Parliament decreed that Urquhart's estates would be forfeited if he could not demonstrate that he deserved to keep possession of them. Urquhart decided to demonstrate that his merits lay in his literary ability, and so he set about publishing four books between 1652 and 1653, all with the express purpose of showing their author to be a heroic figure from a noble family, blessed with extraordinary literary and philosophical gifts. The first, *Pantochronocanon; or, a Peculiar Promtuary of Time* constructs a geneology which takes the Urquhart family back to the sons of Adam; the second, the *Ekskubalauron* (sometimes known by its subtitled gloss, *The Jewel*) sets about introducing the principles of a universal language, the 'jewel' in question; the third, *Logopandecteision, or an INTRODUCTION to the UNIVERSAL LANGUAGE* begins with a book entitled *Neaudethaumata, or, Wonders of the New Speech*. As Craik (1993: 29) observes, this book largely reprints the matter of *Ekskubalauron* and adds to it barely-related attacks on Urquhart's persecutors, namely kirk ministers, judges, and creditors. Finally, in 1653, Urquhart published his translation of the first two books of Rabelais' *Gargantua* and *Pantagruel*. None of the books was particularly successful during Urquhart's lifetime, and the third volume of the Rabelais translation was only discovered in manuscript among his papers, and printed in 1693. Urquhart seems to have been released in 1653, and he spent some of the final years of his life living in Middleburg in the Netherlands. He was dead by 1660.

The bare facts of Urquhart's life not only reflect on the troubled political events of his time, they also give insight into the motives and obsessions which drove his original writings, if not his translation. Urquhart was from an old Scottish family, and grew up in Scotland after the Union of the Crowns, attending Aberdeen University at around the age of eleven. As an adult, however, his focus of concern was London, first as the seat of the court of Charles I, then as the home of his oppressors, the Commonwealth parliament which was his spur to literary activity and his most immediate audience. Like Drummond of Hawthornden, even if Urquhart spoke Scots, he wrote largely in English with a few occasional traces of his spoken linguistic system. And like the Drummond of the *Polemo-Middinia,* Urquhart chose to infuse the vernacular with a plethora of neologisms, mainly deriving from Greek and Latin. The very titles of his prose works bear witness to this exotic grafting onto English of a long-lived Scots classicist tradition. It is possible that the disparity between his spoken and written code gave added impetus to Urquhart's interest in a universal language. However, interest in this topic was widespread in Urquhart's time, as Steiner (1992: 208) observes:

> There are several reasons why these attempts [i.e. to devise a universal language] should have been particularly frequent and sustained during the seventeenth and early eighteenth centuries. The decline of Latin from general currency had created important gaps in mutual comprehension. These deepened with the rise of linguistic nationalism. At the same time, both intellectual and economic relations were developing on a scale that required ease and exactitude of communication. The constant ramifications of knowledge in the seventeenth century, moreover, led to a search for universal taxonomies, for a comprehensive, clearly articulated vocabulary and grammar for all science.

Urquhart's fascination with mathematics and language are, then, typical of philosophical inquiry in his age, although his proposed solutions are idiosyncratic to the point of parody. Inevitably, given the extravagance of his claims for his Universal Language, Urquhart did not go further than offer a descriptive preface, first in *Eskubalauron,* or *The Jewel,* in 1652, later slightly modified and reprinted in *Logopandecteison* (1653). Given that Urquhart must have been aware of a disparity between the speech of his Scottish countrymen and the English medium in which he and his class now elected to write, there is little or no trace of this difference in the preface to his Universal Language. There is the merest hint of Urquhart's Scots in his use if the word 'Bliteri' in the first article of description – deriving from the Middle Scots verb and noun 'bluiter', it is glossed as 'foolish or outrageous speech'. The word survives in Present-Day Scots as 'blether', and in the English collocation 'blithering idiot'. In general, however, Urquart writes in an idiosyncratic English, and in his discussions of the European vernaculars he neglects to mention Scots directly.

Instead he describes English as a dialect of the 'Saxon tongue', with 'dialect' here meaning something akin to 'descendant':

> The French, Spanish and Italians are but dialects of the Latine, as the English is of the Saxon tongue, though with this difference that the mixture of Latine with the Gaulish, Moresco and Gotish tongues make up the three first languages; but the meer qualification of the Saxon with the old British frameth not the English to the full, for that, by its promiscuous and ubiquitary borrowing, it consisteth almost of all languages; which I speak not in dispraise thereof, although I may with confidence aver, that were all the four aforesaid languages stript of what is not originally their own, we should not be able with them all in any part of the world to purchase so much as our breakfast in a market. (Jack and Lyall (eds), 1983: 65)

Urquhart here shows his awareness of the debt English owes to the loanwords which had been flooding into the language for centuries, and indirectly it suggests his belief that there is no 'natural' language which can be described as pure. If all the European vernaculars are impure dialects, then perhaps none can symbolise national character. Elsewhere in *The Jewel,* Urquhart displays scepticism about the very notion of national character – a subject he had a vested interest in, given that he felt he was imprisoned partly on the grounds that he was Scottish:

> True it is, that nothing is more usual in speech then to blame all for the fault of the greater part and to twit a whole country with that vice to which most of its inhabitants are inclined. Hence we have these sayings: the Spaniards are proud; the French inconstant; the Italians lecherous; the Cretians lyers; the Sicilians false; the Asiaticks effeminate; the Crovats cruel; the Dutch temulencious [drunken]; the Polonians quarrelsome; the Saxons mutinous and so forth thorow other territories, nurseries of enormities of another kinde; although nothing be more certain then that there are some Spaniards as humble; French as constant; Italians chaste; Cretians true; Sicilians ingenuous; Asiaticks warlike; Crovates merciful; Dutch sober; Polonians peaceable and some Saxons as loyal as any in the world besides. By which account, all forreigners (for such are all the inhabitants on the earth in relation to those that are not their compatriots) yeelding to the *most* and *some* of each stranger-land in its respective vice and vertue; it may be safely avouched, that there is under the sun

> no national fault nor national deserving whereby all merit to be punished or all rewarded because the badness of most in each destroys the universality of vertue, and the good inclination of some in all cuts off the generality of vice. (Jack and Lyall (eds), 1983: 87–8)

Though casting doubt on the existence of essential national characteristics, and arguing against the existence of pure European vernaculars, Urquhart continues to characterise himself as a patriotic Scot, and he offers his Universal Language as an honest Scotsman's service to humanity in general. The language itself is full of implausible wonders, described in a series of articles, of which the following are simply a typical selection:

> Three and twentiethly, every word in this language signifieth as well backward as forward; and how ever you invert the letters, still shall you fall upon significant words, whereby a wonderful facility is obtained in making of anagrams.
>
> . . .
>
> Seven and twentiethly, in translating verses of any vernaculary tongue, such as Italian, French, Spanish, Slavonian, Dutch, Irish, English or whatever it be, it affords you words of the same signification, syllable for syllable, and in the closure of each line a ryme as in the original. (Jack and Lyall (eds), 1983: 75–6)

Significantly, Urquhart does not refer to 'Scots', only to 'English' or 'the Saxon tongue'. Given his views on the impurity and intermingling of the European vernaculars, it is likely that he regarded the Scots and English linguistic systems as cognate, and both – like the other vernaculars – as imperfect glimpses of a potential, transcendental synthesis:

> Five and fiftiethly, all the languages in the world will be beholding to this and this to none. (Jack and Lyall (eds), 1983: 79)

Although, understandably, Urquhart does not go on to describe his Universal Language in detail, his prose style can be seen as an attempt to put its principles into practice. Although it is undeniably English in its orientation, it is a 'synthetic' English, infused with a wealth of neologisms, mainly classical borrowings, an English that harks back to the dizzy extremes of the Scottish aureate poets, and to the early latinate prose writers. It is an English that is peculiarly suited to the translation of Rabelais.

A.D. Mackie has argued (in Lowland Scots, or 'Lallans') for the inclusion of Urquhart in the canon of Scots translators (Mackie, 1995: 101): 'It wes a Scot, Sir Tam Urquhart, that owreset Rabelais inti a Suthron muckle enrichit bi Lallans.' [I.e. 'It was a Scot, Sir Tom Urquhart, who translated Scots into an English greatly enriched by Lallans.'] It has to be said, however, that, for much of the three books of *Gargantua* and *Pantagruel* that Urquhart completed, his use of Scots is relatively slight. It has been shown that the greatest single influence on the translation, other than the source text itself, was in fact Randle Cotgrave's *Dictionarie of the French and English Tongues* – a formidable early exercise in bilingual lexicography which included and explicitly marked a great number of Rabelais' own neologisms. Craik (1993) shows in considerable detail the use Urquhart made of Cotgrave, observing:

> As Urquhart confers with Cotgrave for even the most familiar words, he must have spent a long time in Cotgrave's company. Plainly the *Dictionarie,* with its lists, classification system, synonyms and, above all, *words,* would have appealed to Urquhart, who was independently interested in all these aspects. (Craik, 1993: 132)

Urquhart's use of Cotgrave is extensive – Craik demonstrates conclusively that Urquhart's often-noted tendency to elaborate on Rabelais by piling synonym upon synonym and meaning upon meaning is frequently a result of his copying or adapting entire entries from Cotgrave's dictionary:

> To the already grotesque and gigantic world of *Gargantua* and *Pantagruel,* the transplanting of Cotgrave's synonyms and variants adds still more colour while leaving unaltered the structural details of Rabelais' tale. Once the reader is familiar with Urquart's expansive methods, he may suspect the occasions when Cotgrave is consulted, especially when he encounters short lists, or pairs of words joined by "and" or "or". (Craik, 1993: 138)

Urquhart's use of Cotgrave as a point of reference is significant in the steady decline in this period of the use of Scots as a formal, public language – Cotgrave's, after all, is a dictionary of French and English. The earliest substantial monolingual dictionary of Scots was not to appear until the nineteenth century, and scholarly bilingual dictionaries of English and Scots have only very recently been published. The great period of codification of English – the climax of the standardisation process – was not to happen until the century following

Urquhart's translation, but even in the seventeenth century a Scottish translator was likely to be thrown back on the resources of the small pool of reference books in English, not Scots.

That being said, it would be surprising if the treasury of words which articulate Urquhart's translation of Rabelais' mock-heroic tales of a family of giants and their adventures among the knights and monks, the con-artists and crooks of a mythological France were to exclude totally the language Urquhart would have spoken (but not written) in his native Scotland. And, if the Rabelaisian translation is not 'muckle enricht' by the inclusion of Scotticisms, there are at least traces of Scots in Urquhart's prose. In some cases, the Scots lexical items are likely to be 'covert' Scotticisms – that is, it is unlikely that Urquhart would have recognised them as particularly Scottish. This probably applies to the common, French-derived word 'tasse' [cup or goblet] in the following list (*Gargantua*, Chap. LI):

> ... eight hundred thousand & fourteen *Besants* of gold, in great antick vessels, huge pots, large basins, big tasses, cups, goblets, candlesticks, comfit boxes, and other such plate, all of pure massie gold besides the precious stones, enameling and workmanship ...

The word 'wezand' [throat] used in the compound 'wezand-slitting' (*Gargantua*, Chap. XXVII), although it derives from OE and is found in Shakespeare, is also by the seventeenth century becoming more confined to English dialects and to Scots. Forms of both 'tasse' and 'wezand' are found in the poetry of Burns, for example.

More overt uses of Scots have several motivations: the word 'quean' [young woman], which is still current in north-east Scotland, is used to preserve the rhyme in *Gargantua* Chap. II:

> Who sitting saw *Penthilesa* tane,
> In her old age, for a cresse-selling quean

> [Who sitting saw Penthilesa taken
> In her old age, for a cress-selling girl]

Like Drummond before him, and Burns after him, Urquhart makes use of the two linguistic systems to extend the opportunities for rhyme, and – in the case of 'quean/queen' – for bicodal punning. Urquhart also follows the time-honoured tradition of Chaucer, Dunbar and others in using northern vocabulary for scatalogical purposes: the Scots term 'skite' [to defecate; from ON skíta, which is cognate with English 'shite', from OE scitan] is intensified with the Latin intensifying prefix 'con-' to coin the expression 'conskite', which appears regularly throughout the text. An echo of the Scots expression 'thrapple' [throat] can also be heard in the tribal name of the 'thirstie Ethrappels' who appear in *Pantagruel* (Chap. II).

However, the most sustained passages of Scots in Urquhart's translation appear in Chapters VI and IX of *Pantagruel.* The latter chapter includes a Scots passage in the 'double dutch' sequence of utterances of obscure languages spoken by Panurge when Pantagruel first encounters him. This is one of Urquhart's typical expansions on his source text, which confines Panurge's languages to German, Italian, Basque, Dutch, Spanish, Danish, Hebrew, Greek, Latin and sundry nonsensical or invented tongues. Urquhart's half-nonsensical addition reads like a parody of sixteenth-century Scots prose:

> *Lard, ghest tholb be sua virtuis be intelligence ass yi body schal biss naturall relvth, tholb suld of me pety have; for natur hass ulss egualy maide; bot fortune sum exaltit hess and oyis deprevit. Non ye less viois mou virtius deprevit and virtiuss men discrivis, for anen ye lad end iss non gud.*

The gist of the passage is that Pantagruel should have mercy on Panurge, because all men are born equal but fortune favours some while it deprives others. The language contains Scots forms (for example, 'sua', so; 'suld', should), Scots grammatical inflexions (the '-it' preterite in 'exaltit' and 'deprevit'), and archaic spellings ('oyis', others). The joke is, of course, that this language is barely comprehensible, and that Scots texts barely a hundred years old should be the butt of such a joke by a Scottish translator is richly suggestive of the way that these texts were beginning to be regarded by the middle of the seventeenth century.

The other Scots passage (in Chapter VI) is even more revealing of Urquhart's attitude to his native speech, and it also shows at its most extreme the self-conscious 'synthetic English' of his written style. In this chapter, the giant, Pantagruel, encounters a pretentious student from provincial Limoges, who, in affecting the manners of the capital city, speaks in a Latinised French, much to the giant's consternation:

> By G-- *(said Pantagruel),* I will teach you to speak, but first come hither, and tell me whence thou art? To this the Scholar answered: The primeval origin of my aves and ataves was indigenarie of the *Lemovick* regions, where requiesceth the corpor of the hagiotat St. *Martial.* I understand thee very well (said *Pantagruel*), when all comes to all, thou art a *Limousin,* and thou wilt here by they affected speech counterfeit the *Parisiens*: well now, come hither, I

> must shew thee a new trick, and handsomely give thee the *comb-feat*: with this he took him by the throat, saying to him, Thou flayest the Latine: by St *John*, I will make thee flay the foxe, for I will now flay thee alive: Then began the poor *Limousin* to cry; *Haw, gwid* Maaster, haw Loard, *my halp and St.* Marshaw, haw *I'm worried:* Haw, *my thropple, the bean of my cragg is bruck!* Haw, *for* gauads *seck, lawt my lean,* Mawster; *waw, waw, waw.* Now (said *Pantagruel*) thou speakest naturally, and so let him go . . .

The code-switching in this passage is fascinating: the dominant narrative is English, as is the direct speech of Pantagruel. This then is the privileged, prestigious code. The direct speech of the Limousin – initially affected, then 'natural' provincial – is first of all the Latinised English Urquhart revels in elsewhere, then specifically the Aberdonian of his university days. The spelling of 'gwid' [good] localises the Scots pronunciation in the north-east of the country, while more general Scots features include the vowels in 'Maaster', 'Loard' and 'gauad', the dropping of the final /l/ in 'Marshaw', and the Scots expressions 'thrapple'/'cragg' [throat] and 'my lean' [= my lane; alone]. The Limousin is the object of linguistic and social mockery in this passage – yet it is difficult not to identify the Limousin with Urquhart himself. Urquhart, like his fellow Scots, would have seemed a provincial at Charles I's court, his native north-eastern speech would have seemed rustic and exotic in London, and in his writing Urquhart often affected an obscurely latinate style. Self-mockery is not widely considered to be one of Urquhart's more obvious virtues, yet he must have recognised aspects of his own personality and history in the character of the Limousin. It is therefore poignant as well as ironic when, a few paragraphs later, we are told that the Limousin died of an enormous thirst, and that this fact is:

> . . . a work of divine vengeance, shewing us that which saith the Philosopher and *Aulus Gellius,* that it becometh us to speak according to the common language; and that we should, (as said *Octavian Augustus*) strive to shun all strange and unknown termes with as much heedfulnesse and circumspection as Pilots of ships use to avoid the rocks and banks of the sea.

Urquhart's shift into north-eastern Scots in order to represent a character's specific social and regional origins signals the beginning of a new trend in the use of Scots in translation, and is an early example of a narrative strategy later exploited in Scottish novels by Walter Scott, John Galt, Robert Louis Stevenson and countless others. As the standardisation process was arrested in Scots, the very non-standard nature of the medium allows it to carry meanings that a deracinated standard variety cannot. Scottish writers who use specific varieties of Scots to pinpoint the regional and social affiliations of their Scottish characters can trace their literary lineage back to Urquhart. Otherwise, it is difficult to gauge his impact on later writers. Certainly, he died disappointed that his translations had found no immediate audience – the lack of response led him to abandon his project of a complete translation of Rabelais. On the other hand, he found favour with later critical writers, and was singled out for praise in the eighteenth century by Alexander Fraser Tytler, despite his Rabelaisian vulgarity. Urquhart has certainly influenced, directly and indirectly, all later translations of Rabelais into English. In the introduction to the Penguin translation, for example, the twentieth-century translator, J.M. Cohen, acknowledges his debt to Urquhart 'for a phrase' (Cohen, 1955: 31). However, in the episode with the Limousin, the debt extends beyond the phrase:

> 'By God,' cried Pantagruel, 'I'll teach you to speak. But before I do so, tell me one thing. Where do you come from?'
>
> To which the scholar replied: 'The primeval origin of my aves and ataves was indigenous to the Lemovic regions, where requiesces the corpus of the hagiotate Saint Martial.'
>
> 'I understand you all right,' said Pantagruel. 'What it comes to is that you're a Limousin, and here you want to play the Parisian. Well, come on, then, and I'll give you a combing.' Then he took him by the throat and continued: 'You murder Latin, by Saint John, I'll make you skin the fox. I'll skin you alive.'
>
> Then the poor Limousin began to plead: 'Haw, guid master! Haw lordie! Help me, St Marshaw. Ho, let me alane, for Gaud's sake and dinna hairm me!'
>
> Whereupon Pantagruel replied, 'Now you're speaking naturally,' and released him.
>
> (Cohen, 1955: 185)

Cohen pays homage to Urquhart by code-switching into Scots to represent the provincial nature of the Limousin's speech – although it is a more generalised Scots in Cohen's translation, not localised in the north-east. Cohen – and Urquhart – could conceivably have used any non-standard English variety to represent the Limousin's 'natural' speech. That Urquhart chose his native Aberdonian is indicative of the way that educated Scots – even Scots who, like Urquhart, were educated at Aberdeen University – now perceived the way they spoke. In writing, it was reserved for contexts associated with provincialism and low comedy. Only seventy years before Urquhart's translation, a Scottish king was commissioning translations into Scots and writing advice for poets in the Scots tongue. Now, for the time being, large-scale translation into Scots was inconceivable, particularly in prose. In a United Kingdom whose centre of gravity was firmly fixed in London, Scots could only be used for local effect, to show the provincial, the rustic, the fool. This potential weakness in Scots was to be turned to advantage in the next century.

Drummond and Urquhart are both transitional figures. They stand at the end of a tradition of translation into a Scots which was a fully-fledged language capable of marking a nascent national identity. However, they also stand at the beginning of another tradition of Scots translating into English, using Scots either to extend their linguistic resources or for local – mainly comic – effect. In the words of Edwin Morgan:

> Drummond's English verse was as important in its way as Douglas's Scots. It acknowledged the reality of the linguistic situation in Scotland, where Gaelic, Scots and English had somehow to live together. Drummond showed that English could be used and that others would use it after him. (Morgan, 1977: 200)

In the seventeenth century, it might well have seemed that English would completely replace Scots as a major medium of translation, and indeed the tradition of Scots translating into English is an distinguished one, taking in such luminaries as the early translation theorist, Alexander Fraser Tytler (1747–1814), and, in the twentieth century, Edwin and Willa Muir. Yet, in the new political union of Great Britain, a nation-state born at the beginning of the eighteenth century, Scots would slowly begin to recover as a medium of literary translation, until, in the twentieth century it burst once more into life.

Chapter 6

'Nae Cotillion Brent New Frae France?': The Eighteenth and Nineteenth Centuries

Towards the Union

Legend has it that Sir Thomas Urquhart died of a fit of laughter on hearing of Charles II's restoration in 1660. The story may be apocryphal, but it is nevertheless appropriate: after his own tribulations, neglect and exile, Urquhart would doubtless have enjoyed knowing of the Scots' part in the reinstatement of the Stuart dynasty after its brief Cromwellian interruption. The king was back in his rightful position in Westminster, and business could continue as usual in Scotland. With the court firmly re-established in London, the late seventeenth century saw the rise in Scotland of the influence of the professions, and in particular, the lawyers who clustered in the courts and clubs of Edinburgh, which was the seat of a separate Scottish Parliament, even if this parliament was, until 1689, 'only a little more than a solemn rubber stamp' for the edicts of Charles II and, later, his brother James VII (Smout, 1969: 201). As Ouston (1987) argues, the Edinburgh lawyers were to play an increasingly influential role in Scotland's cultural life, and, as writers and patrons, they were to act as a substitute for the departed Scottish court. Before the Union of Parliaments, however, these Scottish 'Virtuosi' – professional men whose interests actively embraced the arts and the sciences – consciously looked south for their models and influences, and while they retained some interest in Scottish traditions, the use of written Scots was not part of their cultural agenda. Ouston observes of one such Virtuoso, George Mackenzie, Lord Advocate between 1677 and 1689, and author of *Idea Eloquentia Forensis Hodiernae* (1681):

> It is worth remembering that the Jacobean courtly tradition from which his work derived was both anglophile and nationalist, and

> that this major theme of Virtuoso culture did not involve the tensions to which it was subject after 1707. Indeed it can be argued that one of the reasons for the survival of a distinctive Scottish culture after the Union was the confidence with which English intellectual influences had been imitated and adapted in the late seventeenth century. The use of an English literary style derived from the move of the Scottish Court to London in 1603, and from Scottish writers such as Drummond of Hawthornden, but also, more profoundly, from the Calvinist Reformation, Knox's English prose, and the Authorised Version of the Bible. Use of English as opposed to Scots was the result of a tradition which also made Latin an attractive language. (Ouston, 1987: 19–20)

Mackenzie and his ilk, then, valued a distinctively Scottish tradition within a British, and indeed European, context – external models could be used to provide standards that the native culture could meet, by adoption and adaptation. Mackenzie wrote in both Latin and English, but he continued to value what he saw as the intrinsic merits of Scots – significantly, in the spoken context of legal proceedings. He makes this clear in his essay, *What Eloquence is fit for the Bar*:

> English is fit for haranguing, the French for complimenting, but the Scots for pleading. Our pronunciation is like ourselves, firy, abrubt, sprightly and bold; their greatest wits being employ'd at Court, have indeed enricht very much their language as to conversation, but all ours bending themselves to study Law, the chief Science in repute with us, hath much smooth'd our language, as to pleading ... their language is invented by Courtiers ... but ours by learn'd men, and men of businesse, and so must be massie and significant. (Mackenzie, quoted in Ouston, 1987: 20)

As Scotland moved towards the Union of Parliaments, then, its high culture was driven no longer by courtiers but by the professional classes – self-styled 'Virtuosi' – who prided themselves in their command of Scottish, British and European culture.

However, the self-confidence of the Scottish professional classes was to be fractured by the events closing the seventeenth and opening the eighteenth centuries: the demise of the Stuart dynasty in the Glorious Revolution of 1688, and the amalgamation of Scotland into the newly-created state of Great Britain in 1707. Neither of these events met with universal hostility in Scotland, although obviously each was opposed vociferously, and at times actively, by factions within the country. On the death of Charles II, with no legitimate heir, the succession of his Catholic brother James VII was met with consternation in Protestant Scotland as well as in England. The adoption of William III by Scottish and English nobles showed 'how a British identity of interests could exist outside the personal interests of the monarch' (Smout, 1969: 199). The Protestant succession was ensured, but the nominal Scottish link with the monarch was broken.

The Union of Parliaments in 1707 was resisted by such eloquent figures as Andrew Fletcher of Saltoun, but even so, the Scottish politicians agreed to the treaty, which guaranteed the independence of the Scottish church, education system, and Scots law. In practical terms, the loss of a Scottish Parliament in Edinburgh might not have had much direct effect on Scottish affairs, but for many Scots it would have been at least a symbolic loss, and it prompted a reappraisal of Scottish identity in the new British context. One powerful strategy for reassessing Scottish identity has been dubbed 'applied antiquarianism' (Brown, 1987: 35) – the search for Scottish greatness in the relics of the past, and it is the interest in antiquarianism which, after the Union, began to fuel the Scottish literary revival, and the first signs of a recovery in translation into Scots.

The Status of Scots after the Act of Union

It is impossible to consider Scots translation in the eighteenth and nineteenth centuries without commenting on developments in the relative status of English and Scots. The eighteenth century was, of course, the period in which English completed its long process of standardisation and a fairly homogeneous variety became established as the 'correct' medium of written communication. The completion of this process was made possible by the production of widely accepted reference books, notably Samuel Johnson's *Dictionary* (1755) and Robert Lowth's *Short Introduction to English Grammar* (1762), which established and popularised norms which could then be disseminated through education. Attitudes towards propriety in English spread from the written word to speech, and from the middle-classes in England to their conterparts in North Britain, as the following regulations, published by the *Select Society* in Edinburgh (quoted in Jones, 1995: 9–10) indicate:

> As the intercourse between this part of GREAT-BRITAIN and the Capital daily increases, both on account of business and amusement, and must still go on increasing, gentlemen educated in SCOTLAND have long been sensible of the disadvantages under

> which they labour, from their imperfect knowledge of the ENGLISH TONGUE, and the impropriety with which they speak it.
>
> Experience hath convinced SCOTSMEN, that it is not impossible for persons born and educated in this country, to acquire such knowledge of the ENGLISH TONGUE, as to write it with some tolerable purity.
>
> But with regard to the other point, that of speaking with propriety, as little has been hitherto attempted, it has generally been taken for granted that there was no prospect of attempting any thing with a probability of success; though, at the same time, it is allowed to be an accomplishment more important, and more universally useful, than the former.

Here we have an early indication of the growing use of an anglicised accent as a marker of social status, and a further decline in the number of situations in which Scots – written and now spoken – was considered appropriate and polite. Far from being perceived as the best variety 'for pleading' as George Mackenzie had argued, eighty years earlier, Scots was now considered a mark of vulgarity – or at least that is what the flood of elocution teachers marketing their courses among the aspiring bourgeoisie in Edinburgh would have their prospective clients believe. However, as Charles Jones (1995) has demonstrated, the attitudes of eighteenth-century Edinburgh society to the increasing anglicisation of Scots was much more complex than simple acquiescence in anglicised speech-patterns. If Pittock (1995) has argued that the spirit of Jacobitism endured in British Scotland long after the crushing of the '45, then Jones has also shown that a number of Scots mounted a passionate rear-guard action against the erosion of a keystone in the construction of a separate national identity. Perhaps it is no coincidence that one of the most eloquent supporters of spoken Scots in this period was a Jesuit, and indeed an exiled Englishman, James Adams (1737–1802). While upholding the marriage between England and Scotland, Adams still argues for the retention of symbols of national identity, such as distinctive dress and a distinctive language:

> The sight of the Highland kelt, the flowing plaid, the buskin'd leg, provokes my antagonist to laugh! Is this dress ridiculous in the eyes of reason and common sense? No: nor is the dialect of speech: both are characteristic and national distinctions. National character and distinction are respectable. Then is the adopted mode of oral language sanctioned by peculiar reasons, and is not the result

> of chance, contemptible vulgarity, mere ignorance and rustic habit. (Adams, 1799; quoted in Jones, 1995: 18)

If the social aspirations of the majority of middle-class Scots caused them to succumb, to some degree, to the admonitions of the elocutionists, there were always those who continued to value Scots as a means of expressing national character and identity. As the eighteenth century merged into the nineteenth, many of these Scots articulated this belief by writing sentimental verse – always in a tradition straying little from that of Ramsay, Fergusson and Burns – or by investing energy in antiquarian philological investigations. In 1808, a minister and antiquarian, John Jamieson (1759–1838) published *An Etymological Dictionary of the Scottish Language,* and schoolteacher James Murray (1837–1915) completed his *The Dialect of the Southern Counties of Scotland* in 1873, before embarking on a project which in time was to become *A New English Dictionary on Historical Principles,* later renamed *The Oxford English Dictionary.* Literary imitations of traditional Scots forms retained social respectability, as did philological investigation of Scots, even as the Scottish middle-classes adapted their speech and writing to southern-influenced norms.

This was the climate in which translation into Scots had to survive in the two centuries after the Act of Union. The type of translation which emerged suited the tenor of the times. Classical translation helped relaunch Scots writing, and give it an authoritative written voice at a time when it was being associated primarily with speech. And translations from Scandinavian ballads and German songs fitted into the antiquarian interest in the roots of Scottish traditions and the Scots tongue. Bonaparte's biblical translators, and James Murray, were also motivated primarily by a desire to provide philological illustrations of Scots speech. Probably few of these 'translations' would have impressed Alexander Tytler, whose *Essay on the Principles of Translation* (1790) set out three principles that a good translator should follow:

> I. That the Translation should give a complete transcript of the ideas of the original work.
> II That the style and manner of writing should be of the same character with that of the original.
> III That the Translation should have all the ease of original composition.
>
> In order that a translator may be enabled to give a complete transcript of the ideas of the original work, it is indispensably

> necessary that he should have a perfect knowledge of the language of the original, and a competent acquaintance with the subject of which it treats. (Tytler, 1790; reprinted in Lefevere (ed.), 1992: 128)

As noted earlier, the only Scottish translator deemed worthy of praise by Tytler is Thomas Urquhart, whose Rabelais seemed to him to be marred only by the 'obscurity' and the 'strong tincture of licentiousness' which characterises the original (Tytler, 1790: 397). Of his contemporary Scottish translators, he has nothing to say: presumably their preference for 'imitation' disqualifies them from his attention. Nevertheless, the translations of the eighteenth and nineteenth cenuries contributed more to the literature of their day than their paucity of number would suggest. Furthermore, in their appeal to popular speech on the one hand, and Jamieson and Waddell's conscious experiments in 'synthetic' Scots on the other, they anticipate the strategies used in the renaissance of translation into Scots in the twentieth century.

Homespun Horaces: Allan Ramsay and his Successors

The quintessential eighteenth-century Scots antiquarian was Sir John Clerk of Penicuik (1676–1755). Clerk was another 'Virtuoso', combining interests in archaeology, architecture, landscape gardening, and the Scottish vernacular song tradition, with active patronage of the arts and his own substantial writings – historical studies in Latin and poetic works in English. Brown (1987: 35) writes of Clerk:

> A staunch advocate of the Union, and a Roman antiquary, he employed Roman archaeology in Scotland in such a way as to manifest a nationalism that drew its strength from ancient Caledonian resistance to Rome. This argument, projected forward into the eighteenth century, was deployed in resolving problems of post-Union culture and identity. Clerk sought thereby to find a greatness and a purpose for the smaller nation in face of the political, economic and intellectual power of a Roman England. He wished, paradoxically, to be part of a wider world, and yet to retain the essential character of an independent nationality. He was at once a Roman and a Caledonian, a North Britain and a Scot.

Clerk was a patron of Allan Ramsay (*c.* 1685–1758), an Edinburgh wigmaker and burgess, and the initial inspiration behind the eighteenth-century Scots literary revival. Among Ramsay's works are translations of Horace, a classical poet who would certainly have appealed to Clerk's antiquarian tastes. Ramsay's early poetic compositions were written for the Easy Club, a group of young men who in 1712 founded a literary society which affected hostility to the Union and supported the Stuart king. The Easy Club was modelled initially on English literary societies, which were themselves part of a wider European movement, as Linda Colley has pointed out:

> Voluntary associations of different kinds were breaking out like measles over the face of Britain and the rest of Europe at this time, especially in towns, and almost exclusively among men. There were street clubs, patronised by the leading inhabitants of a particular district, clubs devoted to hobbies, everything from rose-growing to cruel sports and idiosyncratic sex, innumerable masonic and quasi-masonic societies catering to the male delight in secret rituals and dressing up, box clubs, which poorer men joined to provide themselves with a modicum of insurance, clubs devoted to party politics or food, discussion clubs where blue-chinned autodidacts pondered the mysteries of science and philosophy, and more genteel associations where responsible citizens met to dine well and discuss the local poor. (Colley, 1992: 88)

The Easy Club was an early Scottish example of this largely middle-class explosion of social networking and civic and self-improvement. Such literary associations provided the opportunity to improve one's manners and conversation, while advancing one's position amongst one's peers and betters. Significantly, Ramsay's adopted nickname in the Easy Club was 'Gavin Douglas', an early indication of his interest in (and self-identification with) the medieval translator. Ramsay's own *Poems*, first published in 1721, his anthologies of the Scots medieval poets, including *The Ever Green* (1724), and his play, *The Gentle Shepherd* (1725), all helped generate an eighteenth-century revival in the literary use of Scots in poetry and drama. Ramsay's own verses are modelled on the folk poetry of Scotland – for example, the stanzas found in the anonymous *Christis Kirk* tradition – and they range from comic epistles, satires, and mock elegies to addresses, lyrics and epigrams, all in a Scots of varying density (cf. McClure, 1995: 161–70). They include a few translations – or, as Ramsay more accurately styled them, 'imitations' of Horace's Odes, in Scots. Translations of Horace into English, of course, were extremely popular in the late seventeenth century and into the eighteenth. Gillespie (1993: 148) observes, 'It is much more difficult to discover English poets of the later seventeenth century who were not imitators of Horace than to name ones that were. Between 1660 and 1700, new translations and adaptations of poems from the *Odes* alone were written by at least fifty different hands.' But whereas, as Gillespie also notes, the English Horace of the late seventeenth century acts as a spokesman for the period's libertine poses, the Scottish Horace of the early eighteenth century focuses on the Roman poet's moral seriousness and his sense of urbane comradeship. The homespun Horace of Scottish translations is put to work to celebrate the civilised values that can still exist when the individual finds himself at a distance from the metropolitan centre of power, its temptations – and its language. Ramsay's Preface to his *Poems* of 1721 offers a strong justification for the use of Scots rather than English. He conventionally legitimises Scots by indicating a classical antecedent, 'the *Doric* Dialect of *Theocritus*', but he also argues that the linguistic relationship between English and Scots in the early eighteenth century actually favours Scots speakers:

> *the Pronunciation* [of Scots] *is liquid and sonorous, and much fuller than the* English, *of which we are Masters, by being taught it in our Schools, and daily reading it; which being added to all our own native Words, of eminent Significancy, makes our Tongue by far the completest: For Instance, I can say,* an empty House, a toom Barrel, a boss Head, *and* a hollow Heart. – *Many such Examples might be given, but let this one suffice.* (Martin and Oliver (eds), 1945: xix)

Scots, according to Ramsay, is as suitable a medium as English – even a superior medium – for poetic expression. However, the major reason for writing in Scots is hinted at in Ramsay's admission that he knows no Latin:

> *Such Pedants as confine Learning to the critical Understanding of the dead Languages, while they are ignorant of the Beauties of their Mother Tongue, do not view me with a friendly Eye: But I'm even with them, when I tell them to their Faces, without Blushing, that I understand* Horace *but faintly in the Original, and yet can feast on his beautiful Thoughts dress'd in British; – and do not see any great Occasion for every Man's being made capable to translate the Classicks, when they are so elegantly done to his Hand.* (Martin and Oliver (eds), 1945: xviii)

The reference to 'British' rather than 'English' suggests that Ramsay identifies the English tongue with the British state – his 'native Dialect', however, continues to express his identity as a Scot. Despite his membership of the Easy Club, Ramsay left Edinburgh when it was occupied by Jacobite forces – his desire for Scotland's political self-determination found no more active expression than a sentimental nostalgia for the Jacobite cause. In this, as in so much else, Ramsay was the forerunner of later Scots writers of the period.

Five of Ramsay's imitations of Horace are to be found in the 1721 edition of Ramsay's *Poems*, and they are singled out for our attention in Ramsay's Preface to this edition:

> *There are towards the End of this Miscellany, five or six Imitations of Horace, which any acquainted with that Author will presently observe. – I have only snatched at his Thought and Method in gross, and dress'd them up in Scots, without confining my self to no more or no less; so that these are only to be reckoned a following of his Manner.* (Martin and Oliver (eds), 1945: xx)

Ramsay's own qualifications here accurately anticipate critical ambivalence about his competence as a translator. Ramsay's merits and demerits are discussed in some detail by A.M. Kinghorn (Kinghorn and Law (eds),1970: 109–27). Kinghorn argues that Ramsay's versions of Horace are often crude, concrete and obvious when his source is sophisticated, intellectual and lightly ironic. However, he acknowledges that in some passages, Ramsay does capture Horace's spirit. The reason for this lies in the aptness of the classical poet as a literary icon in post-Union Scotland (as indeed he was for rationalists like Pope in Augustan England):

> Horace, with his patronage, his townsman's view of the country, his Sabine farm and his philosophy of popular Epicureanism provided the school of Pope with a mentor having the highest authority who seemed to show them an example of defence against growing materialism, and the gross worship of wealth, and furthermore, appealed to their rationalism as though he were an understanding relative, not blocked from them by centuries of time or by Renaissance deification of the kind given to Virgil. Ramsay, perhaps without more than a vague notion of what he was doing, adapted certain of these attitudes as part of his pose as a young Scottish gentleman, and found in Horace an ancient who was also a modern and as such a suitable model for a self-styled descendant of Dalhousie to imitate. (Kingorn and Law (eds), 1970: 118–19)

Kinghorn here accurately pinpoints much of the attraction that Horace held for Ramsay: the authority of the classical poet, the fact that he combines provincialism with urbanity, and – crucially – his familiar tone of voice. Horace speaks to us more directly than, say,

Virgil, and his first-person construction of lyrical poetic personae was well-suited to the literary revival of Scots, which had for over a century been restricted to the spoken word, and whose cultural expression was by now largely articulated in song. Ramsay could also count on the fact that the recipients of his updated odes would be flattered by the comparison with their classical counterparts. One such ode, 'To R– H– B–', an imitation of Horace's eighteenth ode, illustrates Ramsay's style. The first two stanzas are preceded by a recent, more literal, translation into English, by David West (1997: 41):

> Plant no tree, Varus, before the sacred vine
> in the kindly soil round Tibur and the walls of Catilus.
> For god has put nothing but obstacles in the way of sober men,
> and wine is the only thing that puts biting cares to flight.
>
> (West)

> O B–, cou'd these Fields of thine
> Bear as in *Gaul* the juicy Vine,
> How sweet the bonny Grape wou'd shine
> On Wau's where now, *walls*
> Your Apricocks and Peaches fine
> Their Branches bow.
>
> Since humane Life is but a Blink,
> Why should we its short Joys sink;
> He disna live that canna link *doesn't; can't*
> The Glass about,
> When warm'd with Wine, like Men we think,
> And grow mair stout. *more*
>
> (Ramsay)

Ramsay's typical strategies of domestication and expansion are here evident: since vines do not grow in the Scottish climate, he changes Horace's command ('Don't grow trees, grow vines') into a wish and a compliment ('If only your fine apricots and peaches were vines'). The stanza form adopted by Ramsay here is also markedly Scottish – it is so-called 'Standard Habbie', earlier used by Robert Sempill in his mock elegy to Habbie Simpson, the Piper of Kibarchan, and further popularised by such as Ramsay and, later, Burns. Ramsay's second stanza takes up the idea of wine as a banisher of the cares administered by unkind fate, and transforms this into the more specific notion of wine's ability to inspire virility and courage when faced with the transitoriness of life and happiness. As Ramsay's version continues, he strips away the classical allusions in the original, 'making

Horace's conventional mythological parallels concrete and vital' (Kinghorn, in Kinghorn and Law (eds), 1970: 117).

Horace's odes, then, for Ramsay, were not valuable in themselves, insofar as they had to be faithfully adhered to and reproduced as literally as possible; rather, they served as inspirational models for literary expression in Scots. In this, Horace's own persona was important, as it corresponded with the aspirations of the Scottish bourgeousie in the new 'North Britain' – philosophical, witty, familiar, urbane, yet geographically distant from the centre of power and influence. When we also take into consideration the continuing dominance of Latin and the classics in Scottish education throughout the period, it is unsurprising that Horace remained a popular figure in Scottish translation, and adaptation, for the next century and a half.

Ramsay did venture beyond Horace in his 'imitations' – he adapted the contemporary French poets La Motte and La Fontaine in his *Fables and Tales*, published in the 1720s. It is probable that Ramsay again used a bridging text in English, although his French was probably better than his Latin, allowing him greater access to the original texts. By translating the fables, which had their own origins in medieval fabula, Ramsay not only looked outward to continental Europe, but also backward to the versions of Aesop's fables by the fifteenth-century Scots poet, Robert Henryson. Even Ramsay's choice of contemporary French poets as sources was partly conditioned by his desire to resuscitate a native Scottish literary tradition.

It was Ramsay the classicist, however, who had the greatest impact on his immediate successors. Versions of Horace continued to be written throughout the eighteenth century. One of the most accomplished poets of the revival, Robert Fergusson (1750–74), died tragically young, before he could embark on a project to translate Virgil's *Georgics*. He did, however, 'compose town poems and pastorals after the models of Juvenal, Horace and Virgil' (Freeman, 1987: 141) and he translated Horace's eleventh Ode in a Scots which was considerably denser and more vigorous than Ramsay's:

> Ne'er fash your thumb what gods decree
> To be the weird o' you or me.
> Nor deal in cantrup's kittle cunning
> To speir how fast your days are running.
> But patient lippen for the best,
> Nor be in dowy thought opprest,
> Whether we see mare winters come
> Than this that spits wi' canker'd foam.

> Now moisten weel your geyzen'd wa's
> Wi' couthy friends and hearty blaws;
> Ne'er lat your hope o'ergang your days,
> For eild and thraldom never stays;
> The day looks gash, toot aff your horn,
> Nor care yae strae about the morn.

> [Never pay any heed what gods decree/To be the fate of you or me./Nor deal in magic's fickle cunning/To inquire how fast your days are running./But patient hope for the best,/Nor be in gloomy care oppressed,/Whether we see more winters come/Than this that spits with stormy foam./Now moisten well your leaky walls/ With agreeable friends and hearty boasts;/Never let your hope exceed your days,/For age and servitude never stay;/Today looks ghastly, toot your horn/Nor care a straw about tomorrow.]

If Ramsay's language is a lightly-scotticised English, Fergusson's is a different matter. As his editors, Kinghorn and Law, observe:

> The Old Town [of Edinburgh] was a gathering-place for many regional habits of speech and he drew on whatever resources of vocabulary and pronunciation he could find – living speech, literary usage past and present, thieves' slang, Gaelic borrowings. An adequate glossary to his Scots poems would contain more than 1600 words, of which only about one third were used by Ramsay. (Kinghorn and Law (eds), 1974: xxx)

By reaching beyond his everyday speech in this way, Fergusson's Scots prefigures what would become known as the 'synthetic Scots' or 'Lallans' movement of the twentieth century (see Chapter 7), and he offers an early model for the modernisation of a rich written Scots after the Union.

Fergusson's greater confidence in handling Horatian verse is possibly a result of his classical education at St Andrews University; however, like Ramsay, his gift for vernacular writing was encouraged not in the academy but in the convivial atmosphere of Edinburgh clubs – in particular The Knights Companions of the Cape, founded in 1764, he was known as 'Sir Precenter'. There, almost half a century after the Union of the Parliaments, young Scottish merchants, professionals and artists continued to find expression for their patriotism in Jacobite nostalgia. Fergusson was a Scottish Tory in a period when British politics were dominated by Whigs, themselves descended from the 'Whiggamores', militant Scottish Presbyterians of the late seventeenth century. His opposition to the prevailing political order was articulated in a poetry at once classical and vernacular. Although it is not a translation as such, his pastoral poem 'The Farmer's Ingle' idealises traditional Scottish farm life by perceiving it from a classical perspective:

> Evident in the poem is the influence of Virgil's *Bucolics*, from whence its Latin motto is taken, his *Georgics*, and Horace's *Epodes:* idyllic pictures of farm life in the home, before the ingle. There are also strong traces of Milton and Spenser, and, throughout, a primitivist idealization of the gudeman as the classical stoic ... (Freeman, 1987: 143)

'The Farmer's Ingle' subsequently served as the immediate model for Burns's 'The Cottar's Saturday Night' – indeed, it might be argued that Fergusson's and Ramsay's domesticated Scots adaptions of Horatian personae served Burns as models for his own satirical, lyric and moral poems.

One of Ramsay's best-known Horatian imitations, 'To the Ph--, an Ode' (Horace, I. ix) has been translated several times into Scots. A version which appeared in *Ruddiman's Weekly Magazine,* dated 'Aberdeen, January 22, 1773' was by a poet who called himself 'Vanlu', but about whom nothing else is known. Like Ramsay, 'Vanlu' imitates Horace rather than provides a literal translation – but instead of recreating Horace in Edinburgh, 'Vanlu' shifts him further north. Compare the opening lines of the two Scots versions with a literal English translation (West, 1997: 33):

> You see Soracte standing white and deep
> with snow, the woods in trouble, hardly able
> to carry the burden, and the rivers
> halted by sharp ice.
>
> (West)

> Look up to *Pentland's* towring Taps, *tops*
> Buried beneath great Wreaths of Snaw, *snow*
> O'er ilka Cleugh, ilk Scar and Slap, *each cliff, rock, valley*
> As high as ony *Roman* Wa'. *any . . . wall*
>
> (Ramsay)

> Look up, my friend, look up and see
> The hills of North and Bannochie,
> What heaps of snaw lie o'them! *snow*
> Lord help the bodies of the hills, *folk*
> For neither plows, nor kills, nor mills, *ploughs, kilns*
> Can gang this day amo' them. *go . . . among*
>
> ('Vanlu')

'Vanlu's version of the ode is significant in that its language is specifically that of the north-east; in other words, its Scots has a distinctly regional flavour. This is evident particularly in the third stanza, which contains a stereotypical marker of north-east (or 'Buchan') Scots: 'fat' ('what'):

> But fat care I? The fint a hair,
> Whether the night be foul or fair
>
> [But what care I? The devil a hair
> Whether the night is foul or fair.]

As the Scots literary revival progressed, then, from its origins in Ramsay's verse, two strands begin to emerge, both of them still evident in the twentieth century (see Chapters 7 and 8). The first aims to reconstruct a modern, written Scots, usually on the basis of a central Scots speech, supplemented by expressions from further afield, and from earlier literature. This is the strand associated with Robert Fergusson, and, later, with Robert Burns. The second aims to represent the speech variety of a particular community of Scots, whether that community is bound together by regional identity or social class. This is the strand that is associated with the poet 'Vanlu' and, in the eighteenth century, an increasingly active group of north-east poets, taking their cue from Ramsay, Fergusson and Burns, but reflecting in particular the Scots language of their own region.

In his survey of north-eastern writing, *The Bards of Bon-Accord 1375–1860*, published in 1887, William Walker pays tribute to the influence of Allan Ramsay on Scots vernacular writing, then moves on to praise a north-eastern translation of Ovid by Robert Forbes:

> Among the few real Scottish poems that remain to us between the dates of Ramsay and Ross of Lochlee [i.e. Alexander Ross, 1699–1784], 'Ajax' Speech to the Grecian Knabbs' holds a prominent place; and certainly of all the poems which have been written in 'the broad Buchan dialect' – and since then their number has been very great – very few equal, and none surpass it in pithiness of expression or redolence of home-grown idiom. (Walker, 1887: 210)

Robert Forbes came, like Ramsay and Fergusson, from the merchant classes. Though born and bred in Aberdeenshire, he settled in London to ply his trade as a hosier, and published verse in 'his native dialect' apparently as a hobby. Like 'Vanlu's Horace, Forbes's Ovid is markedly north-eastern. The concluding stanzas of 'Ajax' Speech to the Grecian Knabbs' again have the tell-tale pronunciation of 'what' as 'fat':

But now fat need's for a' this din?
    Lat deeds o' words tak place,
An' lat your stoutness now be try'd
    Just here before your face.

Lat th'armour o' Achilles brave
    Amon' our faes be laid,
An' the first chiel' that brings them back,
    Lat him wi' them be clad.

[But now what's the need for all this din?/Let actions take the place of words,/And let your stoutness now be tried/Right here before your face.//Let the armour of brave Achilles/Be laid among our foes,/And the first fellow who brings them back,/Let him be clothed in them.]

The Bards of Bon-Accord makes mention of various other minor translators and imitators into the Scots of the north-east in the eighteenth and nineteenth centuries. Again, the classical theme is evident in the imitations of Horace's *Epodes*, by John Ogilvie (1797–1867), and in the version of Horace's *Ode, II. xvi* by John Longmuir (1803–83). The last of this line of homespun Horaces, however, was James Logie Robertson (1846–1922), who, under the name 'Hugh Haliburton' enjoyed great popularity among readers of *The Scotsman* newspaper, which published his poems weekly. In his collection, *Horace in Homespun*, which first appeared in 1882 in a volume entitled *Our Holiday*, Horace's urbane and witty persona is reduced to the couthy rusticity of the kailyard. To take one illustration, Horace's address to Virgil, already rendered by Allan Ramsay, becomes 'Hughie's Anxiety For Davy on the Seas'. As the extracts below demonstrate, Robertson's light verse is more a variation on a Horatian theme than a serious attempt to render the Roman poet in Scots:

Daedalus ventured upon the empty air
    with wings not meant for man.
The labour of Hercules burst through Acheron.

(West)

Neist *Dedalus* must contradict — *next*
Nature forsooth, and Feathers stick
Upon his Back, syne upward streek, — *then . . . streak*
And in at Jove's high Winnocks keek, — *windows . . . peek*
While *Hercules* wi's Timber Mell, — *with his . . . club*
Plays rap upo' the Yates of Hell. — *gates*

(Ramsay)

We flew a draigon: an' the spark	*dragon*
Obeys a bairn if need is;	*child*
But look at the mischeevous wark	*mischievous work*
That's wrocht wi' thir torpeedies.	*wrought; torpedoes*
It's lang sin' pouther was fund oot;	*long since gunpowder*
But we've dune weel oorsel' –	*done well ourselves*
We've raised in dynamite, I doot,	*I suspect*
The mucklest deil in hell.	*greatest devil*
	(Robertson)

For all its faults, Ramsay's imitation is at least an attempt to do justice to the Promethean theme of his source: the octosyllabic couplets and the retention of mythological allusions attest to the seriousness of the attempt. In contrast, Robertson's ballad measure, the diminutive familiarity of 'Hughie', and the nostalgia for a pre-industrial idyll have reduced Horace's powerful condemnation of hubris to an occasionally bathetic complaint about the perils of modernity. Colin Milton (1987: 21–25) acknowledges that much of Logie Robertson's work is concerned with evoking an elegaic mood, but he argues that in snatches, *Horace in Homespun* looks forward as well as back. In a very free imitation of *Odes, I. ii,* an exhortation to Mercury, in the guise of Caesar, to restore order to an empire torn by war and natural disaster, 'Hughie' hopes for some *deus ex machina* to restore warmth to a countryside ravaged by winter. Milton remarks approvingly on the early stanzas (which have no close Horatian parallel):

What ance has been may be ance mair,	*once . . . once more*
An' ance – as learnèd clerks declare –	*once*
This planet's fortune was to fare,	
In ages auld,	*old*
Thro' regions o' the frigid air,	
Past kennin' cauld.	*unimaginably cold*
Nae doot but this was centuries gane,	*no doubt . . . centuries*
When human cretur' there was nane,	*creature*
An' this auld warld, her liefu' lane,	*old world . . . all alone*
Bowl' thro' the nicht,	*night*
Wi' tangles hingin' fra a mune,	*hanging . . . moon*
Her only licht.	*light*

(Robertson, 'The White Winter: Hughie Dreads the Return of the Ice Age')

Milton notes that here the juxtaposition of the human and the cosmic

– in a way which is surprisingly untypical of kailyard writing – is a notable precursor to MacDiarmid's early lyrics, and to *A Drunk Man Looks at the Thistle,* a poem whose influence on twentieth-century translation is immeasurable. While admitting that Robertson's verse is largely nostalgic, Milton (1987: 22–23) argues:

> However, it is a mistake to condemn Logie Robertson's verse for its lack of 'realism' or its 'kailyard' character because he is not – or not usually – concerned with the realistic depiction of particulars but with evoking a mood, commending certain values or conveying general truths – truths which are no less true and important for being simple and obvious.

This is a more generous reading of Robertson than critics usually allow. Despite some evocative lines, Robertson's Horatian imitations are finally reductive: they have neither the ambition nor the range of the originals, and they complacently appeal to myths of a pre-industrial society for their moral authority. As vigorous pastoral decays into rural nostalgia, they are the last faint gasp of an energetic and productive tradition of classical imitation and adaptation which Ramsay had begun, over a century and a half before.

It would be misleading to argue that translation, or even imitation, occupied a central place in the eighteenth-century Scots literary revival – numerically, the Scots translations by Ramsay and Fergusson are far fewer than their original poems. Crucially, Robert Burns, while being far from the unlettered ploughman of self-promoted legend, did not translate into Scots, preferring to use Fergusson and Ramsay as immediate models for his original Scots verse, and, to even greater effect, plundering the resources of native Scottish song. Burns's attitude to native and foreign influences in his work can be gleaned from the (however comic) description of the witches' ceilidh in 'Tam O'Shanter':

> Warlocks and witches in a dance;
> Nae cotillion brent-new frae *France,*
> But hornpipes, jigs, strathspeys and reels,
> Put life and mettle in their heels.

Here, imported fashions – symbolised by the brand-new French dance, the cotillion – are discarded in favour of good old native Scottish dances, accompanied by the devil on bagpipes. In Burns's Scotland, even Auld Nick is a cultural patriot. Even so, translation has a small but vital role to play in the literary revival of Scots: translation into Scots revived a distinguished native tradition, while it was in harmony with the classicism and antiquarianism of the early Scottish Enlightenment. The translation of classical authors once again legitimised written literary Scots, and the adoption of Horace in particular gave modern literary Scots an authoritative first-person voice, and a rich seam of appropriate subjects on which to discourse. Directly and indirectly, much of eighteenth-century Scots vernacular poetry is the voice of Horace in homespun, and this voice was to echo well into the nineteenth, and even the early twentieth century.

Homer in a Kilt: James Macpherson's *Ossian*

Conventionally, historians have argued that the initial resentment which accompanied the Act of Union in 1707 gradually ebbed away in lowland Scotland, as the middle and professional classes began to harvest the economic benefits offered by free access to English and, soon, imperial markets. Active enthusiasm for the Jacobite uprisings in 1715 and 1745 was less prevalent in southern Scotland than it was in the Highlands – as noted above, even the Easy Club founder, Allan Ramsay, shunned the Jacobite forces when they occupied the capital. On the whole, it was the Gaels who flocked to support Charles Edward Stuart in the final bid to restore the Stuart dynasty, it was a Highland army which marched to and from England and was destroyed at Culloden, and it was Gaelic culture which was harried and proscribed thereafter. Lowland Scots who opposed the Union found their nationalist hearts and their Jacobite sympathies pulled them in one direction, while their Presbyterian souls and worldly ambitions pushed them in another. Out of the wreckage of the Jacobite risings, there emerged a series of poems which would capture not only the Scottish imagination, but also that of Europe, placing Scotland for the first time at the centre of European literature. The poems were by James Macpherson (1736–96), and they purported to be translations of ancient texts by the Gaelic bard, Ossian.

The Ossianic poems are only indirectly relevant to the present study: they are, after all, composed in English, not Scots, and their alleged provenance is highland rather than lowland Scotland. Even so, their enormous impact on the lowlands of Scotland (not to mention the rest of Europe), and the influence they had of refashioning how Scotland is imagined, both at home and abroad, merits them a brief mention here.

The publication of the Ossian poems was greeted with critical adulation, typified by Hugh Blair's positive comments in his 'Critical Dissertation': in neo-classical Scotland, the points of reference are again to the great writers of antiquity, particularly Homer, with whom 'Ossian' is constantly compared:

> Both poets are eminently sublime; but a difference may be remarked in the species of their sublimity. Homer's sublimity is accompanied with more impetuosity and fire; Ossian's with more of a solemn and awful grandeur. Homer hurries you along' Ossian elevates, and fixes you in astonishment. Homer is most sublime in actions and battles; Ossian, in description and sentiment. In the pathetick, Homer, when he chuses to exert it, has great power; but Ossian exerts that power much oftener, and has the character of tenderness far more deeply imprinted in his works. No poet knew better how to seize and melt the heart. (Blair, 1765; reprinted in Gaskill (ed.), 1996: 358)

Like the translations into Scots of classical writers, then, the poems of Ossian satisfied the home-grown taste for patriotism, antiquarianism and, at least by analogy, classical authority: at last, Scotland had its own epic poet. The Celtic 'Other', long suppressed and even despised in lowland Scotland, had returned with a vengeance, in heroic tales of Celtic kings and princes battling against Norse invaders on the one hand and treacherous usurpers on the other:

> Oscar! said the dark-red Cairbar, I behold the spear of Inisfail. The spear of Temora glitters in thy hand, son of woody Morven! It was the pride of an hundred kings, the death of heroes of old. Yield it, son of Ossian, yield it to car-borne Cairbar.
>
> Shall I yield, Oscar replied, the gift of Erin's injured king: the gift of fair-haired Cormac, when Oscar scattered his foes! I came to Cormac's halls of joy, when Swaran fled from Fingal. Gladness rose in the face of youth; he gave the spear of Temora. Nor did he give it to the feeble, O Cairbar, neither to the weak in soul. The darkness of thy face is no storm to me; nor are thine eyes the flames of death. Do I fear thy changing shield? Tremble I at Olla's song? No: Cairbar, frighten the feeble; Oscar is a rock. (*Temora* Book I; Gaskill (ed.), 1996: 229)

However, the status of the Ossian poems as translations was disputed almost as soon as they were published, and critical indignation at the alleged 'forgery' is still evident over two centuries after the fact. For example, historian Bruce Lenman writes (1981: 120–1):

> Although Macpherson at various points did use scraps of authentic Gaelic tradition, the whole operation appears to have been

> dishonest from the very start and was primarily a means of gaining access to the patronage which would lift Macpherson from poverty and neglect to fame and fortune. *Temora* was too much for many even of his supporters. David Hume experienced grave doubts, while a strong school of opinion in London denounced Macpherson as a shameless forger. That he was, but he brazened it out with all and sundry save the formidable Dr Johnson, never a one to use a rapier where a bludgeon would do, who alone forced the odious Caledonian to crawl away from a literary dog-fight with all the dignity of a well-beaten cur.

Even Lenman, however, grudgingly admits the influence of the Ossianic poems on German and Italian romanticism, and, more recently, the work of Macpherson has been reappraised (cf. Moore, 1997). After all, in lowland Scotland patriotic 'imitations' of classical writers were uncontroversially celebrated, and the longstanding tradition of patronage involved impoverished poets seeking to satisfy the cultural demands of wealthier friends and acquaintances. Ossian spectacularly satisfied a cultural need, not just in Scotland, but across a Europe where new nation-states were seeking models for national heroes. Macpherson's opportunism has recently been considered in a more kindly light:

> In the years following Macpherson's death in 1796, the Highland Society of Scotland set up a Committee of investigation which concluded that, although Macpherson had not produced close translations of individual poems, he had nevertheless drawn on the traditional tales collected in his tours, using certain recognisable characters, plots and episodes. He also developed his own very distinctive measured prose as the medium for presenting the Gaelic material in English, and while this was indebted to the prose tales of Scotland, it also reflected Macpherson's academically influenced preconceptions about the nature of early poetry. For while he undoubtedly came across a large number of heroic ballads in the Highlands, he seems to have regarded his sources somewhat dismissively as the broken remains of great Celtic epics, and to have seen the task of recovery in the light of sympathetic restoration, rather than as a painstaking translation of the miscellaneous mass. (Fiona Stafford, Introduction to Gaskill (ed.), 1996: xiii–xiv)

Macpherson, then, in this view, is seen less as an unscrupulous forger, and more of a combination of two of his lowland literary counterparts: the classical translator, and the collector, refiner and improver of native songs. Moreover, a re-reading of Macpherson's relation to his Ossianic epic has prompted a revision of the conventional history of the eighteenth century, in which 'following centuries of hostility, Scotland drifts into conformity within a couple of generations' (Pittock, 1995: 127). Pittock argues against the grain of 'British' history, saying that lowland Jacobitism was much more widespread and longer-lasting than anglocentric historians have allowed, and that its positive cultural influence on the Scottish Enlightenment has been undervalued. He makes the case that Macpherson's exclusion from the canon of 'English' literature was as much politically as aesthetically motivated: Macpherson transformed the defeated Jacobites of history into the victorious Fianna of myth, a potent symbol that the contemporary anglocentric literary establishment could not stomach.

Certainly, there is much to be said for a view of eighteenth-century Scotland as incorporating a complex set of ideologies in conflict. The Act of Union triggered a crisis for the construction of a Scottish identity: easy markers of national belonging, such as an established monarch, a separate parliament, or even meaningful political borders, had disappeared. The raw materials with which to reconstruct Scottishness in this context – for example, a national language, and a usurped dynasty – were problematical: Scots and Gaelic continued to compete as rival national tongues, and the usurped dynasty was identified with a Catholicism, or at least a Scottish Episcopalianism, that many in the country could not accept. But these icons of Scottishness continued to exert sentimental appeal in an age renowned for its valorising of sentiment, as Scots sought nostalgic solace in their indigenous culture as well as in classical precedents, whether real or imagined.

Rediscovering Roots: Translations of Northern European Songs

Macpherson's 'Ossian' indirectly contributed to a reappraisal of the indigenous in Scottish culture, both in the Highlands and the Lowlands, in the same way as it inspired a new breed of European nation-states to reinvent their own native literatures. The roots of lowland Scots, however, lies not in the Celtic languages but in the Germanic tongues of the Anglo-Saxons and Norse. As the eighteenth and nineteenth centuries progressed, the first stirrings of interest in translating into Scots the folk poetry and songs of Scandinavia and Germany began to manifest itself. This trend can be seen in Robert

Jamieson's translations from Danish, Swedish, German, and 'Prussian Low Dutch' in the *Illustration of Northern Antiquities* (1814), and in Robert Buchanan's Scandinavian translations in *Ballad Stories of the Affections* (1866). As the title of the former volume suggests, the purpose of the work is more philological and antiquarian than aesthetic – in his introduction to his own section, Jamieson modestly asks that he be 'considered rather as a commentator and editor, than a poetical translator' (p. 245). His choice of Scots, he argues too, is not driven by poetic or patriotic considerations – he was, after all, a Scot in exile, and the translations were composed abroad. In his introduction, he also feels the need to defend his use of Scots as a medium of scholarly translation:

> As to the *dialect* adopted in these versions, he [i.e. Jamieson] is under considerable anxiety, being aware that it may be received with diffidence, and its propriety questioned. They were written in Livonia, after a residence of upwards of twelve years in England, and four on the continent; and it will with justice be concluded, that he must have lost much of the natural facility in the use of his native dialect which is above all necessary for poetical narrative. Of this he is himself sufficiently sensible; and therefore would never have attempted to adapt it to original composition; at the same time that he is far from considering it as a valid objection to his undertaking his present task. Having cultivated an intimate acquaintance with the Scottish language in all its stages, so far back as any monuments of it remain, he might be supposed to have some confidence in his use of it. If in his translations he has blended the dialects of different ages, he has at least endeavoured to do judiciously what his subject seemed to require of him, in order to preserve as entirely as possible, in every particular, the costume of his originals. (Weber and Jamieson, 1814: 246)

It is worth quoting this passage at length, for several reasons. First of all, Jamieson feels the need to justify his use of Scots not because it is an inappropriate vehicle for translation – he refers with confidence to 'the Scottish language' – but because he perceives his command of it to be rusty, and he anticipates objections to his use of archaisms. He counters both objections by arguing that his Scots would indeed be mannered if attempting original poetry, but that an archaic Scots best captures the 'costume', or the tone, of the source texts, which themselves have many archaic elements, which, Jamieson claims, contemporary guardians of the oral tradition would not themselves have understood. It is the similarity of the languages which is offered as the main motivation for the translations – exposure to the northern European folk-song tradition through translation is a voyage of *self*-discovery:

> This is one of the strongest features of resemblance between the Northern and Scottish ballad, in which there is found a phraseology which has long been obsolete in both languages, and many terms not understood by those who recite them and for the meaning of which we must refer to the Norse or Islandic of the eighth and ninth centuries. On other points of resemblance, it will not be necessary to say any thing, as they must strike every attentive observer; nor can the style adopted be more satisfactorily justified, than by informing the reader, that the general cast of structure, diction and idiom, has been so sedulously followed that, for whole stanzas together, hardly any thing has been altered but the orthography. (Weber and Jamieson, 1814: 246)

To illustrate this point, Jamieson interlaces one of his Swedish ballads, a version of 'Fair Midel' with a Scots translation designed to point up the linguistic similarities, and, in particular, shared peculiarities of idiom and expression. Two stanzas of the ballad, 'Sir Wal and Lisa Lyle', are given below (Weber and Jamieson, 1814: 375):

> Ridder Wal sadlar up sin gängare grä;
> Sä rider han sig öfwer böljorna blä.
> *Sir Wal saddles up his gangar gray;*
> *Sae rides he him over the billows* (?) *blae.*
>
> Och nær som han kom til en rinnande ström,
> Dær satt en næktergal i et træd, som sjöng.
> *And whan that he cam till a rinning stream,*
> *There sat a nightingale in a tree, that sang.*

Elsewhere in the book, the translations of Danish folk-songs are practically indistinguishable from those being assembled by collectors of indigenous Scottish ballads. One, 'Childe Axelvold', from a Danish text published in 1591, begins:

> The Kingis men they ride till the wold,
> There they hunt baith the hart and the hind;
> And they under a linden sae green
> Sae wee a bairnie find.
> *(I' the loft whare sleeps she, the proud Elinè.)*

In the wake of the highland Ossian 'translations', then (which Jamieson also discusses critically in the introduction to his northern translations), lowland Scots turned towards their roots, seeking out not only indigenous native song, but also similar works from cognate languages. In the case of Scots, the Germanic tongues, particularly the Scandinavian branches, were considered the closest relatives.

Jamieson's example is followed in the mid-nineteenth century by Robert Buchanan, whose *Ballad Stories of the Affections* are translated 'from the Scandinavian'. Buchanan in his introduction refers to Jamieson as a 'veritable singer' whose translations had 'a rugged force and picturesqueness transcending the best efforts in that direction of Scott himself' (1866: viii). Buchanan acknowledges that his own use of Scots is inferior to that of Jamieson's, but claims that this is a deliberate strategy, in part to accommodate English readers. The lively nineteenth-century market for Scottish poetry and novels in England and abroad clearly led to a conscious dilution of the Scots in some work, however reluctant that dilution was:

> My task, on the whole, has been one of no ordinary anxiety. Next to the difficulty of writing a good ballad ranks the difficulty of translating a good ballad, and very few men have succeeded in doing either. Had I consulted my own taste, and translated throughout in broad old Scotch (the only really fitting equivalent for old Danish), I should not only have hopelessly bewildered English readers, but have laid my efforts open to dangerous comparison with those of Jamieson. I have, therefore, done the best I could in the English dialect, using Scotch words liberally, but only such Scotch words as are quite familiar to all readers of our own ballads. (Buchanan, 1866: viii)

Again there are interesting points to note here: the perceived kinship of Scots and Danish, the labelling of English as a 'dialect', effectively equivalent in status to Scots, but more widely known, and the acknowledgement that, although Jamieson's translations are superior to his own, Jamieson's archaic Scots might be wilfully obscure – a criticism that a later translator of Scandinavian ballads, Sir Alexander Gray, was to level at the Lallans writers in the twentieth century (cf. Chapter 8).

Buchanan characterises his own style well enough: it is a thin Scots, basically an archaic 'English dialect' with a liberal sprinking of scotticisms. The opening stanzas of 'Signelil the Serving-Maiden' show it at its densest:

The lady spake to Signelil,
'Signelil, my maiden!
Wherefore, wherefore so thin and ill?'
But the sorrow stings so sorely!

'Sma' wonder I am sae ill and thin,
Malfred, O my lady!
I hae sae muckle to sew and spin.'
But the sorrow stings so sorely!

It is tempting, in these few stanzas, to see the Scots/English distinction as marking the different social status of the lady and her maid (the lady says 'so'; her maid says 'sae'), but later in the poem the situation is reversed:

'My son has plighted his troth to thee,
Signelil, my maiden!
Say, what gifts did he dare to gie?'
But the sorrow stings so sorely!

'He gave me the silver buckled shoon,
Malfred, O my lady!
I wear them when tramping up and doon.'
But the sorrow stings so sorely!

Here the lady uses the scotticism 'gie', while the serving-maid uses the irregular English past tense 'gave', rather than the regular Scots equivalent, 'gied'. The English form is however used alongside the conservative Scots '-n' plural, in 'shoon' (shoes). Buchanan here is taking his cue from the introduction to Ramsay's *Poems* of 1721, by using the Scots system in tandem with the English system in order to enlarge his stock of rhymes, while colouring his Scandinavian tales with a kindred, couthy vocabulary.

A later, more minor, example of what in the twentieth century was to become a growing trend in translation from near-contemporary German is the Rev. Alexander Grieve's 'Songs from the German of Heine', one of which found its way into an anthology *The Bards of Angus and the Mearns* (1897). Its editor, Alan Reid, comments that 'Heine in Scots is novel, and very sweet as Dr Grieve presents him' (p. 207). Unlike Jamieson, Grieve's interest is obviously aesthetic rather than philological, but the ballad form and the theme of love again ensure that the song fits seamlessly into the commercial vogue for native Scots songs and ballads that had continued undiminished since Allan Ramsay's publication of the *Tea-Table Miscellany* (1723–37). Grieve's rendition begins:

Gin at ma dearie's side I be,
    Fu' canty grows ma hairt;
I've rowth o' a' that life can gie
    An' wi' the warl' could pairt!

But when frae her fond airms I gae
    That clespit me sae fain,
Then a' ma gear flees far away –
    An' puir am I again.

[When I am at my sweetheart's side/Full cheerful grows my heart;/I've plenty of all that life can give/And with the world could part!//But when from her fond arms I go/That clasped me so lovingly,/Then all my goods fly far away/And poor am I again.]

The investment of patriotic fervour into the discovery and refashioning of native songs again meant that there were considerable constraints on translation into Scots in the later eighteenth and nineteenth centuries. Such poetic translation as existed had to place itself in respect of this perceived native tradition: there was little room for cotillions – 'brent new frae France', or indeed from anywhere else – which did not directly participate in the re-imagining of the Scottish nation.

Yet the Scottish nation had changed profoundly and continued to change. In an anthology entitled *The Scottish Minstrel: The Songs and Songwriters of Scotland subsequent to Burns*, published in 1885, Jacobite laments (such as John Grieve's 'Culloden; or Lochiel's Farewell') sit cheek-by-jowl with rousing anthems to English and American patriotism (such as exiled Scot, Thomas Cambell's, 'Ye Mariners of England', and John Bathurst Dickson's 'The American Flag'). By the late nineteenth century, Scotland's partnership in the British imperial adventure, and its contribution to the North American diaspora allowed its citizens to adopt multiple nationalities – Scottish, English, British – as seemed appropriate to the time and circumstances. The refashioning of Scottish identity now took place within a British and an imperial context – Scots could now resist this alignment or accept it, but they could not ignore it.

Pulpit Paraphrases: Victorian Bible Translations

The last, great, distinctively Scottish institution to survive the Act of Union was the Church of Scotland. In the first half of the nineteenth century, the General Assembly of the Kirk served as an arena for debate on a range of Scottish concerns. Christopher Harvie (1988: 31) writes:

> The Kirk could indeed claim jurisdiction over what Henry Cockburn, a fairly representative figure in both groups, called 'the whole Christian and civic economy' of Scotland. Its annual General Assembly looked more like a parliament than many of the provincial assemblies of continental Europe, and acted as the *locus* of a type of transactional politics.

Even if the power of the Kirk was shaken by the Disruption of 1843, when almost 500 of the 1200 ministers walked out of the General Assembly in protest against what they saw as a compromise to the Kirk's autonomy, its social influence only gradually declined over the next half century and more. It is therefore unsurprising that the most significant translations into Scots of this period came from Kirk ministers, or were renderings of parts of the Bible into Scots.

Tulloch (1989) has given a more detailed account than is possible here, as well as generous illustrations, of the beginnings of biblical translation into modern Scots. As noted in Chapter 4, the lack of a Scots Bible during and after the Reformation has long been seen to have contributed greatly to the decline in the use of Scots as a public language. The effects of this decline are evident in later Scottish literature – Murison (1977: 5) mentions the 'classic example' of code-switching from Scots to English in Burns's 'The Cottar's Saturday Night' when the rural patriarch takes the big ha' Bible down to read from the Scriptures. Nisbet's scotticised Bible was not widely distributed, or even known about, until the final decade of the nineteenth century, and it was not published until 1901. There was, however, a certain amount of Scots translation of biblical texts in the nineteenth century, inspired by a diverse set of motives.

The principal motive was philological, and it sprang from an unexpected source: Prince Louis Lucien Bonaparte (1813–91), whose uncle, Napoleon Bonaparte, had had scenes from the Ossianic cycle painted on the walls of Malmaison. Prince Louis turned his attention to Europe's minority languages, including Scots, as objects of interest. One of his projects was to translate books of the Bible into minority languages and dialects – including Basque and various Celtic tongues – and to this end he commissioned various Scottish (and English!) translators to render biblical passages into Scots. The first of Bonaparte's translators was Henry Scott Riddell (1798–1870), a one-time shepherd and aspiring minister whose ecclesiastical ambitions were frustrated by bouts of mental ill-health. In 1856, 1857 and 1860, Riddell published, at Bonaparte's expense, scotticised renditions of *The Gospel of St Matthew, The Book of Psalms* and *The Song of Solomon* – both closely modelled on the Authorised Version. These small-scale publications, which were explicitly for philological rather than religious purposes, were accompanied by an anonymous *Song of Solomon* (1860), a further *Song of Solomon,* by Joseph Philip Robson (1860) and yet another *Song of Solomon,* this time by George Henderson (1862). All were based on the Authorised Version, all were commissioned by Bonaparte, and Riddell's early renditions set the tone for his successors. As Tulloch observes, all Bonaparte's translators found great difficulty in rendering such a revered text as the Authorised Version into Scots, particularly since the now-longstanding association of Scots with speech, comedy and song mitigated against the construction of a formal register of decorous written prose. As a result their translations founder on several counts – they are too literary to be accurate representations of nineteenth-century Scots speech, and they are too close to the Authorised Version to be distinctive models of modern Scots prose. A later 'philological' rendition, not commissioned by Bonaparte, but inspired by Riddell, is appended by the eminent linguist and lexicographer James A.H. Murray (1837–1915) to his *The Dialect of the Southern Counties of Scotland* (1873). Here he renders the first chapter of the Book of Ruth in three regional varieties of contemporary spoken Scots, before embarking on the full book in his own dialect of Teviotdale. Despite lacking Bonaparte's direct sponsorship, Murray is more in tune with his original project of giving an accurate rendition of Scots speech, always recognising that Scots was a patchwork of spoken varieties, each of which had to be differently represented.

For the shorter chapters, Murray in fact uses 'palæotype', an early phonetic script invented by A.J. Ellis, while for his full version of Ruth, he uses a specialised 'phonetic spelling', the technical details of which he is at pains to explain. Tulloch (1989: 53–4) observes:

> Murray's work stands well apart from the Bonaparte translations which preceded it in that Murray has an absolutely clear idea of what he means by Scots and consistently adheres to it regardless of either the properties of English grammar of the familiar renderings of the Authorised Version. Murray knows exactly what he is doing. He is reproducing contemporary spoken Scots, not a literary register of Scots. He accepts that modern Scots has rejected most of the earlier Latinate borrowings and is thus essentially informal. He makes it quite clear, too, that he is using Scots in

spite of knowing that the normal religious language of Scotland is English.

An academic interest in the linguistic illustration of an endangered minority language variety, using *the* canonical text in western civilisation was therefore an important early impulse in nineteenth-century biblical translation. However, although Bonaparte's and Murray's translations were clearly intended for a small scholarly readership, as examples of an endangered language variety, there is evidence of a wider demand for these texts. Significantly, Henderson's rendition of the *Song of Solomon,* was republished anonymously, with some alterations, some time after 1879, in a two-penny pamphlet entitled *The Song of Solomon Printed in ye olde Scottish Dialect.* (Given that Bonaparte's translators were commissioned expressly to supply examples of contemporary Scots, the title of the pamphlet is either carelessly misleading, or it is indicative of attitudes towards Scots by the late nineteenth century – even modern Scots seemed 'old'.) Even so, a wider public than the purely academic evidently existed for scriptural translations into Scots, and in the versions of the *Psalms,* and of *Isaiah,* by P. Hately Waddell (*c.* 1817–91) there is a definite attempt to fashion an acceptable modern literary Scots prose.

Waddell was another minister, first in the Free Kirk and then in the Church of Scotland, but he also led an active literary life, editing Burns and Scott, and writing a dissertation to prove the authenticity of the Ossian poems, as well as original literary tracts (Tulloch, 1989: 38). Unlike Bonaparte's translators and Murray, Waddell translated from the Hebrew into Scots, and his style is substantially different from a faint echo of the Authorised Version, as can be seen by comparing the beginnings of Riddell's and Waddell's versions of the twenty-third Psalm (reprinted in Tulloch, 1989: 110, 111):

> The Lord is my shepherd; I sallna inlak.
>
> He maks me til lye doun in green an' baittle gangs; he leeds me aside the quæet waters
>
> He refreschens my saul; he leeds me in the peths o' richteousniss for his næme's sak'.
>
> Yis, thouch I wauk throwe the vallie o' the skaddaw o' deæth, I wull fæer nae ill: for thou art wi' me; thy cruik an' thy staffe thaye comfirt me.
>
> (Riddell)

> The LORD *is* my herd, nae want sal fa' me:
>
> He louts me till lie amang green-howes; he airts me atowre

> by the lown watirs:
>
> He waukens my wa'-gaen saul; he weises me roun, for his ain name's sake, intil right roddins.
>
> Na! tho' I gang thro' the dead-mirk-dail; *e'en thar,* sal I dread nae skaithin: for yersel *are* nar-by me; yer stok an' yer stay haud me baith fu' cheerie.
>
> (Waddell)

While Riddell largely confines himself to substituting the familiar phrases of the Authorised Version with Scots equivalents, Waddell in contrast disrupts the well-worn rhythms with new-fashioned phrases, and at times new-fashioned words, like 'dead-mirk-dail' ('valley of the shadow of death'). In attempting such an ambitious translation, Waddell recalls problems faced by Gavin Douglas in the early sixteenth century – the lack of a wide Scots vocabulary, and the lack of a tradition in a formal written register. These problems did not overly tax the poets and translators of the Scots revival, mainly because their adoption of a Horatian first-person persona, or, alternatively, their focus on folk-inspired song, allowed them to restrict themselves to the kind of Scots which would be spoken. When Allan Ramsay wished to raise the register of his Horatian odes, he diluted the Scots and anglicised his verse. Waddell is one of the first modern translators of Scots to reject the anglicising solution, and his strategies for modernisation anticipate those adopted by Lallans writers in the twentieth century (see Chapter 7). As Tulloch clearly shows (1989: 40–47), when a suitable Scots word does not exist for a concept he wishes to express, Waddell compounds two or three simple items (as in 'dead-mirk-dail', which literally means 'death-dark-valley'), or he borrows from another language, or he gives a literal translation a foreign word (i.e. a 'calque'), usually from German, which he viewed as the ancestor of Scots. Tulloch (1989, 42) observes:

> The Romance languages prefer to create new words with affixes, to derive rather than combine. In pointing out Germanic elements in 'Auld Lang Syne' Waddell noted their equivalents in German and it is clearly German of all the Germanic languages that has particularly influenced him. The words for *judge* . . . show clear German influence: *righter* is from the German noun *Richter* and *right* from the German verb *richten.* Waddell's *to-flight* meaning 'refuge' (Ps. 62: 8) is a calque of German *Zuflucht* and it seems possible that the word *torne* may be taken from German *Zorn* 'anger' with the initial letter changed to allow for the same phonetic difference as between *to* and *zu.*

Again, in the twentieth century, Lallans translators will use similar strategies to expand their vocabulary, invoking Scots' kinship with the Germanic languages. Like the Lallans translators, too, Waddell uses archaisms, though more sparingly than the later 'dictionary-dredgers' were to be accused of doing, and he extends the semantic range of words by putting them in unexpected contexts, often metaphorical. For example, Tulloch (1989: 43) notes that he uses 'misfaur' (literally, 'misfortune') in the sense of 'sin'. In short, all of these strategies were employed to construct a formal, modern, literary Scots – and without exception, they were to be employed by twentieth-century writers bent on following Waddell's example. His biblical translations take literary Scots out of the eighteenth-century Enlightenment, and the kailyard nostalgia of the Victorians, and into the modern age.

Chapter 7

'Mongrels of Fire and Clay': Lallans Translations in the Twentieth Century

Making it New: Hugh MacDiarmid and his Successors

If translation into Scots endured a relative famine from the Union of the Crowns to the turn of the twentieth century, thereafter it enjoyed a feast. Twentieth-century Scots translations have been the subject of numerous books, and interest seems to be growing (see, for example, Findlay, forthcoming). This chapter and the one following cannot deal comprehensively with the astonishing amount of translation into Scots over the past hundred years; rather they pick out some major trends and significant figures. The present chapter considers mainly those translations which are written in a 'synthetic Scots' or 'Lallans' – that is, a Scots which although it is based on the everyday speech of the translator, might also incorporate archaisms, neologisms, borrowings, and calques to extend the range of vocabulary. This literary variety of Scots tends to be regarded by its advocates as a unifying symbol of a distinctive Scottish identity – Lallans is a 'nation language'. The final chapter considers those translations which are written in a variety of Scots which is limited to a more 'accurate' representation of the writer's immediate speech community. For the sake of convenience, I have termed these as 'vernacular' translations. In one sense, of course, all Scots translations are vernacular translations in relation to Latin, the lingua franca of educated Europe in the Middle Ages. However, the term 'vernacular' also captures the modern distinction between those translations which attempt to represent the speech of an actual community and those non-vernacular translations which attempt to reconstruct a synthetic Scots. The 'vernacular' varieties of Scots reject the notion of a 'nation language' in favour of a form of speech and writing which is rooted in a particular locality and social class. Linguistically, the line between Lallans and the 'vernacular' Scots is far from absolute – the most synthetic of Scots usually has a basis in everyday speech, and the most 'representational' of vernacular Scots often resorts to some vocabulary-extending strategy associated with the Lallans movement once it is written down, especially if some unfamiliar concept has to be communicated. However, there is an ideological distinction between the two camps, insofar as they tend to have different conception of what Scots is, and why there should be translations into it. It is these ideological tensions that will be the focus of our attention here.

The renewed impetus towards a broad range of translations into Scots – of any kind – can be credited to Christopher Murray Grieve, 'Hugh MacDiarmid' (1892–1978), and in particular to one of his poems, the lengthy *A Drunk Man Looks at the Thistle* (1926). In this collage of ballad, parody, philosophy, polemic, satire, and occult mysticism, the eponymous 'Drunk Man', a self-confessed 'mongrel o fire and clay' addresses the thistle, an equally ambivalent symbol of Scotland's fortunes. Incorporated into the whole are sections 'suggested by' prominent European contemporary poets – the Russians, Alexander Blok and Zinaida Hippius; the Belgian, Georges Ramaekers; and the German, Else Lasker-Schüler. These 'suggestions' derive from MacDiarmid's reading of contemporary poetry in English translation, and his versions are in places very close to the English renditions by Deutsch, Yarmolinsky and Bithell (see the notes to Buthlay (ed.), 1987 to compare the English and Scots wordings). At times, though, MacDiarmid alters some lines of his source considerably, in order to incorporate the translation better into the themes, images and concerns of his poem overall. Consider, for example, MacDiarmid's reworking of Deutsch and Yarmolinsky's translation of Else Lasker-Schüler's 'Sphinx' (cf. Buthlay (ed.), 1987: 34–6):

She sits upon my bed at dusk, unsought,
And makes my soul obedient to her will,
And in the twilight, still as dreams are still,
Her pupils narrow to bright threads that thrill
About the sensuous windings of her thought,

And on the neighbouring couch, spread crepitant,
The pointed-patterned, pale narcissus fling
Their hands toward the pillow, where yet cling
Her kisses, and the dreams thence blossoming, –
On the white beds a sweet and swooning scent.

The smiling moonwoman dips in cloudy swells,
And my wan, suffering psyches know new power,
Finding their strength in conflict's tortured hour.
(Else Lasker-Schüler, trans B. Deutsch and A. Yarmolinsky, in *Contemporary German Poetry*, London, 1923)

The Mune sits on my bed the nicht unsocht,
An' mak's my soul obedient to her will;
And in the dumb-deid, still as dreams are still,
Her pupils narraw to bricht threids that thrill
Aboot the sensuous windin's o' her thocht

But ilka windin' has its coonter-pairt
– The opposite 'thoot which it couldna be –
In some wilde kink or queer perversity
O' this great thistle, green wi' jealousy,
That breenges 'twixt the munelicht and my hert ...
(Hugh MacDiarmid, *A Drunk Man Looks at the Thistle*, ll. 401–10)

[The moon sits on my bed tonight unsought/And makes my soul obedient to her will;/And in the dead of night, still as dreams are still/Her pupils narrow to bright threads that thrill/About the sensuous windings of her thought.//But each winding has its counterpart/– The opposite without which it could not be/In some wild kink or queer perversity/Of this great thistle, green with jealousy/That plunges between the moonlight and my heart ...]

The first stanza is a near-verbatim re-working of the English 'crib', while the second is a substantially transformed version: the narcissus mutates into the Scots poem's dominant image, the thistle, and the concept of the windings of the moon's thought reappear in the second stanza as their mirror-image, represented by the wild perversity of the thistle's shape. Thus the 'suffering psyche' and the 'tortured hour' of the source text are not so much translated as articulated by the psychomachia of moon and thistle.

All this is a far cry from the cosy Horatian imitations of 'Hugh Haliburton', although, as noted in Chapter 6, in brief passages the earlier 'Hughie' anticipates the later 'Hugh' in the articulation of a cosmic perspective. MacDiarmid acknowledges his European sources (while coyly remaining ambivalent about their status as 'translations') in his own footnotes to *A Drunk Man Looks at the Thistle* – if this was stealing, he wanted to draw attention to the theft. In particular, he wished to demonstrate that Scots poetry could take its place in the *contemporary* canon of European poetry, although, as W.N. Herbert

(1995: 139) observes: 'we have the peculiar sight of a socialist poet in the 1920s citing and translating from Russian symbolists like Ivanov and Blok, rather than focusing on an actual contemporary like Mayakovsky'. Herbert argues convincingly that MacDiarmid was strongly influenced by the example of Ezra Pound as poet and translator, and that MacDiarmid's sense of the modern in European poetry was filtered through the sensibility of the expatriate American poet. Even so, MacDiarmid's versions of recent European poems signalled a break from the prevailing Scottish traditions of classical imitation and ballad translation. These traditions continued to construct Scotland as a couthified neoclassical arcadia – a construction which MacDiarmid considered sentimental and degenerate.

Many of MacDiarmid's developing views on Scots at the time he was writing *A Drunk Man Looks at the Thistle* are recorded in the pages of 'Contemporary Scottish Studies', a series of articles and reviews written for the *Scottish Educational Journal* between 1925 and 1927. A selection of the articles was published in book form in 1926, the same year as *A Drunk Man Looks at the Thistle* appeared. The articles also prompted a lively correspondence in the *SEJ*'s letters page, and in 1976, the articles and the letters they prompted were republished to mark the centenary of the *SEJ* (McIntyre, 1976). In the articles, MacDiarmid's antagonism to the successors of the nineteenth-century school of Scottish writing is vividly expressed; for example, in a review of *Swatches o' Hamespun* (1921) he argues that 'A Vernacular revivalist who is not also a Scottish separatist is a contradiction in terms', before embarking on a vilification of much of current writing in Scots (MacDiarmid, 1926; McIntyre (ed.), 1976: 83):

> If Braid Scots is to become a living thing again it must be developed to correspond to the suppressed elements of Scottish psychology in ways of which English is incapable, and not be identified exclusively with the cult of mediocrity to which Aberdonians in particular have so largely committed themselves. Any young Scot with literary powers which he wishes to dedicate to his native country can have no more disheartening experience than to come in contact with the kind of ideas on cultural matters entertained by the London Vernacular Circle and their equivalents in Scotland, and will certainly receive no encouragement from these people unless he falls in both with their petty moral prejudices and lack of interest in anything that is not of a wholly kailyaird order. From the [Scottish] Renaissance point of view, on the contrary, it is claimed that it is utterly wrong to make the term

> 'Scottish' synonymous with any fixed literary forms or to attempt to confine it to any particular creed or set of ideas – let alone to such notions as are really part and parcel of Scottish degeneration and provincialisation.

MacDiarmid here is clearly setting out a personal manifesto in which he, as a representative of the 'Scottish Renaissance' is breaking with a tradition which has become unionist, nostalgic and complacent. As we saw in Chapter 6, this tradition had been born in Jacobitism, but over the course of two centuries, strands of it had been gentrified and tamed, as its rebelliousness had been romanticised, and its intellectual antiquarianism had been transmuted into easy nostalgia and narrow philological enquiry. MacDiarmid's attack on the 'kailyaird' ethos may well entail a selective view of the Scots tradition, but it does explicitly set his own project apart: MacDiarmid's Scottish poetry will be nationalist, not unionist; European, not parochial; free-thinking, rather than narrow-minded; and experimental, not enslaved by tradition. In this project, translation will play a part, as indicated by MacDiarmid's approving quotation from Professor Hugh Walker (McIntyre (ed.), 1976: 83):

> 'People who keep pigeons have discovered that from time to time they must bring eggs from a neighbouring dovecot if they wish to keep up the excellence of their birds. If pigeon fanciers are too exclusive, and refrain from all exchange of eggs, their stock will weaken and ultimately die out. A like fate, De Quincey thinks, awaits the literature of any country which is preserved from all foreign intercourse. He says that every literature, unless it be crossed by some other of a different breed, tends to superannuation.'

Clearly, MacDiarmid's incorporation of Blok, Hippius, Lasker-Schüler and Ramaekers into *A Drunk Man Looks at the Thistle* is part of his attempt to reinvigorate Scots poetry by 'bringing in eggs from a neighbouring dovecot'. In this attempt to follow Ezra Pound's dictum and 'make it new', MacDiarmid's poetry signals a return to the attitude towards translation adopted by James VI and his court poets: native literature would be stimulated and strengthened by translation into Scots of the best of recent European poetry. But in making a break with the immediate past, MacDiarmid also antagonised the 'philological' school of vernacular poetry. Cumming, the editor of the series, *Swatches o' Hamespun*, which occasioned MacDiarmid's bile, defends himself by arguing that his intention was to produce '"dialect, literature if possible, but dialect first and foremost" ' (McIntyre (ed.), 1976: 90). Defending the humble, Burnsian nature of the verse he has printed, Cumming continues:

> Furthermore, when an architect proceeds to plan a but-and-ben, he is entitled to kick when he is told that his building is unsuitable as a kirk. His views as to his intention must be considered. Mr Grieve applies a literary standard to a linguistic effort.

Cumming's comparison of his literary endeavours to building a 'but and ben' – that is, a two-roomed country cottage – betrays his lack of ambition. The hugely ambitious MacDiarmid positions himself in opposition to those whose main priority is aimed at, in Cumming's words, 'recording the dialect as it is'. His strategy is to follow the example of Waddell's translations of the *Psalms* and Jamieson's translations of the Northern ballads, and create a 'synthetic' Scots, a literary medium which will transcend the vernacular, and which will be capable of articulating the 'suppressed elements of Scottish psychology in ways of which English is incapable'. This new variety of Scots was effectively a synthesis of different contemporary dialects with archaisms adopted from earlier varieties of Scots, alongside new coinages. While the vernacular poets strove to record the 'authentic' Scots of a particular place, and others, like Lewis Spence, strove to be faithful to the 'the old Court Scots' of the medieval and renaissance makars, MacDiarmid constructed a Scots that was deliberately 'inauthentic' – it could not be identified as Scots from any one time or any one place. As we can see from the letters and poetic parodies, published in the *Scottish Educational Journal* throughout 1926 and 1927, MacDiarmid was not without his critics. Writing in August 1926, six months after his attack on *Swatches o' Hamespun*, in an article entitled 'Towards a Synthetic Scots' (McIntyre (ed.), 1976: 117–18), MacDiarmid defends his new literary medium by – again – appealing to European models:

> The development of the *Landsmaal* movement in Norway –as of the Provençal movement – was coterie work. No coterie of sufficient calibre has yet emerged in Scotland. The few poets and theorists who have so far advanced and the new synthetising tendencies are a very heterogeneous handful – at such different stages of development that useful co-operation between them is scarcely possible; while there is no non-creative worker for Scots with anything of value to bring to such a suggested symposium. Practically all so-called vernacular enthusiasts are still bogged in

> considerations of dialectal demarcation. Nevertheless the movement has begun, and the ultimate outcome is assured. The history of dialect developments in most other European countries makes it clear that the synthetic principle is bound to triumph in the long run – if complete desuetude is to be avoided; and since the Burns Federation and other bodies are pledged to the revival of Scots, it follows that however improbable any such development may still appear to them, they must sooner or later come round to realise that a synthetic Scots is the only way out.

MacDiarmid's words here are an early, explicit articulation of views which were to be taken up and repeated again and again by proponents of the Lallans movement, and later, the Scots Language Society: a new, literary medium, synthesising past and present Scots, is necessary for the robust expression of a separate national identity. However, the poet and polemicist has other advantages in mind when writing this defence of what would come to be known as 'Lallans': MacDiarmid goes on to argue that the time is ripe for the establishment of synthetic Scots to 'give Scotland a short cut into the very forefront of contemporary creative experimentalism' and he comments 'A Scottish Mayakovsky at this juncture would be a Godsend' (McIntyre (ed.), 1976: 117, 118).

Although MacDiarmid's longed-for 'Scottish Renaissance' took two decades to attain critical mass, his rallying-cry proved in time to be irresistible, and a 'coterie' of Lallans poets slowly began to evolve, though it never quite lost its heterogeneous quality. Even MacDiarmid's call for a Scottish Mayakovsky was eventually answered in Edwin Morgan's Scots translations of the Russian poet, *Wi the Haill Voice* (1972). Indeed, in the wake of *A Drunk Man Looks at the Thistle*, translation was to become one of the major projects of the Scots synthesisers.

MacDiarmid set the tone of much that was to follow, not only in his literary and linguistic technique, but in his socialism, his nationalism and his internationalism. The First World War and the Russian Revolution had begun to unravel the ideological certainties which tied together the constituent parts of the British Empire, and the early decades of the twentieth century saw the beginnings of a reorientation in Scotland's relationship with England. As early as 1928, MacDiarmid was a founder member to the National Party of Scotland (he was later expelled for his communism; just as the Communist Party in Scotland expelled him for his nationalism), but it was not until the close of the Second World War and the final stages of the dissolution of Empire that a recognisable coterie of writers in synthetic Scots really began to make their mark. Much of the translation of these twentieth-century 'makars' was as aggressively contemporary as MacDiarmid's, and, like MacDiarmid, they were keen to demonstrate that Lallans was a suitable Scottish medium for rendering the best of modern European culture.

William Soutar (1898–1943) published a series of poems entitled 'Theme and Variation', written between 1934 and 1941 and, in the manner of MacDiarmid, his contemporary and friend, they were 'suggested by' usually contemporary European sources. 'Recognition', written in 1940 and suggested by Heinrich Lersch, attests to Soutar's pacifism and internationalism, and yet in its conclusion, it also echoes the proto-socialism of Robert Burns' 'Is there for honest poverty'. The narrator, a soldier in the trenches, believes he sees his brother lying in no-man's-land, and resolves to bury him. The poem ends:

> I brocht mysel' to bury him, and had sma' mind o' fear;
> But the face that met me in the mirk was no my brither dear.
> It was my e'en that wrang'd me; my blinded hert was richt:
> There is nae man but aye will be a brither in my sicht.
>
> [I brought mysef to bury him, and had little thought of fear;/But the face that met me in the dark was not my brother dear./It was my eyes that wronged me; my blinded heart was right/There is no man but he'll always be a brother in my sight.]

In his introduction to a selection of Soutar's poems, Aitken describes Soutar's translation technique in a way that is very reminiscent of MacDiarmid's (Soutar, 1988: x):

> The variations Soutar played upon his themes range from a more or less literal translation of the theme-poem ino Scots to the creation of a new poem altogether or occasionally to a rewriting of the poem from a different point of view. It is not merely a prejudice in favour of a Scottish poet writing in Scots that makes one think that Soutar almost invariably improved on his originals. Frequently, of course, he was working from English translations, sometimes rather pedestrian translations, of poems originally written in Russian, Sanskrit, Yiddish, German, or Hungarian, and the comparison is therefore not with the true original. Further, Soutar was not setting out to give a translation, but to play a free variation on a chosen theme.

MacDiarmid set a precedent that Soutar was happy to follow in his own, quieter way. Soutar's own experience of warfare was with the Navy between 1916 and 1919; by the time of the Second World War, he was bedridden with a crippling disease which was finally to take his life. By the time of his death, a younger generation of Scots makars was emerging from the Second World War with an enhanced sense of social injustice and an even more jaundiced view of the legacy of British imperialism. Like Soutar, they looked to MacDiarmid as a political and poetic guru.

Sidney Goodsir Smith (1915–75) was born in New Zealand, and educated privately and at Oxford; yet, he adopted the left-wing nationalism of MacDiarmid, and opted to write in the synthetic Scots which could now represent the modern aspirations of his chosen culture. Among his translations are renditions of the nineteenth-century French poet, Tristan Corbières, and – significantly – Alexander Blok's 'The Twelve'. Unlike MacDiarmid and Soutar, Smith is more concerned to recapture in his translations the polemical intensity of the source material, and less concerned with incorporating them into an original poem or sequence of poems. His Scottish Twelve still march in revolutionary Russia:

> Quaet is aa the citie now,
> Neath Nevski Touer aa is calm,
> There's deil the polis in the toun –
> Cheer up, fellies! – tho we haena a dram!
>
> The bourgeois stands at the street corner
> His neb weill-happit in his collar,
> By him a scruntie tyke is standan
> Chutteran wi tail dounhingan.
>
> The bourgois stands like the stairvan tyke,
> Stands speakless like a question-mark –
> Wi'ts tail atween its legs, at his back
> Stands the auld world, like the hameless tyke.
>
> [The city is all quiet now/Beneath Nevski Tower all is calm/ There's not a policeman in the town –/Cheer up, fellows! – Though we haven't got a drink!//The bourgeois stands at the street corner/His nose well-wrapped-up in his collar,/By him a scruffy dog is standing/Trembling with tail hanging down.// The bourgeois stands like the starving dog,/Stands speechless, like a question-mark –/With its tail between its legs, at his back/Stands the old world, like the homeless dog.]

In the post-war years, MacDiarmid's predicted coterie continued to grow, its swelling numbers including William Montgomerie (1904–94), and Alastair Mackie (1925–85), both of whom continued the trend of translating from contemporary poetry into Scots – with a strong emphasis on Russian. As the language of international socialism, with a powerful and resolutely modern literary tradition, Russian of all the European languages exerted the dominant influence on the Lallans translators. Mackie, for example, has translated from the Russian of Fyodor Tyutchev, Osip Mandelstam, and Anna Akhmatova.

However, not all translation of contemporary poetry originated from outwith Scotland. For the first time, Gaelic literature found itself being translated into Scots. MacDiarmid's growing interest in Celtic culture prompted him to translate Gaelic poems, such as 'Bizerta' by George Campbell Hay (1915–84), and once again his example was enthusiastically followed. Work by the great modern Gaelic poet, Sorley MacLean (1911–96), has been translated by Douglas Young and Robert Garioch, and others, like William Livingstone and Derick Thomson have been translated by Douglas Young and Alexander Scott (cf. McClure, 1988, 1994). It is interesting to compare two versions of one of Sorley MacLean's poems, 'Camhanaich/Dawn', an English version by MacLean himself, and a Lallans translation, 'Ye were the Dawn', by Douglas Young:

You were dawn on the Cuillin
and benign day on the Clarach,
the sun on his elbow in the golden stream
and the white rose that breaks the horizon.

Glitter of sails on a sunlit firth,
blue of the sea and aureate sky,
the young morning in your head of hair
and in your clear lovely cheeks.

My jewel of dawn and night
your face and your dear kindness,
though the grey stake of misfortune is
thrust through the breast of my young morning.

(MacLean)

Ye were the dawn on the hills o the Cuillin,
The bousum day on the Clarach arisan,
the sun on his elbucks i the gowden flume,
the whyte rose-fleur that braks the horizon.

Gesserant sails on a skinklan frith,
gowd-yalla luft and blue o the sea ...
the fresh mornan in your heid o hair
an your clear face wi its bonnie blee.

Gowdie, my gowdie o dawn and the derk
your loesome gentrice, your brou sae rare ...
albeid wi the dullyart stang o dule
the breist o youth's bee thirlit sair.

(Young)

McClure (1988) offers a close examination of this poem among other translations by Young of MacLean's poetry, concluding '*Ye were the Dawn* faithfully conveys the literal meaning of its original, and is worthy to stand on its own merits as a poem in Scots' (p. 141). Its Scots is highly synthesised: rare and archaic words in the Scots poem include 'flume', 'gesserant' (a kind of armour made of small strips of iron – thus, here, 'sparkling'), 'blee' (as McClure notes, an English rather than a Scots archaism, meaning 'complexion') and 'dullyart' (mentioned only in Jamieson's Scottish dictionary, and meaning 'of a dirty, dull colour). 'Skinklan' ('glittering') originates in central Scotland and western Caithness, but is now also largely literary. The '-an' inflexion in 'arisan', 'skinklan' – and, less appropriately, 'mornan' – derives from the Older Scots present participle, '-and' rather than the anglicised '-ing'.

Douglas Young's literary Scots is an extreme example of Lallans. McClure (1988: 145) comments:

> Young's choice of vocabulary items is often highly individual: not only in his Gaelic translations but throughout his Scots poetry he shows a greater fondness for archaic and unusual words than any other of the major post-MacDiarmid poets. Nearly always in his translations of MacLean, however, his rare words are judiciously chosen to give an effect suggested by, or at any rate appropriate to, his originals.

Young was an accomplished linguist, who also translated from Scots into Latin and Greek. Though he could read Gaelic, he was not fluent in the language, and he composed no original Gaelic poetry himself. George Campbell Hay and William Neill (b. 1922) are among the few Scots poets equally at home in Gaelic, Scots and English, and both are accomplished translators in and out of all three languages and more. Twentieth-century translation has nevertheless seen a greater effort than ever before to cross-fertilise the Gaelic and Scots literary traditions, no doubt because linguistic rapprochement is seen to be in the interests of building a sense of a national community. In 1994 an anthology of translations between Scots and Gaelic, *Twa Leids/Dà Chànan* (i.e. 'Two Tongues'), edited by George Philp and Ian MacDonald, was published as part of an ongoing project to bridge these two distinct – and often oppositional – strands in the Scottish cultural patchwork.

The most accomplished Scots translator of the twentieth century, Edwin Morgan (b. 1924) defies categorisation as purely as a 'Lallans' poet, if only because his substantial body of work includes poetry and drama in English, as well as more localised Glaswegian (see Chapter 8). By 1972, the year of the publication of his Scots Mayakovsky, much of the original, post-war impetus behind the Lallans movement had faded. Even MacDiarmid had abandoned poetry in Scots for a scientific style, which he dubbed 'synthetic English', a jargon reminiscent of the excessively latinate passages found in Urquhart (see Chapter 5). Fifty years on, the sheer novelty of reading and writing contemporary poetry in Scots had long worn off, and Morgan is drawn to synthetic Scots when translating Mayakovsky partly by mutual political sympathies, but equally by a delight in not-so-simple linguistic playfulness:

> There is in Scottish poetry (e.g. in Dunbar, Burns, and even MacDiarmid) a vein of fantastic satire that seems to accommodate Mayakovsky more readily than anything in English verse, and there was also, I must admit, an element of challenge in finding out whether the Scots language could match the mixture of racy colloquialism and verbal inventiveness in Mayakovsky's Russian. (Morgan, 1972; reprinted in Morgan, 1996: 113)

The ever-so-slightly grudging reference to MacDiarmid unobtrusively anticipates a distanced, ironic stance towards the synthetic Scots of the Renaissance makars – and this ironic stance was in turn to influence younger generations of Scots poets and translators, such as Roderick Watson, Robert Crawford, W.N. Herbert and Donny O'Rourke (cf. France and Glen (eds), 1989). In an article comparing English translations of Mayakovsky with Morgan's Scots version, Hyde (1992: 89) comments:

> If we were to try to define what this literary Scots can do that is peculiarly suited to Mayakovsky, the answer would take us into questions of history, culture, and traditions, as well as into the fascinating domain of the nature of synthetic, or quasi-synthetic,

> language. Literary Scots is an ever-emergent language, devised in response to the specific needs of a national voice, consciously different from English. There are inescapable political concomitants: Lallans, as it is called, in some way defies the Act of Union, and is the voice of a suppressed popular consciousness. But Scotland has always had a powerful urban culture, which has strikingly re-emerged at various points in history in order to redefine a tradition going back to the medieval *makars* Dunbar and Henryson, and circling awkwardly around Burns, a great poet and an ambivalent cultural institution. Lallans draws upon this, but ironically, at any rate as Morgan and others use it.

The self-conscious irony of the latter-day makars is one possible response to the fact that 'the voice of a suppressed popular consciousness' is articulated in a medium which a dwindling number of the Scottish populace find easy to understand. (Other possible responses to this dilemma are considered in the following chapter.) It has been suggested (Macafee, 1986) that in such a circumstance, Scots, and Lallans in particular, has the surface appeal of nonsense poetry – at first sight, or hearing, its meaning is as opaque and playful as Lewis Carroll's 'Jabberwocky', although with some effort, of course, meanings are laid bare. Poets like Robert Crawford and W.N. Herbert have explicitly played with half-nonsensical Scots/English 'translatorese' in their collaboration *Sharawaggi* (Crawford and Herbert, 1990; cf. Crawford, 1995) but the roots of the ironic turn in Lallans translations lie in Edwin Morgan's poetry. An example of Morgan's ironic playfulness is well demonstrated in 'Eupatoria', in which Mayakovsky's linguistic variations on 'Yevpatoriya', the name of the holiday resort, are exuberantly equalled by Morgan's. The opening lines of the Scots version are:

> O for the souch o the seas
> and the glory o
> the breeze
> that waffs owre Eupatoria!
> (By-ordnar kindlike
> in its peripatorium
> it kittles
> the cheek o the haill Eupatorium.)
> We'se lie
> on the *plage*
> and plouter at the sandy-pats,
> broichin and bronzin

wi the broon Eupadandycats.
Skellochs
and splish-splash
and the skraich o rollocks!

[O for the sigh of the seas/and the glory of/the breeze/that wafts over Eupatoria!/Extraordinarily kindly/in its peripatorium (wanderings?)/it tickles/the cheek of the whole Eupatorium./We'll lie/ on the beach/and splash at the sandy-pats,/sweating and bronzing/with the brown Eupadandycats./ Screams/and splish-splash/ and the screech of rollicks!]

Many of the elements of Lallans poetry are indeed present: the portmanteau neologisms, usually based on 'Eupatoria' (such as 'Eupatorium' and 'Eupadandycats'), the different regional provenances of the Scots terms (south-western 'kittles', tickles, and 'broichin', sweating, are mixed with north-eastern 'skellochs', screams), and the occasional archaism, such as (later in the poem) 'kyte' (= belly), which, according to the *SND*, had fallen out of popular usage by the early twentieth century. However, the high-spirited subject matter here contrasts with the high seriousness of earlier Lallans renditions of Russian poetry, and marks a new, post-modern phase in translations into Lallans. Synthetic Scots is no longer the natural medium for articulating 'the suppressed elements of Scottish psychology' – but it is one of a range of media which can articulate the many-faceted, fractured elements which go into constructing the dynamic, malleable identity of the Scots. The underlying seriousness of Morgan's linguistic experiments should not be underestimated, however, just as it should not be laboured. As Wood (1987: 343) observes of the Mayakovsky translation:

> Morgan's interest in the Russian poet is not solely linguistic; it is related to the value Morgan places in Mayakovsky's work as 'an attempt to incorporate into verse something of the urban, industrial and technological dynamism of the modern world.' It is interesting in this connection that Morgan frequently links Mayakovsky with the American, Hart Crane, whose work he admires for similar reasons: for its linguistic energy and as a positive response to twentieth-century urban culture. Like some of Morgan's other linguistic experiments, the Mayakovsky translations have influenced his work elsewhere and contributed to the development in his work of a more direct representation of city life.

As Horace provided a voice for serious Scots poets of the eighteenth and nineteenth centuries, it can be said that Russian poets like Blok and Mayakovsky have dominated a strand of twentieth-century translations into Scots: they have given the Lallans poets in particular a wider range of voices than their indigenous tradition had hitherto allowed, and overlaid the translations with desperately needed cultural connotations – in the eighteenth century it was the authoritative classicism of imperial Rome; in the twentieth century it has been the revolutionary modernism of Russian literature.

Unironic translations of contemporary and near-contemporary poetry into Lallans continue to be written and published, mainly in the magazine of the Scots Language Society, *Lallans*. In *Mak it New* (MacCallum and Purves (eds), 1995), an anthology celebrating twenty-one years of *Lallans*, a considerable number of poems are translations of twentieth-century poets: including Neil MacCallum's 'owresetting' of the Flemish of Hugo Claus and the French of Jacques Borgeat; Alastair Mackie's translation from the modern Greek of K. Karytlokes; and Lilian Anderson's rendition of the Russian poet Evgeny Vinokurov. The anthology also reprints a short survey of Scots translations, written in Lallans by A.D. Mackie, and entitled 'Frae Ither Leids' (MacCallum and Purves (eds), 1995: 99–102). A slightly earlier anthology of Scots poetry, also mainly in Lallans, *The New Makars* (Hubbard (ed.), 1991) likewise contains its fair share of translations, including T.S Law from the Afrikaans of Uys Krige, David Angus from the Tamil of Kalporu Cirunuraiyár, Robert Crawford from the German 'of the Austrian Erich Fried', and – a very free translation! – Matthew Fitt from the English of Led Zeppelin. Evidently, more than seventy years after MacDiarmid started the trend, the pigeon eggs are still being swapped and cross-fertilised.

'The Auld an Nobil Tung': Revisionist Translations

Not all Lallans translators, however, have been thirled to the contemporary. MacDiarmid's purpose may have been to drag Scots poetry kicking and screaming into the twentieth century and therefore to focus on the modern; however, those who picked up his baton very quickly began to turn their attention not only to their contemporaries but to the literatures of past times and foreign lands. Lallans translators returned to themes which had been treated by earlier Scots translators and also broadened their outlook to include languages and writers never before rendered into Scots. There were a variety of reasons for this activity – MacDiarmid's insistence on the modern may have seemed too narrow a focus for educated Scots makars who were the products of an educational system that still valued the classics. For those whose education did not include sufficient instruction in the preferred classical or modern languages, the publishing industry ensured that there was now a greater than ever availability of 'cribs' in English to draw upon. Partly, too, the modern makars wished to draw attention to their internationalism by associating themselves with the recognised canon of world literature. If the 'philological' translators of the eighteenth and nineteenth centuries had wished to point out their linguistic roots by translating from German and Scandinavian folk literatures, then the Lallans poets wished to indicate their intellectual and emotional roots by drawing on a wide range of writers with whom they felt empathy and shared concerns. Moreover, as we have seen demonstrated again and again, the exploration of foreign literature has been seen as a challenge to Scots and as a way for Scottish translators to extend their poetic voices by experimenting with registers which Scots had lost but which were long-established elsewhere. Finally, the very name 'modern makars' and 'Scottish Renaissance' indicates a concern to reconstruct the conditions of the past, to emulate in particular the court poets of the sixteenth century, the prelapsarian epoch before the Union of the Crowns, when Scots was a prestigious linguistic medium and its writers fashioned a poetry that ranked alongside the best of European literature. The makars of the new renaissance wished to burst open the dams of the English centuries, and let the rivers of literature in Scots – including translation – flow again.

In this enterprise, Latin and Greek remained favoured sources, although translations need not be in classical Latin. J.K. Annand (1908–93) translated *Songs from Carmina Burana,* a medieval manuscript containing Latin as well as macaronic poems in Latin mixed with German, French, Italian or Provençal. The songs are humorous observations on monastic life, in tune with the iconoclastic spirit of Burns's satires: indeed, 'Come All Ye Boozers' (*Potatores exquisiti*) uses a stanza form familiar from the poetry of the eighteenth-century Scots poets:

> Ye that canna tak a dram
> Frae this table rise and scram,
> This is nae place for namby-pam.
> Teuchter feardie-gowks inside
>   Are ye, and we
> Bauld drinkin fellas canna bide
>   A man T.T.

> [You who cannot take a drink/Rise from this table and scram/ This is no place for the wishy-washy./Highland scaredy-cats inside/Are you, and we/Bold drinking fellows can't abide/A man teetotal.]

A more sober, and less anachronistic, note is struck in Annand's rendition of Ronsard's 'Elegy on the Depairture o Mary Queen o Scots on her Retour til her Kinrick o Scotland'. Here the echoes of the sixteenth-century makars are evoked in the aureate latinisms and the dignified parallelism of the syntax:

> Gif the fury o your hands, sae cruel,
> Has sic pouer owre things beautiful,
> Gif aa the virtue, pitie, gudeness,
> Douceness melled intil demureness,
> Sanctlike weys and puritie
> Didnae resist your cruel envie,
> Let's hope in our humanitie,
> Nocht waur arise nor vanitie.

> [If the fury of your hands, so cruel/Has such power over beautiful things,/If all the virtue, pity, goodness,/Gentleness mixed into demureness,/Saintlike ways and purity/Didn't resist your cruel envy/Let's hope in our humanity,/Nothing worse should arise than vanity.]

Annand's Scots translations are a conscious blend of present and past, and he neither scorns nor rejects the legacy of the sixteenth, eighteenth and nineteenth centuries. In this he is spiritual kin to Robert Garioch (1909–81), whose twin muses were the ghosts of Robert Fergusson and Giusseppe Belli (1791–1863). Garioch draws on both Fergusson and Belli to find a voice appropriate to his pin-pricking satires on institutional and individual pomposity. Scots, a symbol of the plain speech of the common man, is an ideal vehicle for this kind of satire; for example, in 'The Wee Thief's Mither' the eponymous narrator justifies her son's petty criminality thus:

> Plenty fowk, Excellency, that git on fine,
> Steal hunners mair nor him, and niver falter,
> and they win reverence, and dine, and wine.
>
> I've aye gien this advice til him: Son Walter,
> lift hauf a million; fir the churches, syne,
> ye'll be a sanct, wi lillies on yer alter.

[Plenty of folk, Excellency, who get on fine,/Steal hundreds more than him, and never falter,/and they win reverence, and dine, and wine.//I've always given this advice to him: Son Walter,/lift half a million; for the churches, then,/You'll be a saint, with lillies on your alter.]

Garioch also translated from the Greek of Hesiod, and from the French of Apollinaire and Michaux, but it is the Belli poems in particular which help him recapture the hard-edged satirical voice which had become softened in the post-Burnsian slide into sentimentality.

As Garioch recaptures the spirit of Belli, so Tom Scott (1918–95) aims to recapture the sympathy for society's outcasts that he finds in the poetry of François Villon (1431–*c.* 1463). For Scott, translating Villon allows him to recall the medieval Scottish makars while articulating sentiments in tune with his own fiery brand of Christian socialism. In 'Ballat o the Hingit', the narrators speak, literally, with gallows-humour:

And gin we caa ye brethren, dinnae scorn
The humble claim, even tho it's true
It's juist we swing: ye ken weill nae man born
No aa the time is blest wi mense enou.
Sae for our cause, guid-hertit brethren, sue
Wi the Virgin's Son they hingit on Calvary's bou,
That grace devall afore our judgement's due
An kep us up in time frae hell's gret maw.
Sen we are deid, ye neednae gird at's nou
But pray the Lord has mercie on us aa.

[And if we call you brothers, don't scorn/The humble claim, even though it's true/It's just we swing: you know well no man born/Is blessed all the time with enough sense./So for our cause, good-hearted brothers, sue/With the Virgin's Son they hanged on Calvary's bough,/That grace should fall before our judgement's due/And keep us up in time from hell's great mouth./Since we are dead, you needn't strike at us now/But pray the Lord has mercy on us all.]

Tom Scott, like his peers, translated from a range of sources – including Dante, Baudelaire and Meleager – and he is one of several Scots poets to render Old English poetry into Lallans. McCulloch (1998) suggests that Alexander Scott's adaptations of the 'The Seafarer', 'The Wanderer' and 'The Battle of Maldon' – as 'Seaman's Sang', 'The Gangrel', and 'Sang for a Flodden' – are effectively his war poetry: the

Scottish poet responds to the themes of alienation and loss in the source texts, and finds in it a way of expressing his experience as a soldier in the Second World War. It is interesting to compare the opening lines of two different Scots versions of 'The Seafarer' with an English version by Edwin Morgan:

> This verse is my voice, it is no fable,
> I tell of my travelling, how in hardship
> I have often suffered laborious days,
> endured in my breast the bitterest cares,
> explored on shipboard sorrow's abodes,
> the welter and terror of the waves ...
>
> (Edwin Morgan, 'The Seafarer')

> A suthfast sang I can sing o my life,
> Vaunt o vaigins, how I vexious tyauvin
> In days o sair darg hae dreeit aften.
> Bitter the breist-pangs I hae abydit,
> Kent abuin keels care-trauchlit wonnins,
> Mangset o the mainswaw ...
>
> (Tom Scott, 'The Seavaiger')

> Anent mysel I'll tell ye truly:
> hou, stravaigin the seas in trauchlesome days,
> aye tholan the dunts o time,
> I've borne strang stouns in my breist,
> kennan my ship the hame o mone cares.
> Amang the coorse girn o the swaws I've taen my pairt ...
>
> (Alexander Scott, 'Seaman's Sang')

Alexander Scott's translation is more comprehensible than Tom Scott's, mainly because it is less inclined to compound words to form neologisms ('seavaiger', 'care-trauchlit', 'mainswaws') and less inclined to invert the syntax – although it should be noted that compounding and inverted syntax, alongside the strong alliteration which pervades all three versions, are of course characteristics of this period of Old English literature. However, it is to the very name 'Old English' that both Scots writers would object: Tom Scott labels his source 'Anglo-Saxon', while Alexander Scott labels it simply 'West Saxon'. In these translations, the Scots poets are going beyond the recaptured Enlightenment of Garioch's Belli, and the new medievalism of Annand's monks and Tom Scott's Villon, to reclaim the roots, not only of English, but of Scots language and poetry. The 'West Saxon' translations implicitly proclaim that 'Old English' could equally well be renamed 'Old Scots', and indeed that present-day Scots is in many ways truer to its Germanic origins than present-day English.

There is a strong sense in which some twentieth-century Scots translators are concerned with making good the missed opportunities which partly constitute Scotland's past, in order to offer a revisionist picture of Scottish history. There is a sense of 'what if' about many translations mentioned above – 'what if Dunbar had translated Villon?'; 'what if Alexander Montgomerie had translated Ronsard?'; 'what if Fergusson had translated Belli?' If the Scottish literary tradition – impressive though it is – has nevertheless involved a series of missed opportunities, then it is the patriotic and literary duty of today's crop of Scots writers to supply the lack. This patriotism is invoked in the introduction to *Tales frae the Odyssey o Homer* (1992) owerset, or translated, by Willaim Neill (b. 1922):

> The aim o this buik wes tae mak sic a tellin o a gret tale as wad gae ower eithlie intil Scots an tae gie a heize tae the hairts o thir fowk wha still tak pleisure in the auld an nobill tung.
>
> Gin I'm tellt that Scots is no a leid but a 'mere dialect' I will mak repone that it's the yae 'dialect' on the isle o Britain that hes a literarie tradeition raxin back ower mair nor sax hunner year. R.P. itsel is nocht but a dialect stellt up bi the establisment. A leid is a dialect wi its ain government, an thare's fouth o ensaumples o yon sempil meisure. (Neill, 1992: 10)
>
> [The aim of this book was to make such a telling of a great tale as would go easily into Scots, and to raise the spirits of these folk who still take pleasure in the old and noble tongue.//If I'm told that Scots is not a language but a 'mere dialect' I will reply that it's the one 'dialect' on the isle of Britain that has a literary tradition reaching back over more than six hundred years. RP itself is nothing but a dialect propped up by the establishment. A language is a dialect with its own government, and there's plenty of examples of that simple maxim.]

Neill's project is overtly to raise the status of 'an auld an nobil tung' by translating 'a gret tale' into it. The intention, the subject matter, and even the language Neill employs, immediately bring to mind Douglas's translation of the *Aeneid*. Compare the Cyclops episode in both translations:

> An than he yellocht oot a fearsome skraich
> sae the lang echoes dirled atour the craig,
> an feart we ran awa while he pluckt oot

the slockened stob frae oot his bluidie ee.
Clean gyte wi pyne he heized it oot an cried
tae aa the etins on yon wundie heichts.

(Neill, 1992: 40)

[And then he yelled out a fearsome screech/so that the long echoes rung beyond the crag,/and frightened we ran away while he plucked out/the soaking spike from out his bloody eye./Clean mad with pain he lifted it out and cried/to all the giants on those windy heights.]

Skars this was said, quhen sone we gat ane sicht
Apoun ane hill stalkand this hidduous wicht
Amang his beistis, the hird *Poliphemus*
Doun to the coistis bekend draw towart vs:
Ane monstour horibill, vnmesurabill and mischape,
Wanting his sicht, and gan to stab and grape,
With his burdoun, that was ane grete fir tre,
Fermand his steppis, becaus he micht not se.

(Douglas, 1513: III)

[Scarce was this said when soon we got a sight/Of this hideous fellow, stalking upon a hill/Among his beasts, the shepherd Polyphemous,/Down to the coast's beacon draw towards us:/A horrible monster, unmeasurable and misshapen,/Lacking his sight, and he began to stab and grope,/With his staff, that was a great fir tree,/Supporting his steps, because he could not see.]

Neill dispenses with Douglas's rhyming couplets in favour of blank verse. Both translators employ a plain style here, but each is willing to adopt rarer vocabulary items when the occasion demands; for example, Neill's 'etin' is an archaic word for giant, deriving from OE 'eoten'. The similarities between the translations are obvious – but there is an important difference. Whereas Douglas was attempting to render a Latin text into the vernacular to extend access to it, Neill is rendering a Greek text into the vernacular to satisfy the aesthetic and political desires of a minority. English translations would serve most Scottish readers well – perhaps even better – than a Scots text if they simply want to read the *Odyssey* but don't read Greek. The Scots translation is there largely to fill in a perceived gap in a distinctively Scottish tradition of translating. Kenneth Farrow's translation of the *Iliad* into Lallans prose fulfils a similar function – if literature in Scots is to have any credibility, then it should have its own versions of the great literature of the world. Farrow's ambitious undertaking is still seeking a publisher at the time of writing, although a brief excerpt appears in the *Lallans* retrospective, *Mak it New* (MacCallum and Purves, 1995). The unpublished manuscript contains episodes which, again, have powerful resonances with older Scottish literature: the fall of Troy, after all, provides the backdrop to perhaps the greatest of all Scots poems, Robert Henryson's 'The Testament of Cresseid', a tragedy which makes use of the same raw material as Chaucer's earlier 'Troilus and Criseyde' and, later, Shakespeare's 'Troilus and Cressida'. In these stories, the Greek hero, Diomedes, diverts the affections of the beautiful Cresseid from her Trojan lover, Troilus. Farrow's prose translation revisits the source of the medieval and renaissance reworkings of the classical tale:

> Whan Aeneas saw the dirdum Diomedes gart kythe, he set oot throu the fell stramash for ti seek Prince Pandarus. Whan he wan til thon buirdlie chiel, the son of Lykaon, he says til him braid oot: 'Whaur nou yeir skeil wi the bou? Whaur ir yeir wingit flains? The'r nae man ferrer kent nor you, an nane can tak a swatch o ye in Lykia. Haith, lad! Pit up a wurd or twa ti Zeus, syne hae a gae at that fallae thonder, the maister o the battil, whaever he be. See the skaith he's duin areddies, killin aw oor guid freins. Yit caw cannie tae! Aiblins he's ane o the ayebydin gods, fasht ower sum skantin o wurship an mebbe wantin a sacrifice'. (Farrow, unpublished MSS; 'Buik Fyve')

> [When Aeneas saw the uproar Diomedes made manifest, he set out through the great tumult to seek Prince Pandarus. When he won through to that burly fellow, the son of Lykaon, he said to him straight out: 'Where now is your sill with the bow? Where are your winged arrows? There's no man better known than you, and none is a match for you in Lykia. Faith, lad! Put up a word or two to Zeus, then have a go at that fellow yonder, the master of the battle, whoever he is. See the harm he's done already, killing all our good friends. Yet be careful too! Perhaps he's one of the immortal gods, angered by some lack in our worship and maybe wanting a sacrifice'.]

Farrow is conscious of the two-way mirror his translation holds up to the Scottish literary tradition: while translating Homer, he has also 'endeavoured to make the text bristle with allusions to Scottish Literature, history and culture' (personal correspondence). The modern translation of the classical text thus reworks it so that, effectively, Homer prophesies the vernacular Scots tradition of later centuries.

Homer is, therefore, not only appropriated by the Scottish literary canon, he is seen to be its source and fount.

Farrow's mammoth project to translate into prose the entire *Iliad* is undoubtedly influenced by the most ambitious attempt to emulate and extend the work of earlier writers, and to compensate for perceived historical lacunae – *The New Testament in Scots* (1983), translated from the Greek by William Lorimer (1885–1967). The manuscript was edited and published posthumously by his son, Robert. The tradition of the Victorian Bible translators, discussed in Chapter 6, had continued intermittently well into the twentieth century, with William Wye Smith's *New Testament in Braid Scots* (1901), Thomas Whyte Paterson's *Proverbs* (1917), Henry Paterson Cameron's adaptation of Thomas à Kempis's *Imitation of Christ* (1912) and *Genesis in Scots* (1921), and Alex Borrowman's *The Buik o Ruth and Ither Wark in Lallans* (1979). All the translators were church ministers, and, with they tended to base their Scottish Bible translations on the English Revised Version (Tulloch, 1989: 54–72). William Lorimer's translation of the New Testament can be seen as the climax of this tradition, being based not on an English intermediary text but on the Greek sources. Lorimer was not a minister, but a professor of Greek at St Andrews University, with an active interest in Scots lexicography. Implicit in the Lorimer *New Testament* is the question: 'What if King James had commissioned the Authorised Version of the Bible in Scots rather than English?' In other words, the Lorimer *New Testament* aims to combine an authoritative vernacular version of the gospels with the incipient language-planning project of Waddell's Scots *Psalms*. Robert Lorimer is in no doubt about his father's realisation of the importance of his translation for the modern development of Scots:

> it was while reading the neutral press in 1916–1919 that he had first become keenly interested in the problems encountered by linguistic minorities in reviving or developing their languages. Before the beginning of the Second World War further study convinced him that, if Scots was ever to be resuscitated and rehabilitated, two great works must first be produced: a good modern Scots dictionary, and a good modern Scots translation of the New Testament, with which (it might be assumed) all well-educated general readers, and many others, were already familiar. In September 1945, soon after I returned from the War, he told me that he had recently been considering what to do when he retired, and had tentatively decided to undertake the task of making his own Scots translation of the New Testament. (R. Lorimer, in W. Lorimer, 1983: xiv)

In the event, William Lorimer spent twenty years translating the New Testament, combining this task with voluntary work for the *Scottish National Dictionary* as an external contributor. The result is a work of considerable scholarship and linguistic virtuosity, which deservedly became a Scottish best-seller on its publication. Lorimer devised his own orthography to convey the particularities of Scots pronunciation; for example, an accent over <y> or <i> indicates the phoneme /i/, (corresponding to the English, 'machine') as in 'wídow' or 'líar'. However, despite his recognition that his translation of the New Testament would potentially act as a normative guide for written Scottish prose in the twentieth century, Lorimer consciously varied the language he used in the gospels: 'I have deliberately refrained from writing in a uniform 'standard' Scots. On the contrary, I have made differences between different writers' (Lorimer, 1983: xvii). The Scots translation, then, seeks to record the differences between different authors of the New Testament by varying the language, not regionally, but by a fairly consistent system of differences in spelling (which reflects pronunciation) and vocabulary. This subtle variation is evident when corresponding passages of the gospels are compared – witness the changes rung on 'servant-girl' in the passages below (emphases added):

> Meantime, Peter wis sittin furth i the close, whan a *servan-queyn* cam up an said til him, 'Ye war wi the man frae Galilee, Jesus, tae, I'm thinkin.'
> But he denied it afore them aa: 'I kenna what ye mean,' said he; an wi that he gaed out intil the pend.
>
> (Matthew, 26)

> Aa this while, Peter wis doun ablò i the yaird. As he wis sittin there beikin himsel at the fire, ane o the Heid-Príest's *servan-queans* cam in an, seein him, tuik a guid luik o him an said, 'Ye war wi the man frae Nazareth, this Jesus, tae, I'm thinkin.'
> But he wadna own wi it: 'I kenna buff nor sty what ye'r speakin o,' said he; an wi that he sloppit out intil the fore-close.
>
> (Mark, 14)

> They war aa sittin round a fire they hed kennelt i the pailace close, an Peter wis sittin amang them, whan a *servan-lass* saw him whaur he sat i the lowe o the fire, an, takkin a lang vísie o him, said, 'This ane wis wi him, tae.' But he wadna own wi it: 'Na, na, wuman,' said he, 'I haena nae kennins o him.'
>
> (Luke, 22)

> The *servan-lass – the janitress,* like – said tae Peter, 'Ye'll no be ane o this man's disciples, tae, na?'
> 'No me,' said he.
>
> (John, 18)

Lorimer's *New Testament* is a linguistic *tour de force,* which seeks literally to enshrine the concept of tolerable dialectal diversity at the heart of the modern Scots revival; but perhaps the most audacious moment in this translation is partly the result of an editorial decision. In the apocryphal version of Christ's temptation in the wilderness, William Lorimer had intended to cast the devil's speech in a phonetic representation of an English accent. Finding this too heavy-handed, Robert Lorimer substitutes the conventional English spelling of the Authorised Version, noting that 'the Deil reminds us how much influence it has exerted in Scotland during the last three hundred years or so':

> Syne Jesus wis led awà bi the Spírit tae the muirs for tae be tempit bi the Deil.
>
> Whan he hed taen nae mait for fortie days an fortie nichts an wis fell hungrisome, the Temper cam til him an said, 'If you are the Son of God, tell these stones to turn into loaves.'
>
> Jesus answert, 'It says i the Buik:
>
> *Man sanna líve on breid alane,*
> *but on ilka wurd at comes*
> *furth o God's mouth.'*
>
> Neist the Deil tuik him awà til the Halie Citie an set him on a ledgit o the Temple an said til him, 'If you are the Son of God, throw yourself down to the ground. For it says in the Bible:
>
> *He shall give his angels charge concerning thee,*
> *and in their hands they shall bear thee up,*
> *lest at any time thou dash thy foot against a stone.'*
>
> Jesus answert, 'Ithergates it says i the Buik: "*Thou sanna pit the Lord thy God tae the pruif.*"'
>
> (Lorimer, 1983: 455)

Lorimer's *New Testament* is a monumental piece of work, which comes, as Paul Scott (1983;1991: 140), observes, '300 years too late'. The cultural centre of most Scots' lives today is not as fixed on the kirk as it was in the century following the Reformation, and, in the interim period, normative standards of written English have been widely disseminated through the Scottish education system. Still, as Scott continues (p. 141):

> It is certainly too late in the day for a *New Testament* alone to make the major impact on speech habits which it once would have done. Even so, a successful work on this scale and level could still radically transform attitudes to the language, and its chances of survival, usage and development.

The existence alone of the Scots *New Testament* – as with the existence alone of any Scots translation – cannot guarantee the revival of the use of Scots outwith the literary sphere in today's Scotland. There has to be the political will, popular acceptance and – even today – a sea-change in educational values and a commitment to providing educational resources. Current changes in the Scottish political system and ongoing developments in the Scottish school curriculum, to allow the more direct articulation of Scottish desires and experiences, might conceivably bring about the fulfilment of Paul Scott's prophecy. However, it is still to be seen whether the Scottish people are ready to endorse a public role for Scots outwith the charmed circles of literature and the local, familiar, intimate speech communities which still use it for everyday communication.

The Word Spoken: Lallans Translations on Stage

Numerous modern translations into Scots aim to address a further historical missed opportunity – namely, the suppression by the Presbyterian kirk, from the Reformation to the eighteenth century, of the Scottish theatre. It was indeed Allan Ramsay, the poet, dramatist and translator, who attempted to revive the pre-Reformation traditions of Scottish drama by opening a theatre in Carubber's Close, Edinburgh, in 1736, only to have it closed down again in 1739. The twentieth-century Scottish Renaissance signalled a renewed interest in Scots drama, in which – once again – translation played a significant role.

Original Scots plays with historical themes had become popular in the wake of the twentieth-century Renaissance: Robert McLellan's *Jamie the Saxt* (1937) was an early offering, and the popular success of this play was followed by the often-revived *The Flouers o' Edinburgh* (1948), a satire on the desire of the eighteenth-century gentry to adopt anglicised pronunciation. R.S. Silver dramatised the story of Robert the Bruce between 1948 and 1951 (*The Bruce* was eventually published in 1986); and a decade later Sidney Goodsir Smith followed this up with *The Wallace* (1960). Translations into Scots tended also to toe the historical line. Robert Kemp followed up his adaptation of Sir David Lindsay's medieval Scots play, *Ane Satire of the Thrie Estaitis*, performed at the second Edinburgh international festival, in 1948, with vigorous translations of Molière, *L'Ecole des Femmes* (*Let Wives Tak Tent*, 1948) and *L'Avare* (*The Laird o' Grippy*, 1958). *Tartuffe* (1986) joins a long line of Molière translations, this time by Liz Lochhead (b. 1947). In her introduction, Lochhead revels in the range of sources for her own 'synthesised Scots':

> Actually, it's a totally invented and, I hope, theatrical Scots, full of anachronisms, demotic speech from various eras and areas; it's proverbial, slangy, couthy, clichéd, catch-phrasey and vulgar; it's based on Byron, Burns, Stanley Holloway, Ogden Nash and George Formby, as well as on the sharp tongue of my granny; it's deliberately varied in register – most of the characters except Dorine are at least bi-lingual and consequently more or less 'two-faced'. (Lochhead, 1985: Introduction)

The register shifts in the translation are evident both in the contrast between Tartuffe's Scots and Cléante's English, and in the internal variations in Tartuffe's language. The social differentiation between Tartuffe and Cléante is dramatised by the English/Scots divide:

CLÉANTE: And it is written, sir, that on Orgon's whim
Valère be dispossessed and you should usurp him?
Taking his bride, her inheritance and his good name?
Accepting property to which you have no claim?

TARTUFFE: Ah jist maun trust that those that ken me best
Ken better than Ah'd act oot o' self-interest.
A' the glisterin' riches in the warld mean nut a thing tae me.
Ah'm the last wan tae get dazzled by their glamourie . . .
(IV. ii)

[**TARTUFFE:** I just must trust that those that know me best
Know better than that I'd act out of self-interest.
All the glittering riches in the world mean not a thing to me.
I'm the last one to get dazzled by their witchcraft/glamour . . .]

If Tartuffe's own speech shifts towards English when he is at his prayers, then the irony is double-edged, since the situation and the rhythms and rhymes allude to the Scots of Burns's 'Holy Willie's Prayer' – the ghost of deflatory Scots haunts Tartuffe's anglicised religiosity:

TARTUFFE: May merciful heaven grant to thee and thine
Health, wealth and grace baith temporal and divine.
I, God's humblest servant ask, and ask in all sincerity,
May He crown you all your days wi' bountiful prosperity.

(III. iii)

Peacock (1993) observes that Molière is one of the most-translated playwrights into Scots – his adaptations suit the Scots' taste for satire, complement the music hall tradition of larger-than-life stereotypes, and are set in a period in which many Scots of both the middle and working-classes would have used the vernacular quite naturally. Fitting equally well into this vein of popular comedy, satire, and a historical setting is the tantalising glimpse of a Lallans version of Dario Fo's *Mistero Buffo/Comic Mysteries*, translated by Stuart Hood and appended to Ed Emery's English version (Hood (ed.), 1988, 1992). Although Hood calls his translation a 'Lallans' version, there are elements in it which mark it as specifically north-east Scots, as the following extract from the Resurrection of Lazarus indicates: the words 'fitever' and 'fit' ('whatever' and 'what') again demonstrate stereotypical north-eastern Scots pronunciation. And arguably the north-eastern Scots' stereotypical concern with lucre is evoked as the bystanders at Lazarus' resurrection begin betting on whether or not Jesus will be able to raise him from the dead:

Richt than! Saxpence! A sheelin. Fitever ye like.
I'll haud them. Dae ye trust me? He dis. We aa trust each ither. Fine than, I'll tak the money.
Richt, than, tak tent though. Doun on yer knees, aabody.
Fit's he daein?
He's there prayin.
Wheesht will ye?
Hey there, Lazarus, git up noo.
Oh, he cin haud forth and he cin sing if he likes – aa at'll come oot is the worms he's fou o.

(Hood (ed.), 1992: 121)

[Right then! Sixpence! A shilling! Whatever you like./I'll hold them. Do you trust me? He does. We all trust each other. Fine then, I'll take the money./Right, then, take care though. Down on your

> knees everybody./What's he doing?/He's there praying./Shhh, will you?/Hey there, Lazarus, get up now./Oh, he can hold forth, and he can sing if he likes – all that'll come out is the worms he's full of.]

The long Scottish tradition of classical adaptation is continued in the translations of Aristophanes by Douglas Young, *The Puddocks* (1957) and *The Burdies* (1959). The first play was performed by students at St Andrews' Byre Theatre in 1957, and the second received a professional production – and mixed reviews – at the Lyceum Theatre during the Edinburgh Festival of 1966. Christopher Small in *The Glasgow Herald* (23 August 1966) had few qualms about the transposition of Athens to Edinburgh:

> In fact, as those who have already seen Douglas Young's Aristophanic exercises will know, 'The Birds' turns most readily and happily to Scots language and circumstance; and classicists will surely agree that this exceedingly gay, irreverent, gaudy and melodious version is a faithful realisation of the original script.

However, the drama critic of *The Times*, writing on the same day, endured 'a dismal evening':

> Searching for some argument in defence of this production one can at least say that it fits logically into the festival drama programme as a local variation on the main theme of Greek theatre: and that unlike many past Lyceum shows it is not a try-out for London. Nowhere else in the country is Aristophanes likely to fall into the hands of the Scottish Nationalists.

More worrying, perhaps for Young was that his translation of *The Burdies* and its subsequent Festival production drew criticism from Alexander Scott, a fellow Lallans poet and dramatist, with whom Young engaged in a latter-day flyting in the pages of *The Scotsman* (August/September 1966). This correspondence prompted Scott to write a squib, 'Supermakar Story' (Robb (ed.), 1994: 101–4), based on the correspondence, and in this poem it is Young's use of Scots which is most at issue:

> Supermakar pit it [i.e. *The Burdies*] in print
> (He loo'd yon coorse creation),
> Ae page had Burns's rhymin in't
> On 'burdies' – wrang quotation –
> The t'ither pages aa were tint
> In mirkest mystification.

Supermakar had praise o the beuk
    Frae dominies gleg at the Greekin,
That kent the classics at ilka neuk –
    But Scots? They'd started keekan,
Yet couldna learn to tell the look
    O' cauldest kail frae reekan.

[Superpoet put it in print/He loved that coarse creation,/One page had Burns's rhyming in it/On 'burdies' – wrong quotation –/The other pages all were lost/In darkest mystification.//Superpoet had praise of the book/From teachers smart at Greek/Who knew every corner of the classics–/But Scots? They'd started peeking,/Yet couldn't learn to tell the look/Of coldest kale from steaming.]

The criticism here may seem ironic – one Lallans poet criticising another for using mystifying language – but it is symptomatic of a general problem in presenting 'synthetic Scots' for a live audience. As McClure noted in the discussion of Young's Gaelic translations, above, Young was one of the most eager of the Lallans makars to extend his vocabulary by using archaisms, compounds, borrowings and calques, and there is still an element of these strategies for linguistic modernisation in his stage-Lallans, as the following excerpt from *The Puddocks* illustrates. The Chorus is commenting on the rivalry between Euripides and Aeschylus for the Chair of Tragedy in Athens:

Chorus: Siccar the dunneran makar'll herbour a terrible anger,
suin as he sees his rival sherpan his tusk wi a clangour
shill and dirlan. Wud wi gram and teen,
Aeschylus will rowe his een.

Hech! sic a flytin we'll see – bress helmets' gesserant flashin,
wallopan horsemane phrases, and skelves frae the chariots'
  bashin,
whan the chiseler fends the architect's
stallion-muntit word-effects.

[*Chorus:* Surely the thundering poet'll harbour a terrible anger,/as soon as he sees his rival sharpen his tusk with a clangour/shrill and piercing. Mad with grief and sorrow,/Aeschylus will roll his eyes.//Hah! such a verbal duel we'll see – brass helmets' shining flashing,/walloping horse-mane phrases, and splinters from the chariots' bashing/when the chiseller resists the architect's/ stallion-mounted word-effects.]

(Young, 1958; ll. 814–21)

The reader of these verses obviously has more time to process them than the watcher and listener in a theatre audience, a fact that Young himself recognised in his Introduction to *The Puddocks,* when giving guidance to possible producers:

> the Scots vocabulary used by me was not all such as to be readily recognised at first hearing even by habitual speakers of Scots, much less by Americans and other English-speakers in a random audience .... I would emphasise that producers have my entire goodwill in discreetly watering down my Scots reading version with whatever English, American, Irish or other expressions they may think proper to their purpose, provided always that on any programme they will state that their acting version is based on, but in actual wording does not fully represent, my printed text. (Young, 1958: ix)

Audiences' unfamiliarity with 'high-style' Lallans makes it less of a commercial proposition for stage performance, and more recent Scots drama tends to take the route of reproducing something much closer to an urban idiom (see Chapter 8). However, a few Lallans dramatic translations are still being published and produced, either of texts which gravitate towards the colloquial and away from the 'high style', or of texts which are so well known that they require little explanation. For example, *Klytemnestra's Bairns,* a Scots translation of Aeschylus's *Oresteia* by Bill Dunlop, was performed at the 1990 Edinburgh Festival Fringe, and it is perhaps significant that in 1992 there were two published versions of Shakespeare's 'Scottish play', one by Robert Lorimer and the other by David Purves, past editor of *Lallans* magazine. These full-length adaptations appeared in the wake of Edwin Morgan's brief extract, 'The Hell's-Handsel o Leddy Macbeth' (*Macbeth,* I.5: 16–55). Purves's 'scotticisation' of the Shakespeare text is less dense than the Morgan version, which is meant to be read rather than watched and listened to. The Lorimer version lies somewhere between them:

> Glamis ye are, an Cawdor, an ye sal be
> what is promised ye. Yit A am feart
> yeir naitur is ferr owre fou o the milk
> o human kyndness ti uise the quickest wey.
> Ye wad be gret, ye hae th'ambeition for't,
> but ye are ferr owre sachless for't.
>
> (Purves, 1992: 10)

> Aye, ye are Glamis, ye are Cawdor, and ae thing mair

ye sall be, ae thing mair. But och, I traistna
sic herts as yours: sic fouth o mense and cherity:
ower-guid for that undeemous breenge! Ye'd hae
the gloir, the gree, the tap-rung, but ye want
the malefice the tap-rung taks.

(Morgan, 1976; reprinted in Morgan,1997: 227)

Glamis ye're ense, an Cawdor, an will be
what ye've been hecht. Yit I misdout your naitur,
o man-kin's mither-milk it's fulled owre fou
tae cleik the shortest road. Ye'r keen o gryteness –
no scant o ambítion, but scant o'th'illness
o will tae gae wi'd.

(R. Lorimer, 1992; 25–6)

Purves's, with its sparser use of obscure Scots vocabulary, and less complex syntax, is better suited to performance than either of the other two. Morgan's is written to be read, like much Lallans verse, with a glossary or reliable Scots dictionary close at hand. Morgan's Scots here makes interesting comparison with the 'Glaswegian Scots' he adopts for his translation of *Cyrano de Bergerac* (see Chapter 8). Lorimer's version is closer to the lexical density of Morgan's version, and the complex syntax and surprising collocations ('keen o gryteness', 'scant o th'illness o will'), while paralleling the linguistic ingenuity of Shakespeare, make the language even more difficult for a modern audience to comprehend in performance. Nevertheless, like the Scots versions of 'The Seafarer' discussed above, the several Scots *Macbeths* attempt to reappropriate cultural property: Shakespeare's play, after all, has its origins in Bellenden's translation of Boece's *Scotorum Historia* into Scots, and in the *Daemonologie* by Shakespeare's Scottish patron, James VI and I (cf. Farrow, 1994; Mapstone, 1998). This reappropration is combined with a mischievous appeal to the authority of canonical literature – here to *the* English playwright. Moreover, the play is so familiar that the unfamiliarity of the Scots language should not be perceived as a barrier – indeed, like Lorimer's *New Testament*, these translations might even be considered ways of reteaching the Scots their own language, as well as making English speakers look afresh at the Shakespearian text. In his 'Translator's Note' Purves records his hope that the defamiliarisation involved in translating English into Scots will prompt just such a re-examination:

> Inevitably, there have been gains and losses in translating Shakespeare's English into Scots, but since performances of this great

> play have in modern times become ritualised, the use of Scots serves to restore meaning to important passages which have tended to become worn-out and hackneyed. (Purves, 1992: xviii)

Shakespeare's Scottish play is not the only one which has been appropriated by Scots. Ellie McDonald (b. 1937) has adapted both Hamlet's soliloquy and Act 3, Scene 1 of *A Midsummer Night's Dream* in her collection *The Gangan Fuit* (1991). It is a strange but somehow heartening irony that a process that begins by plugging the gaps in the discontinuous history of Scottish drama comes full circle by prompting renewed appreciation of the English national bard. The impulses and articulations of Lallans poetry, prose and drama are complex, varied and dynamic over time. Alongside the impulse to modernise Scots, the Lallans writers aim to elevate the status of the language, and – so far as is possible – to restore to Scottish literature some of the riches that history has denied it. As we have seen, in this ambitious project, acts of translation have played a crucial part.

The Status of Synthetic Scots

The excerpts from translations given above show that, linguistically, 'synthetic Scots', or 'Lallans' is quite diverse. At one end of the continuum is the relatively plain style of J.K. Annand, Robert Garioch, or Stuart Hood, which seldom strays far from the vocabulary of the Scots speech of the translator's place and time; in the centre would be the Scots of David Purves, William Neill and Kenneth Farrow, none of whom are afraid to use a considerable number of words which are now confined to written literature rather than speech; while at the other end is the experimental, high style sometimes adopted by Douglas Young, Robert Lorimer and even Edwin Morgan, all of whom stretch the resources of the language by playing with established meanings, and frequently incorporating expressions never before encountered in Scots. This 'high-style' Lallans is an expression of a cultural dilemma: here, after all, is a variety which claims to be 'the language of the people' but which nobody ever actually spoke. In contrast, the plain-style of Lallans can seem very close to the 'vernacular' Scots to be discussed in the following chapter; indeed, the difference between plain-style Lallans and vernacular Scots lies less in the language used in any particular text and more in the writer's attitude to the general ethos of moving beyond an 'accurate' representation of the speech variety of a particular community, rooted in a time and place, in order to construct a linguistic medium able to articulate national aspirations. Lallans writers value their language because it is the language of the nation; vernacular writers value their language because it is the language of a more immediate speech community, socially and geographically. The label 'synthetic' or 'plastic Scots', used by MacDiarmid and Young to indicate modernity and high technology, is now sometimes used derisively to indicate a variety of Scots which rejects its roots in an identifiable speech community. However, its proponents vigorously defended their right to synthesise Scots. In an address to the St Andrews Society, with Hugh MacDiarmid in the chair, in 1945, Douglas Young compares his own attitude to Scots with that of Gavin Douglas:

> First, it seems to me ridiculous to restrict oneself to words heard. It is important to keep contact with the living racy spoken language of all sorts and conditions of Scots, but no literary creator in English, Russian, or French would restrict himself to words heard. Words read may be as good as words heard, and even a Methuselah would never hear all the words which are still used. I even adopt words read in a dictionary, or words I make up for myself from Scots and kindred roots by old Scots principles, such as my words '*Ice-flumes*' for glaciers.
>
> Secondly, I think that enough harm has been done by the practice of Gawn Douglas and Allan Ramsay of introducing English vocables into Lallans. We have already too many strangers within our gates and are risking the loss of our citadel. It is just like the controversy about admitting Poles, Englishry, and such like to Scots citizenship. Admit a few of many nationalities, but do not allow too large a quota to any one breed of immigrant. If Lallans fails, coin something from Latin or Greek if you like, as King's English does; if all else fails admit a Hottentotism rather than another Anglicism. This should be our intransigent policy for the next five hundred years or so.

The linguistic and racial exclusivism smacks of the unsavoury side of nationalism; nevertheless, the basic argument that there is nothing illogical or unprecedented in modernising a language variety is a fair one, and it is not surprising that there is a small, but lively, group of people in Scotland who continue to write in Lallans. And, as the proportion of 'owresettins' which pepper anthologies and the regular issues of *Lallans* magazine show, translation remains a key method of promoting this variety of Scots. In an interview, one of the 'new Scottish poets', Donny O'Rourke (b. 1960), observes that he finds it easier to write 'good thick Scots' when translating, and he admits that his adaptations of twentieth-century French poetry in his collection, *Eftirs*, contain words recovered from the Scots and Ulster dictionaries. Challenged on the artificiality of the exercise, he responds:

> Truthfully, I would now, without self-consciousness, use words that I found initially for use in a poem in conversation, because they are such beautiful words, it is a great language. I used to be very critical of some people who spoke Scots in public with a kind of quaintness, a slight affectedness, but I'd be much less hard on them now. I really do think that finding opportunities to use these very precise, very resonant words is something that Scots people should do more often. There is a mixture of the sincere and the artificial. I think you can end up with very beautiful lyric poetry. I'm not talking of my own work in this instance. I think people like David Kinloch, especially, and Bill Herbert are able to combine a kind of sincerity with artifice based on recovered words, you know, retreived language. (MacGillivray, 1997: 10)

The boundaries which have long held between 'plastic' and 'realistic' Scots are shifting, in a world in which we have been taught to re-evaluate the roles of essence and artifice in the construction of complex social identities. Nevertheless, if younger poets are returning to Lallans with a renewed sympathy, then their influence is as much the ironic, playfulness of Edwin Morgan as the strident nationalism of Hugh MacDiarmid. For some of today's writers, Lallans continues to hold out the promise of a reconstructed language for a re-imagined nation; for others, it provides an apt means of literary experimentation in a world which views identities as necessarily contingent, and always artificial.

Chapter 8

The Cult of the Real: Twentieth-century Scots Vernacular Translations

Regional Voices

In the discussion in the previous chapter of Edwin Morgan's translation of Mayakovsky, and its impact on younger Scots poets, we saw that a latter-day, ironic use of Lallans is one possible response to the dilemma facing writers in synthetic Scots; namely, that they were compelled to construct a variety of Scots that no-one had ever actually spoken in order to voice 'a suppressed popular consciousness' (Hyde, 1992: 89). No matter how valid the project of modernising Scots so that it can act as a vehicle for twentieth-century national aspirations, the dilemma remains: how can 'the people' be authentically represented, when the language put into their mouths is synthetic? As was noted, one response is simply to acknowledge the dilemma and treat Lallans with post-modern irony, by questioning the very nature of authenticity. Alternatively, though, the Lallans project can be rejected, and writers can attempt to offer a more accurate representation of how Scots now speak. This is generally offered as a 'real' Scots in opposition to the 'synthetic' Scots of the Lallans writers. In the eighteenth and nineteenth centuries, we observed that there was a growing concern to represent the 'natural dialect' of the writer, what I shall call for want of a better term 'vernacular' Scots, whether that was 'Vanlu's north-eastern Scots, James Murray's Borders Scots, or the Scots of Bonaparte's 'philological' Bible translators. The bridge between the Victorian and the modern vernacular translators was Sir Alexander Gray (1882–1968).

It is significant that, unlike the Lallans radicals of the early twentieth century, Sir Alexander Gray was very much a pillar of the establishment. His publishing career began in 1915 when he was working as a government translator of German and Dutch for what he called 'the

Lie-Factory' (Gray, 1966: 150). As part of his duties as a civil servant, he translated a book entitled *J'accuse, von einem Deutschen,* in which a Swiss author attacked German government policy. The book contained passages of poetry, which Gray duly versified in English. By his own account, this forced introduction to literary translation led Gray to experiment with German songs and ballads, and led in time to his publication in 1920 of *Songs and Ballads, chiefly from Heine,* and in 1928 to *Songs from Heine for Schumann's Dichterliebe.* In these early renditions, Gray aims for 'transplantation' rather than literal translation, thus emphasising the commonality of the north European folk and song traditions which had been so much a theme of nineteenth-century translations into Scots (see Chapter 6). Thus the Rhine becomes the Forth in the following song:

Im Rhein, im heligen Ströme

The Forth, the hallowèd river,	
By Stirlin's wa's glides doon;	*Stirling's walls*
And in its waters are mirrored	
The Castle, the Kirk, the toon.	*town*
In the Kirk there hangs a picter,	*picture*
Painted on cloth sae bricht;	*so bright*
In my life's darkened places,	
It has shone wi' friendly licht.	*with friendly light*
Afore oor lady o' sorrows	*Before*
The blessed angels boo.	*bow*
Her lips and her ee-broos, her haffets	*eyebrows, locks*
Are the marrows o' hers I lo'e.	*equals of, love*

Gray went on to publish several volumes of translations of European ballads and songs: *Arrows* (1932) – of which he later ruefully remarked that his introduction, on the German ballad tradition and its translation into Scots, was better remembered than the poems themselves – *Sir Halewyn: Examples in European Balladry and Folklore* (1949), *Four-and-Forty: A Selection of Danish Ballads Presented in Scots* (1954), and *Historical Ballads of Denmark* (1958). In his concentration on the ballads and songs of Scandinavia and Germany, Gray is evidently continuing the tradition of encompassing kindred literatures through translation, established by Robert Jamieson, Robert Buchanan and the Reverend Alexander Grieve – indeed, Gray notes in his introduction to *Four-and-Forty* that while he enjoys the civilised balladry of the Romance languages, he feels his Scots translations are more suited to 'the ballads of the tougher North' (Gray, 1954: xii–xiii). When challenged that he is simply translating 'one incomprehensible into another incomprehensible', Gray's response is to point to the simplicity and directness he finds in the Scots vernacular (Gray, 1932; reprinted 1966: 119):

> In short, these poems, if converted into English, would reek to me of artificiality; but those which interest me, by some obscure kinship of language or sentiment, seem capable of being clothed in dialect without violence or constraint. This, and no perfivid patriotism (though I trust I am not lacking in this), is my reason for using the medium of dialect in these versions. It is the virtue of dialect, when properly used, that it permits the use of the simplest words without lack of dignity; and consequently the writer in dialect may with safety say what in the standard language would savour of bathos and banality.

Here in the introduction to *Arrows*, there are hints (in the qualifying phrase, 'dialect, when properly used') that Gray is discreetly opposing those he later described as 'his youngers and betters' in the synthetic Scots movement (Gray, 1950; published 1966: 146) – with his emphasis on simplicity and directness, Gray strove to adopt a style of Scots which avoided obvious archaisms, neologisms or borrowings. Gray's family roots were in Angus, to which he dedicates his early translations from Heine, and his translations are evidently based on the regional speech of that area in his own time. One of his criticisms of Jamieson's renderings of the Scandinavian ballads was that 'He is far more archaic, and therefore more difficult to read, than there is any need to be' (1954: xiv), and by the time he came to write *Four-and-Forty,* in the mid-1950s, with the Scottish Renaissance in full bloom, he could no longer conceal his irritation with 'those who had acquired their Lallans in the course of an English public school education' (1950; published 1966: 146). While he again praises Scots as the medium best suited to the translation of ballads, he attacks the Lallans poets' explicit or implicit rejection of English as an alien tongue:

> The identification of 'English' and 'England' tends to suggest in ultra-patriotic circles that the English language is something we have got from England, one of those things imposed on us by the 'auld enemie', that it does not really belong to us and that accordingly it is, or would be, a patriotic act to reject or repudiate the imposition. It is not so, and neither Henryson nor Dunbar ever

> suffered from this illusion. I am, I imagine, as good an Anglo-Saxon as anyone who strides by the banks of the brawling Arun (and probably less of a Norman) – though who among us knows what he is? – and I claim the English language in the widest sense as part of my indubitable and inalienable birthright. Nor am I prepared to sell this part of my birthright for a pre-fabricated dish of Lallans pottage which neither I nor any of my ancestors ever spoke. (Gray, 1954: xxi)

Here we can see a typical displacement of anxieties about the construction of personal identity, based on affiliations to nation and class, into a typically forceful debate about 'authentic' and 'inauthentic' language. For all his sincere Scottish patriotism, Gray was equally an unashamed Briton: a civil servant, then a professor of economics, his literary outputs were offered with all the modest disclaimers of the stereotypical English gentleman amateur. In the heat of this ideological opposition, Gray ignores the fact that much Lallans poetry is little removed from vernacular Scots (cf. Purves, 1997); yet his rejection of synthetic Scots, and his craftsmanlike translations of the Scandinavian and German folk-songs, leave open the door for other poets and translators to continue to adopt varieties of Scots which owe more to regional solidarity (within a national framework that can be either Scottish or British) than to a national aspiration that is explicitly separatist.

Two of the most active regional centres of Scottish writing are the north-east, around Aberdeen, and even further north in the islands of Shetland and Orkney. Both centres have a long tradition of vernacular literature that reflects the particularities of north-eastern and insular speech. Gavin Douglas, for one, is claimed as an Aberdonian by modern writers of 'the Doric' (a term which, although originally broader in application, has latterly come to be associated particularly with north-east Scots). Alexander Hutchison (b. 1943) is one north-eastern translator who combines the eclecticism of the Lallans makars, with a voice that is identifiably Doric. His translations derive from all periods, and include versions of Catullus, Ronsard, and the contemporary French poet, Raymond Queneau (see France and Glen (eds): 1989: 180–82). The poem below, translated from Queneau's 'Sourde est la nuit', captures particularly modern anxieties about social disintegration and the paralysis wrought by fear:

FROM THE FRENCH OF RAYMOND QUENEAU

Deef the mirk, the shadda, the haar,
deef the birk, the cassay-stane;

deef the haimmer t' the anvil-heid,
deef the sea, the houlat his lane.

Blin the bumlick, blin the mirk,
blin the girss, the barley-heid;
blin the mowdie aneth the grun,
blin the roddan, blin the seed.

Dumb the mirk, the deepest dool,
dumb the sangs, an dumb the laich;
dumb the the glimmer o the lift,
dumb the wid, the watter, the craik.

The hale hypothec's totteran noo:
totteran baists, totteran stanes;
totteran tae the likeness drawn,
a totteran yaff t'shift yer banes.

Bit faa glisks, faa kens,
faa spiks a wird o't yet?

(Hutchison, in France and Glen (eds.), 1989: 182)

[Deaf the dark, the shadow, the sea-mist,/deaf the birch, the cobblestone;/deaf the hammer to the anvil-head,/deaf the sea, the owl alone.//Blind the stumbling-block, blind the dark,/blind the grass, the barley-head;/blind the mole beneath the ground,/blind the rowan, blind the seed.//Dumb the dark, the deepest sorrow,/ dumb the songs, and dumb the laugh;/dumb the glimmer of the sky,/dumb the wood, the water, the bird-cry.//The whole lot is tottering now:/tottering beasts, tottering stones;/tottering to the likeness drawn,/a tottering yelp to shift your bones.//But who glimpses, who knows,/who speaks a word of it yet?]

This translation demonstrates that just because a Scots poem is written in the modern vernacular, it is not necessarily easier to understand than a poem in 'synthetic' Scots. Here the problem is not the archaic or rare nature of the vocabulary, but the highly localised nature of the forms, some of which would be weel-kent in the countryside of north-east Scotland, but less well-known outwith that region. Such words would include 'bumlick' (or 'bumlack', a stumbling-block; restricted to Aberdeenshire and Banff); 'mowdie' (a mole; now north-eastern in provenance) and 'rodden' (rowan-berry; now also confined to the north). The spellings also conventionally represent Doric pronunciation, in particular the /f/ realisation of what elswhere in Scotland would be spelled <wh-> and usually pronounced /ʍ/, although in urban areas anglicised /w/ is becoming more common. The idiom, 'hale hypothec', meaning 'the whole lot', is derived from an expression in Scots law, referring to a creditor's right to hold a debtor's effects as security, without actually taking possession of them.

Hutchison's translation is as modern and as apocalyptic as MacDiarmid's early lyrics, but the insistently north-eastern Scots used resists easy identification with a pan-Scottish nationalism. This is a translation that celebrates a region as much as a nation.

A celebration of locality equally pervades the work of Sheena Blackhall (b. 1947), and, like Alexander Gray, she explicitly rejects the ideology of the Lallans movement, preferring the 'real' language of her kith and kin:

> Twis a stammygaster fin a wee Scots pedant screived tae me (fair set on garrin me agree wi him) that the grammar an spellin o Lallans wis fit Scots poetry *sud* be aa aboot! An here wis me, thinkin poetry wis aboot rhythm, an souns, an feelins, an picturs! Bit then, I'm a Scots illiterate. I didna learn Doric frae a buikie. I learned it frae ma bluid kin, at kistins, at waddins, at wark an at play, in the howfs an parks an glens o Deeside, Skene an Cromar. I dinna recollect ae relation, stoppin mid-ben a spikk an wheekin oot a dictionar tae see gin a wird wis richt standard Scots or nae! (Blackhall, 1996: iii–iv)
>
> [It was a shock when a little Scots pedant wrote to me (fully set on making me agree with him) that the grammar and spelling of Lallans was what Scots poetry *should* be all about! And here was I, thinking poetry was about rhythm, and sounds, and feelings, and pictures! But then, I'm a Scots illiterate. I didn't learn Doric from a book. I learnt it from my blood-relatives, at christenings, at weddings, at work and play, in the taverns and fields and valleys of Deeside, Skene and Cromar. I don't recollect one relative, stopping in mid-speech and whipping out a dictionary to see if a word was proper standard Scots or not!]

The admonishments of the 'wee Scots pedant' referred to here bring to mind the critical remarks of MacDiarmid on the mediocrity of Scots vernacular literature at the turn of the century, and particularly that emanating from Aberdeen, which he portrayed as the locus of a debased variety of Scots. Blackhall's vigorous defence is again predicated on the 'reality' of her Doric as opposed to the artificiality of Scots learnt 'frae a buikie'. Sheena Blackhall, however, cannot be accused of restricting her topics to 'wee comic verses tae please the easy-pleased' – her collection of stories, *Wittgenstein's Web* (1996) includes three translations into the Doric of Italian tales by Italo Calvino, Alberto Moravia and Italo Svevo. English bridging texts have also been consulted, and in her version of Calvino's 'Pesci Grossi, Pesci Piccoli' Blackhall acknowledges her debt to Archibald Colquhoun's rendering of the tale (in Trevelyan (ed.), 1965: 70–87):

> BIG FISH, LITTLE FISH
>
> Zefferino's father never got into bathing-dress. He stayed in rolled-up trousers and vest, with a white linen cap on his head, and never moved away from the rocks. He had a passion for limpets, the flat clams which stick to rocks and become with their very hard shells almost a part of the stone. To prise them off Zefferino's father used a knife, and every Sunday he would scrutinize the rocks on the headland one by one through his spectacled eyes. On he would go until his little basket was full of limpets; some he ate as soon as gathered, sucking the damp bitter pulp as if from a spoon; the rest he put into his basket. Every now and again he would raise his eyes, let them meander over the smooth sea and call out: 'Zefferino! Where are you?'

> MUCKLE FUSH-TEENIE FUSH
>
> Zefferino's faither nivver wore dookers. He keepit on his rowed-up trooser legs an sark, wi a fite linen bunnet on his heid, an nivver traivelled awa frae the rocks. He'd a saft spot fur lempets, yon fat clams clappit teetle the rocks that grow (wi their byordinar teuch shells) near-like pairt o the steen. Tae yark them aff, Zefferino's faither made eese o a knife, an ilkie Sabbath he'd glower at the rocks on the heidlan, ane bi ane, throw his glaisses. He'd cairry on till his wee pailie wis fu o lempets: some he galloched doon as sune's he preed them, sookin the sappy wersh soss as if frae a speen; the lave he stappit into his pailie. Ilkie noo an again, he luikit up, his een reengin ower the smeeth sea, an skelloched, "Zefferino! Far are ye?"

Again, the translation contains peculiarly north-eastern characteristics; for example, the /f/ in 'Far are ye?'; and the /i/ phoneme in what elsewhere in Scotland would be /u/ – 'speen/spoon', 'smeeth/smooth'. Blackhall transforms the formal standard English which distances the Colquhoun translation into a representation of spoken Doric – complete with diminutives, such as 'pailie', and colloquialisms such as 'dookers'. The result, given the important qualification that the Doric here is probably much more lexically dense than even most north-eastern Scots would use for everyday purposes, is a concrete, highly specified characterisation through language. This simply would not be possible in the 'high style' of Lallans, owing to its characteristic synthesis of Scots of different places and times.

Although north-eastern Scots has the best-established tradition of local Scots literature outwith the central belt, there is other, similar, regional activity elsewhere. Insular Scots – the Scots of Orkney and Shetland – deserves a mention if only because its lively tradition of vernacular writing is in a Scots highly influenced by Norn, a Scandinavian variety spoken on the islands and in Caithness up until the end of the nineteenth century. William Tait (b. 1918) 'transplants' the French of contemporary poet, Georges Brassens' 'La Mauvaise Réputation', to the Shetland of the Scottish pipes and the festival of Up Helly Aa:

> On Up Helly Aa nycht, snug I lay
> Soond asleep i my seck o hay.
> Da skirlin pipes at goed dirlin by
> Hed naethin ta doe wi me, tocht I.
> Wrang, bi my will, I never did ta nonn,
> Toh I never heard da euphonium gronn.
> But de braa sheelds is whick ta blem,
> If ye tak a different gait fae dem.
> Aabody points da finger at me –
> Aa bit da haandless, dat you'll see!
>
> (Tait, in France and Glen (eds),1989: 83; stanza 2)

> [On Up Helly Aa night, snug I lay/ Sound asleep in my sack of hay./The skirling pipes that went ringing by/Had nothing to do with me, thought I./Wrong, by my will, I never did to anyone,/ Though I never heard the euphonium groan./But the handsome lads are quick to blame,/If you take a different path from them./ Everyone points the finger at me – /All but the handless, that you'll see!]

Here instead of north-eastern characteristics we see the plosives /d/ ('da/de/dat') and /t/ ('tocht/toh') for what elsewhere would be the fricatives /ð/ (in 'the/that' and, devoiced, in 'though') and /θ/ (in 'thought'). Insular Scots pronunciations are also reflected in 'sheelds' (i.e. 'chiels', or 'lads'), and 'whick' (i.e. 'quick'). Although the lexical content of this stanza is less obviously regional than the passages by Hutchison and Blackhall, the poem is still strongly local, a translation into a variety of Scots designed to serve a clearly defined speech community within the Scottish nation.

Again, in the past it has often been too easy to set up the synthesisers of Scots in opposition to those whose voices aim to represent 'the language of the people' with a greater degree of regional and social particularity. The success the Lallans poets helped raise the profile, and broaden the themes and ambition of the vernacular poets, while there is often less linguistic difference between the products of the different 'schools' than some of their propaganda would lead us to expect. Lallans texts can often be read as vernacular texts with the very obvious local markers stripped out and a few archaisms or neologisms thrown in. It is symptomatic that a range of surface linguistic features should be so energetically invested with conflicting ideologies of national and regional identity. Sheena Blackhall (1996: iii) observes that 'Dugs merk their territory wi dug-pish. I merk mine bi drawin or scrievin ... ' [Dogs mark their territory with dog-piss. I mark mine by drawing or writing ...'] The territorial analogy seems vividly apt: Scotland can reasonably be seen not as a homogeneous nation but as an arena in which contesting communities jostle for position. Furthermore, the question of how language indicates affiliations and constructs identities becomes even more aggravated when social class is added to the complex of nation and region.

Urban Voices

The dilemma of how a synthesised Scots can represent the 'real' social struggles of contemporary Scots, when it is not perceived to be an 'authentic' representation of the way they speak and write becomes even more pointed when the focus of attention moves from the country to the city. Macafee (1983, 1994) and Macaulay (1991, 1997) have demonstrated that working-class speech in west central Scotland is both conservative and innovative: much more than middle-class speech, it is a repository of features from older Scots, and it has also been enriched by contact with mainly Irish immigrants in the nineteeth century. The working classes, however, are also the most likely to reject the middle-class pieties imposed upon them by 'genteel' Scots whose attitude to Irish innovations is less than generous. Tom Leonard (b. 1944) has sought to rediscover and bring to wider attention a radical strain of poetry published in smaller magazines and broadsheets in nineteenth-century Scotland. In his introduction to the anthology, *Radical Renfrew* (1990), Leonard attacks the attitude of the middle-class contributors to Scottish poetry anthologies towards the working-classes who still used Scots in their speech:

> Those most active in promoting this [Victorian literary] Scots were often those most opposed to what was happening in areas like Glasgow and Paisley. It was not a simple matter of locality and national culture. For with the industrial revolution had come the emergence in Britain of the proletarian urban dictions, and diction had become in Renfrewshire, as elsewhere in Britain, what it has never ceased to be since: not simply a matter of locality, but of class. The proletariat of the West of Scotland, Protestant or Catholic, freethinking or of any other religion, of immigrant stock or not – all could be seen as forming linguistically a colony within a colony. The new middle class of the towns and city – who identified most with Queen's English in their diction – were often those most insistent on 'good Scots' in their literary hobbies. The contempt that was heaped on the speakers of the new urban diction of the West of Scotland was based on class, and sometimes, religious, prejudice as much as a desire for a return to the mythical 'pure' diction of a pure race of pre-proletarian Scottish folk.
>
> This carried into the twentieth century, as some of it has carried to this day. (Leonard, 1990: xxiii)

The kind of middle-class Victorian promoters of 'good Scots' are kin to the ballad translators, Buchanan and Jamieson, and a modern counterpart would be Sir Alexander Gray, whose no doubt sincere devotion to Scots was nevertheless presented as a hobby – his collection, *Four and Forty* is partly dedicated to *British* Railways, as provider of a genial place in which to compose. In contrast, the working-class poets championed by Leonard wrote out of a desire to subvert the anglocentric political status quo. Unsurprisingly, for a genre which is focused on the local, none of the radical commentators that Leonard includes in his anthology are translators, and practically nothing of Leonard's own 'Glasgow' poetry is a translation, with the possible exception of the poem 'Jist ti Let Yi No', which is 'from the American of Carlos Williams' (Leonard, 1984: 37):

> ahv drank
> thi speshlz
> that wurrin
> thi frij
>
> n thit
> yiwurr probbli
> hodn back
> furthi pahrti

awright
they wur great
thaht stroang
thaht cawld

Leonard's language in this and other poems signifies a break from the middle-class representations of Scots which go back to the nineteeth century and beyond: his phonetic spelling gives primacy to the 'real' voice, and the few instances where he departs from standard grammar (in the simplified verb paradigm, 'ahv drank', and in the use of 'thaht' as an intensifying adverb) are exactly those instances which would be stigmatised as 'bad Scots' by the stereotypical middle-class Scot. Leonard, in his own poetry as well as in his anthology, forces us to reconsider the status of proletarian Glasgow speech, as well as the values that it embodies and which are imposed upon it.

Leonard's choice of Carlos Williams as inspiration is significant: in 'The Locust Tree in Flower, and why it had Difficulty Flowering in Britain' (1976, reprinted 1984: 95–102), Leonard praises Williams's 'inclination to see and treat language as an object in itself' (p. 96). The American's poetry is important to Leonard because in his eyes it focuses on language for its own sake, without reference to the knee-jerk social, economic, class-based evaluations that the British inevitably indulge in:

> What I like about Williams is his presentation of voice as a fact, as a fact in itself and as a factor in his relationship with the world as he heard it, listened to it, spoke it. That language is not simply an instrument of possession, a means of snooping round everything that is not itself – that's what I get from Williams. (p. 95)

Leonard's response to Williams's 'Just to Let You Know' presents Leonard's voice as 'a fact in itself, and a factor in his relationship with the world as he heard it, listened to it, spoke it'. The phonetic spelling and the non-standard grammar are ways of getting at the reality, the factuality of the voice; the change from plums to beer ('thi speshlz') and from apology ('Forgive me') to acknowledgement ('awright') is neither mocked nor celebrated. The voice just is: its authenticity is all that matters.

Leonard is ambivalent about the achievement of Hugh MacDiarmid, and, like Sheena Blackhall, suspicious of the motives of later Lallans makars. On the one hand he acknowledges that MacDiarmid's obsession, in both Scots and English, with testing the boundaries of lexis corresponds to Carlos Williams's concern with language as object; on the other, he sees this obsession as partly a desire to appropriate cultural property by the process of naming. Leonard's antipathy to such appropriation by any dominant class is at the foundation of his rejection of Lallans. His poster poem – 'MAKARS' SOCIETY/GRAN' MEETIN' THE NICHT/TAE DECIDE THE SPELLIN' O' THIS POSTER/ADMISSION: THRITTY PEE (A HEID)' – is celebrated as a lampoon of the nit-picking, navel-gazing obsessions of some in the Scots language movement, an obsession that implicitly seeks to exert social control by imposing a 'correct' Scots spelling. Leonard's position is that language – including poetry – is an object in the real world which can uniquely express real-world problems of poverty, oppression and injustice. Given the burden of social responsibility with which language is imbued, accuracy of representation, the cult of the real, is primary.

Those who have followed Leonard in translating into something approaching a working-class Scots vernacular have tended not to be poets but dramatists. With some notable exceptions, unlike their compatriots in the Lallans school of historical drama, the vernacular playwrights have tended more towards addressing contemporary social and economic problems in their translations. While Tom Leonard must undoubtedly be a profound influence on many writers representing the urban voice in Scotland today, there are other influences at work too, not least the tradition of variety shows and music-hall comedy in Scots.

Bill Findlay, himself a prolific translator into Scots, has written of the sudden wave of Scots dramatic translations from the early 1980s (Findlay, 1996a, 1998). Although some of the pre-eminent Scottish translators, such as Robert David Macdonald at the Citizens' Theatre in Glasgow, prefer to use standard English as their linguistic medium, Findlay argues that the distinguishing factor of this upsurge in translations is the willingness to use some variety of Scots. He attempts to account for the fact that the fifteen years between 1980 and 1995 have seen more theatrical translations into Scots than existed in the first eighty years of the twentieth century:

> One partial explanation might lie in a kind of delayed effect arising from the burgeoning of indigenous drama in the 1970s and playwrights' new harnessings of the particularities of Scottish speech at this time. A further reason perhaps lies in the even greater expansion of indigenous theatre activity that was witnessed in the 1980s, and a related rise in confidence in the distinctiveness and health of Scottish theatre culture – a confidence

> that was expressed partly in a wish to forge direct contact with contemporary happenings in foreign theatre. Given the linguistic distinctiveness of most of these translations, a further reason might appear in a more general trend discernible over the same period to assert with new-found confidence the validity of Scottish voices on our stages in performing non-Scottish plays, whether translations or English-language plays ranging in period and place from Shakespeare to Mamet. That this shift was accomplished without alienating audiences – indeed, quite the reverse – suggests that a similar change was taking place in audience attitudes, perhaps as a reflection of the wider cultural and political nationalism that was evident in the Scotland of the 1980s. (Findlay, 1996a: 190)

Ironically, this cultural and political nationalism followed hard on the heels of the failure of the first devolution referendum in 1979 to secure an increased measure of home rule for Scotland. The collapse of James Callaghan's Labour government as a consequence of the referendum debacle led to eighteen years of Conservative rule, mostly under that archetype of English nationalism, Margaret Thatcher. It is possible that the Conservative Party's explicit pro-English, anti-foreigner stance fostered an implicitly contrasting openness to international influences in the Scottish arts of this time. Theatre was probably best-placed among the Scottish arts to reflect this adoption of international influences. As Randall Stevenson notes:

> It's rare to hear Scots spoken in the media: it's likewise rare, in film or television particularly, to find much focus on Scottish issues or affairs, however much Hollywood may recently have rediscovered the romance of Scotland as a moneyspinner. Theatre offers one of the last public arenas – and maybe one of the best – for raising and debating issues of immediately local, regional or national concern. (Stevenson, 1996: 17)

The language used in this debate inevitably dramatises political and cultural issues, either explicitly or implicitly. The very use of an 'authentic' vernacular Scots serves to localise the speakers, regionally and socially; just as the choice of Lallans raises awkward questions of compromised national identity. Again, the distinction between Lallans and the vernacular voices can become blurred, as we saw in Stuart Hood's north-eastern 'Lallans', used in his translation of Dario Fo. Fo effectively became an honorary Scot, as *Mistero Buffo* was joined by translations of *Accidental Death of an Anarchist, Female Parts,*

Trumpets and Raspberries, *The Virtuous Burglar* and *An Ordinary Day* by writers such as Ian Brown, Joseph Farrell, Morag Fullerton, Robert Walker and Alex Norton. Some of the published translations, for example by Joseph Farrell, do not reflect the degree of 'localisation' they enjoyed in the theatrical productions. Perhaps the most apposite of the Dario Fo plays in 1980s Scotland was *Can't Pay? Won't Pay!* adapted by Alex Norton and Robert Walker, which tuned into Scottish protests against the reorganisation of local government taxation – the notorious 'poll tax' – which was to focus resentment against the Thatcher government of the time. In these plays, contemporary national issues were dealt with in an urban Scottish voice that could represent the 'real' language of the people – a language that was possibly marked off from English largely by accent and subtle speech rhythms, but which nevertheless was distinctive in its social, regional and national character.

Urban voices can also be heard in more recent Scots translations of historical plays, for example, in Edwin Morgan's *Cyrano de Bergerac* (1992). This bears comparison with Liz Lochhead's *Tartuffe* (see Chapter 7); however, where Lochhead states that her Scots is 'totally invented', a synthesis of old and new, demotic and literary, English and Scots, Morgan claims that the contemporary Glasgow vernacular is the basis of his translation:

> Various English versions of the play have been made, but it is one of those rich and challenging works which need to be translated again and again, in different circumstances and for different purposes, readerly and actorly. The time seemed ripe for a Scottish version, but one that would be thoroughly stageworthy, and not incomprehensible to audiences at the Edinburgh International Festival. I decided that an urban Glaswegian Scots would offer the best basis, since it is widely spoken, can accommodate contemporary reference, is by no means incapable of the lyrical and the poetic, and comes unburdened by the baggage of the older Scots which used to be thought suitable for historical plays. (Morgan, 1992: xi)

The crucial sentence is the last: what exactly is 'the baggage of the older Scots'? Presumably, Morgan here is following Tom Leonard's rejection of Lallans as an inauthentic mode of expression – although he uses it (ironically) in his Mayakovsky translations, and, perhaps less ironically, but still playfully, in his excerpt from *Macbeth* – a 'readerly' translation. Moreover, in explicitly identifying Cyrano as a Glaswegian, Morgan here restates his 'otherness' (in Rostand's play,

Cyrano is a Gascon, an outsider in Paris); and in valorising his Scots, Morgan is exhibiting civic rather than national pride. Morgan's Glaswegian, however, is not the phonetic representation of 'real' voices found in Leonard's poetry, but something approaching the synthesis of colloquial and literary found in the lower registers of Lallans. This is evident in Cyrano's 'flyting' with Valvert, who has insulted his appearance, but without wit or imagination. Cyrano shows him how a long-nosed man *could* be insulted:

> CYRANO: Yer *canto*' s no *bel* , young man!
> Ye could have said – oh, lotsa things, a plan
> For each, tae suit yer tone o voice, like so:
> *Thuggish:* 'If Ah'd a nose like yours, Ah'd go
> Straight to the surgery fur amputation!'
> *Freen-like:* 'Dinnae dunk it in a cup, fashion
> Yersel a Munich tankard for tae slurp fae.'
> *Descriptive:* 'A rock? A peak? A cape? The survey
> Shaws the cape's a haill peninsula!'
> *Pawky:* 'If it's a boax and no a fistula,
> Whit's in it, pens or pins or penny needles?'
> *Gracious:* 'Ye're a right Saint Francis, ye wheedle
> The burds o the air tae wrap their gentle tootsies
> Roon yer perch an rest their weary Guccis!'
> *Truculent:* 'Puff yer pipe until the smoke
> Comes whummlin oot yer nose, and the big toke
> Has awe yer neebors cryin "Lum's on fire!"'
>
> (I. iv)

The Scots here is close enough to English not to require glossing for a wider audience – the differences are largely in pronunciation. However, there are a few lexical items, like 'pawky' (sly) or even 'lum' (chimney) which are falling out of general use and thus becoming 'literary'. In any case, the whole style of the piece – which is after all verse drama – represents a merging of the colloquial and the literary.

The dichotomy – whether real or imagined – between vernacular, authentic Scots and literary, artificial Lallans derives from the ambiguous nature of the Scottish nation: region, class and nation become conflated and at times confused. Urban Scots stands for the 'real' Scot, the male, working-class city dweller, against the anglicised Scot of the middle classes, who, as Alexander Gray observed, could as easily have learnt his Lallans in an English public school as at his mother's knee. In this environment, it is not surprising that in the wake of Lorimer's *New Testament in Scots* (1983) came *The Glasgow*

Gospel (1992), and *Auld Testament Tales* (1993), later combined and expanded into *A Glasgow Bible* (1997) – all by Jamie Stuart. More retellings of the gospel and Old Testament stories than translations as such, Stuart's biblical adaptations nevertheless continue a key project of the Reformation, begun by Nisbet in the sixteenth century, deflected by the Geneva and King James Bibles, restarted in the nineteenth century, and reaching its climax in the Lorimer *New Testament:* the rendering of sacred texts in 'the language of the people'. Stripped of the daunting scholarship of the Lorimer *New Testament*, and of its secular aim to revive written Scots, Stuart's *Glasgow Bible* perhaps comes nearer to the evangelical goal of the original reformers. Indeed, the earlier *Glasgow Gospel* was at least partly prompted by the Church of Scotland, as Stuart's publisher, Lesley Ann Taylor, recalls in her 'Publisher's Preface'. Stuart initially reacted to the Kirk's suggestion with some scepticism:

> Jamie had some doubts. Many people love the pithy nature of the Glaswegian vernacular, while others have little regard for it. The Revd John Campbell, Church of Scotland Adviser on Mission and Evangelism, and a good friend of Jamie's, had few doubts. To him the Patter [i.e. Glaswegian Scots] was a real joy. Why shouldn't the greatest story ever told be presented in the language of the people? After all, as John Campbell pointed out, Jesus Himself must have conversed in the ordinary language of the people. (Taylor, in Stuart, 1997: viii)

The implication of Campbell's words, coming only seven years after Lorimer's successful translation, is that the Lorimer translation is still removed from 'the language of the people', at least from the language of Scotland's urban proletariat. Stuart's rendition of Peter's denial illustrates the differences between his version and Lorimer's (see Chapter 7):

> Meantime Peter wis sittin oot in the coortyard. This burd comes up tae him an says, 'Wir you no a pal o thon Jesus, the man fae Galilee?'
>
> 'Ah don't know whit you're bletherin aboot,' said Peter.
>
> Then he went oot inty the porch an anither lassie spots him. She cries tae the folk staunin aroon, 'See this yin here? He wis alang wi that Nazarene!'
>
> Wance mair Peter denies it, sweirin at them, 'Ahve telt ye – ah *dinny* ken the man!'

The elements of Scots here are those which are partly indicative of the innovatory, and thus stigmatised, Scots that grew up in the melting pot of immigrants into the new cities in the industrial revolution: the topic marker 'see this yin' [note this one] and the general slang item 'burd' [young woman]. Other features are more traditional: the demonstrative 'thon', the verbs 'bletherin' and 'ken' have long histories in Scots. But much of the passage's distinctiveness comes from spellings which indicate Glaswegian pronunciations of words common to both Scots and English: 'wir/were', 'whit/what', 'anither/another', 'wance/once', and so on. Lexically, in fact, there is little to distinguish the two language varieties, Scots and English; the burden of difference is carried largely by the orthography signifying a distinctive phonology. Given a more idiosyncratic orthography, this statement is equally true of Tom Leonard's Glasgow poetry. Such representations reflect the phenomenon of 'dialect levelling' which is continuing, particularly in the cities of Scotland's central belt (see, for example, Macafee, 1994; Macaulay, 1997).

Some promoters of Lallans mourn this haemorrhaging of Scots terms, regarding Glaswegian as a form of 'broken English'; while supporters of the vernacular again counter that it is a real rather than an idealised Scots. The polarisation of the debate is a pity: the different varieties of Scots do slightly different things, and their interdependence is greater than is sometimes acknowledged. On the one hand, Lallans promoters can exploit the fact that their synthesis of a range of Scots is able to fulfil the functions of a full national language; while the basis of most Lallans texts in some form of spoken Scots nevertheless allows it to retain its street credibility. The vernacular writers might adopt a variety that never strays far from the speech of a given place and time, yet they trade on the fact that, from the sixteenth century on, there is an established and honourable tradition of literary translation into Scots – including, at crucial points, Lallans Scots. This tradition raises even writing in vernacular Scots above the status usually accorded to non-standard varieties of English in England. As we saw in the previous chapter, there are welcome indications that younger Scots poets and translators are following the lead of Edwin Morgan and are becoming more inclined to blur the categories and refuse to be backed into one corner or the other.

Mixed Voices

The range of possible Scots voices is a strength in Scottish writing, and in translation into Scots. The clearest single indication of this comes in the translation by Bill Findlay and Martin Bowman of Québécois writer Michel Tremblay's *La Maison Suspendue* (*The House Among the Stars*), first performed at the Traverse Theatre in Edinburgh in 1992, then later in Perth Theatre. Like Dario Fo, Tremblay has effectively become an honorary Scot through translation, Bowman and Findlay having enjoyed critical and popular success with performances of *The Guid Sisters* (1989, 1990, and 1992), *The Real Wurld?* (1991), *Hosanna* (1991), *Forever Yours Mary-Lou* (1994) and *Albertine in Five Times* (1998). In most of these plays an urban Scots is employed as a Scottish correlate to the urban Québécois known as 'Joual' (literally, 'horse language'). However, in *The House Among the Stars*, the stories of three generations of a dysfunctional French Canadian family are told using different varieties of Scots. Three different time-zones are presented simultaneously on-stage, and we learn of the family's move geographically from country to city, and socially from peasantry to the urban working classes, to middle-class academia. The language used by each generation is an index of the family's history: the oldest generation uses a rural Scots, sometimes near-literary in its lyrical passages, the middle generation speaks a vigorous urban dialect, and the youngest generation employs a standard English with distinctive Scots traces, as the following extracts (set in 1910, 1950, and 1990 respectively) illustrate:

VICTOIRE: Dreams . . .
JOSOPHAT: Whitwey dreams? It's you's jist duin sayin Montreal's fu' ae fowk frae the country deein ae boredom. A' ah'm ettlin is tae brek thir boredom. The lang stories ah kin tell, an thit you're aye tellin me aff fur, ah kin mak fit the city tae. Ah kin mak the mune rise in the city jist as easy as here!

EDOUARD: Ah dae things ma wey, Bartine! Naebody else has ma style . . . and, listen, I bloody well enjoy bein different fae ither folk! . . . We need watter fur the moarn, so it'll be me his tae go'n git some fur us, wulln't it? But ah'll go fur the messages ma ain wey. Naebdy in Duhamel wull've ivir went fur watter ma wey afore – ivir! Gaun fur a pail ae watter's borin, but ah'll turn it intae somethin extra special! That's where ah am the clever alec, Bartine!

MATHIEU: When I was a boy my favourite dream was that I'd have a huge family . . . not unlike yours, in fact. I didn't know that my mother had thrown my father out and had chosen to bring me up on her own in a tiny wee flat . . . I'd invent brothers and sisters for myself and multiply the rooms in our house . . . I invented a father for myself, too . . . A loving father who lived with us . . . A magic prince I could love . . . in the same way that I love my own son today . . . to the extent that I could hug him to death . . .

[JOSOPHAT: What do you mean, dreams? It's you who's just finished saying that Montreal's full of folk from the country dying of boredom. All I'm trying to do is to break their boredom. The tall tales I can tell, and that you're always scolding me for, I can make fit the city too. I can make the moon rise in the city just as easy as here!

EDOUARD: I do things my way, Bartine! Nobody else has my style . . . and, listen, I bloody well enjoy being different from other folk! . . . We need water for tomorrow, so it'll be me who has to go and get some for us, won't it? But I'll run errands my own way. Nobody in Duhamel will have ever gone for water my way before – ever! Going for a pail of water's boring, but I'll turn it into something extra special! That's where I'm the smart alec, Bartine!]

The slightly literary resonances of Josophat's register ('ettlin', 'mune') contrast with the urban idioms of Edouard's ('go fur the messages', 'clever alec'), while Mathieu's generation slips into only the occasional scotticism ('wee'), usually to signal intimacy or affection. In the code-switching that occurs between generations in this play, the entire family history is dramatised in a way that would not be possible in standard English, or even in a single, standard Scots. It is a remarkable play that exploits the full range of Scots voices, easily achieving Bowman and Findlay's intentions:

> The play was a gift for us as it allowed for three distinct idioms: a rural Scots for 1910, and urban variety as in *The Guid Sisters* for 1950; and a Scottish English for the 1990 characters. With family roots in Banffshire and Angus, the translators welcomed the opportunity to try and suggest the sound of the Northeast in the rural characters' voices. Curiously, *The House Among the Stars* has had more success in Scotland than Quebec, having had two professional productions within a year (the Traverse in October, 1992; Perth in August, 1993) whereas in Quebec it has not been produced professionally since its *création* in 1990. (Bowman and Findlay, 1994: 66)

The play's success in Scotland is possibly because it speaks to the shifting identities of many Scots today – the fractured affinities that many have with an idealised image of rural life, the ambivalent attractions of the cities, and the love–hate relationship with standard English. It relativises the cult of the real by putting urban Scots into a historical context – the rural, the urban and even the anglicised speech of the generations speak of different but equally valid Scottish experiences, as they affect a single family over time.

'Real' Voices?

In twentieth-century translations into Scots, the use of an urban or rural vernacular tends to indicate a community within a community, a region within a nation; or, as Tom Leonard puts it, a 'colony within a colony', an oppressed proletariat within an oppressed Scotland. There can be a range of reasons for adopting a vernacular idiom; for example, to celebrate a clearly defined region or social class, or to support that region or class's resistance to domination from within or without Scotland. Even more so than Lallans Scots, the vernacular varieties can be represented in different ways. Tom Leonard's phoneticised Glaswegian might be seen as the heir to James Murray's transcriptions of the Book of Ruth into his Borders' speech. Jamie Stuart's *Glasgow Gospel*, like Edwin Morgan's *Cyrano de Bergerac* adopts a spelling which owes something to older Scots, and something to modified English orthography. Sheena Blackhall's Doric, and William Tait's Shetlandic retain specifically regional usages, many of which would be edited out of a standardised Scots variety.

The relatively high status accorded to vernacular translations into Scots, as compared with translations into varieties of non-standard English, is perhaps due to there being no single widely accepted standard Scots available. The promotion of Lallans is still a minority pursuit, and the codification of Lallans is not so far advanced that – even given the political and social will – it could easily be disseminated through the Scottish educational system. One of the functions of a standard variety of language is to suppress variation, to edit out forms distinctive to particular localities, to establish 'correct' norms for written grammar, vocabulary and spelling, and, to a certain extent, to promote 'polite' ways of speaking. Given that the establishment of these linguistic norms inevitably disadvantages those who do not subscribe to them, there has been a long history of resistance to the standardisation of Scots which runs counter to the ambitions of the Lallans promoters. The main weapon in the armoury of the supporters of vernacular writing, particularly the urban vernaculars, is that it is 'real' – in the often-repeated words, it more accurately represents 'the language of the people'. However, as the translations discussed in this and the previous chapter show, constructions of 'the real' are always ideologically predicated, and they imply social, political and cultural positions which are dynamic, and which continue to be negotiated as the Scottish nation evolves.

This book has attempted to chart the cultural negotiations and tensions – literary, linguistic, political and historical – which have shaped and been shaped by translations into Scots over the past half-millennium. As the story moves on, old questions resurface. Chapter 1 considered how Scots has been used in translation by non-Scots, for whom standard English acts as a cloak of invisibility. The problem non-Scots face when confronted by a vigorous variety of Scots arose once again, early in 1998, when the Scottish playwright John Byrne's Scots adaptation of Gogol's *The Government Inspector* was the hottest ticket in London, where it was produced by the Almeida Theatre. On a brief tour to the King's Theatre in Edinburgh, Scottish critics took the opportunity to join in the acclamation – although some worried that Byrne's use of Scots as a marker of corrupt provincialism pandered to English prejudices. Joyce McMillan in *The Herald* (13 February 1998), resolved this dilemma by arguing that Scottish audiences understood the play better than their English counterparts:

> When this production first opened at the Almeida in London it baffled some critics, who are used to regarding the various accents of London as 'neutral' – capable of representing any city or country, anywhere – whereas other accents from around these islands are seen as local and specific, suggesting one particular setting. But the audience at the King's seems to grasp right away that Byrne meant his version of *The Government Inspector* to remain in nineteenth-century Russia; and that he is using a Scots demotic language to represent a certain kind of small-town culture.

In other words, what the English critics didn't realise was that the provincial corruption portrayed in the play was not to be identified with Scottish culture as a whole, but with a particular set of small-town attitudes that might exist anywhere. There is a nagging sensitivity in Scotland to what the English might be thinking, and this undercuts McMillan's call, elsewhere in the review, for a confident, distinctive Scots literary culture. Of course any translation will be interpreted in different ways in different contexts – and doubtless most Londoners would be surprised to find a Scottish critic observing that *all* London's various accents are considered 'neutral'. After all, Venuti's claimed invisibility of the translator was predicated on the perceived neutrality of standard English rather than, say, Estuary English or Cockney. It is perhaps also significant that McMillan, a critic for a Glasgow-based newspaper, goes on to compare a Glasgow audience's response to the Scots used in a Tremblay translation favourably to the Edinburgh audience's more negative response to the Scots of the Gogol adaptation: there is 'no barrier of disapproval' in Glasgow to the use of Scots:

> Edinburgh audiences confronted by a Scots language production will often say to one another, half-apologetic, 'It's very Scottish isn't it?'; sure enough, I heard a woman saying exactly this during the interval of *The Government Inspector.*
>
> And the only remedy for this attitude is for actors in Scots productions to focus so cleanly and perfectly on the meaning of the text that the audience simply ceases to be conscious of accent or idiom and becomes wholly absorbed by what is being said. Actors who are used to using Scots as a lingua franca for all kinds of 1990s drama usually manage this well; others find it more difficult.

McMillan is here looking forward to a time when Scots will still seem such a natural choice for public communication that it will bestow the cloak of invisibility currently enjoyed by standard English. Until that time Scots will not emerge from 'the same strange – and sometimes highly creative – limbo it has occupied for the past 200 years' (ibid.). The implication is again that Scots will not become a 'real' language until it is the natural language of choice in the public sphere in Scotland – to the extent that it is recognised as such in the nation's anglicised capital.

Polyphony

Ultimately, debates about the 'reality' of respective varieties of Scots are futile. As the foregoing chapters have shown, it is more fruitful to consider who is using a particular variety, how it is being used, why it is being used, when it is being used, and to whom. Only then can we assess the wider cultural context of the construction and reconstruction of national, social and personal identity through language. And in this task, as we have seen, the spotlight falls again and again on translations into Scots – they provide a sensitive and fascinating case study of the way one nation continually refashions its own culture in relation to the cultures of others.

Translation Studies, too, has gone through several identifiable phases in its short existence. Bassnett (1996: 24) associates the 1970s with polysystems theory, the 1980s with a culturalist turn, and the 1990s with the question of the translator's visibility. All three phases have direct relevance to the study of translations into Scots. Polysystems theory derives from the writings of Even-Zohar (1978, 1990) and may be briefly characterised as an approach to translation that downplays the question of equivalence between the source and target text; instead, the scholar situates the translation within larger systems of literary and cultural production. Thus the Scandinavian and German ballad translations of the nineteenth and twentieth centuries might be seen in the context of the contemporary interest in indigenous folksong, and the mid-twentieth century taste for Molière on stage might be related to the Scottish passion for music-hall and pantomime. In politicised form and modern dress, this passion re-emerges in the adaptations of Dario Fo.

According to polysystem theory, the function of translation is to reinforce current genres and offer opportunities for stylistic extension. According to Even-Zohar, translations tend to be central to literary activity in nations which are emergent, while they are more marginalised in nations which are established and settled. While disputing the marginalised status of translations in established nations, Gentzler (1996: 118) allows that translations are crucial to the construction of a new or revitalised national consciousness: 'Polysystem theory, as a tool for studying the literatures from emerging nations, from developing countries, or countries undergoing radical change, is becoming increasingly indispensable.' As a case study, Scotland fits neatly into the parallels Gentzler draws between present-day Israel and Quebec, the Czech republic in the nineteenth century, fifteenth-century England, and the early years of Latin American nations. The translations of Gavin Douglas in the sixteenth century, Allan Ramsay in the eighteenth century, and the Scots Renaissance writers in the twentieth century can all be seen as responses to fundamental political changes in Scotland: the emergence of the state, the Act of Union, and the rise of modern nationalism. For all Scottish translators down the centuries, the use of Scots has been a political act – as Gentzler (1996: 118–19) says of Québècois, translation into the vernacular is 'less a way of introducing a foreign text and more a way of legitimizing a distinct ethnological and political entity'. Translations have given a stylistic range and a sense of authority to Scottish literature, and they have validated the identity of the Scots language and, by implication, the Scottish people.

But, of course, such a sweeping statement requires qualification. In the 1980s, as Bassnett (1996: 22) observes, 'with a rethinking of cultural history and the formation of literary canons well under way, the emphasis shifted to the question of power relationships between writers, translators and readers'. Gentzler invokes the cultural historian Michel De Certeau in a plea to consider the everyday realities of how texts get chosen for translation, for publication and for consumption:

> While many sociologists and system theorists have attempted to generate totalizing models that describe and incorporate consumers (the extra-literary) into their systems and explain their behaviour, such generalizing claims tend to conceal and cover-up multiple differentiating activities. In fact, De Certeau would go so far as to argue that the practices of everyday life do not conform to any laws of any coherent system. (Gentzler, 1996: 123)

The individual engages in acts of 'evasive conformity' (ibid.), surreptitiously employing his or her creativity to disrupt the activities of a repressive system. The attractive notion of evasive conformity can be applied to many Scottish translations. The epitome would be Sir Thomas Urquhart, whose version of Rabelais was a strikingly inappropriate peace offering to a puritanical regime whose goal was to establish God's commonwealth in England. Scots translations have bubbled up from colourful, largely male, subcultures: from the elite community of James VI's court poets to the gentlemen's clubs of the eighteenth century and the fractious synthesisers of the modern Scots Renaissance. Throughout, the Scottish nation, like the Scots language, has been a site of contention more than consensus. Translators into Scots are active in this contest for the nation's soul, producing texts that subvert the status quo by endlessly redefining the speech community (or, rather, communities) by which the nation is represented.

The instability of the Scots language becomes a virtue in this task of endless redefinition. The fact that Scots exists only in variety complicates the issue of the translator's 'visibility' – the keyword of Translation Studies in the 1990s (Bassnett, 1996: 22). This subject has been touched upon, in Chapter 1 and earlier in this chapter, but it is worth returning to in conclusion. To recapitulate, Venuti (1995a, 1995b) argues that translation habitually effaces the linguistic and cultural foreignness of texts, assimilating the Other:

> Translation is thus an inevitable domestication, wherein the foreign text is inscribed with linguistic and cultural values that are intelligible to specific domestic constituencies. This process of inscription operates at every stage in the production, circulation, and reception of the translation. It is initiated by the very choice of a foreign text to translate, always an exclusion of other foreign texts and literatures which answers to particular domestic interests. It continues most forcefully in the development of a translation strategy that rewrites the foreign text in domestic dialects and discourses, always a choice of certain domestic values to the exclusion of others. (Venuti, 1995b: 9–10)

As we have seen, issues of domestication and foreignisation are complicated when the 'domestic dialect' is not standard English. The choice of Scots – and particularly the choice of literary Scots, or Lallans – allows the Scottish writer a medium of translation that is simultaneously foreignising and domesticating. Dense Scots is not unlike a foreign language to many Scottish people, although it is a language that is nominally 'theirs'. And even given the enormous energy directed towards translation into Scots over the past century, texts in Scots are still vastly outnumbered by texts in English. The act of reading a text in Scots, then, is an experience curiously familiar and strange for a Scot. Translating into Scots, therefore, seems to fulfil Venuti's call for translation strategies which 'risk unintelligibility, by decentering domestic ideologies too far, and cultural marginality, by destabilising the workings of domestic institutions' (Venuti, 1995b: 23). Scots translations frequently skirt with unintelligibility, even to Scots, yet they simultaneously represent the domestic for those same Scots. This process mirrors Orientalism, in which the exotic Other is articulated within a frame of reference determined by western values (cf. Said, 1978). In the words of Carbonell (1996: 83):

> Said's main argument is that the Orient is an imaginary space construed by the ideology, the cultural set of values and norms of the West: an 'imaginary geography' where the Orient is 'orientalized', pictured as it ought to be, rather than as it actually is. In 'orientalist' writing, both the familiar and the alien co-exist.

The lack of a widely accepted standard variety allows Scots translations to represent both the familiar and the strange: instead of looking at the alien and finding it familiar, we look at ourselves and discover our exoticism. An Aberdonian sailor can be wandering Aeneas, a Lothian bourgeois can be Horace at the gates of Rome, a Borders journalist can be Alexander Blok, downing vodka in a Moscow tavern, and dreaming of his own dark lady. In these literal 'translations', the prevailing ideologies are indeed inverted, and Aberdeen, Edinburgh and Langholm – rather than Rome, Moscow, or even London – are located not at the margins, but at the centre.

In translations into Scots we reinvent our own 'imaginary geography' in a medium which allows no invisibility to the translator. The absence of a fixed standard variety necessitates the continual reinvention of the language of the Scottish nation; the translator must choose from the unfocused norms of an urban demotic, a rural Doric, or a literary synthesis, and each choice is pregnant with historical, cultural and political connotations. Each translation is a redefinition of what it means to be Scottish, and as Scotland's political structure undergoes another of its periodic transformations, ready for the new millennium, we can confidently expect this process to continue with energy unabated.

Bibliography

Aitken, A.J. (1977) How to pronounce older Scots. In Aitken, McDiarmid and Thomson (eds), pp. 1–21.

Aitken, A.J. (1996) *The Pronunciation of Older Scots*. Dunfermline: The Robert Henryson Society/Scotsoun Publications.

Aitken, A.J., McDiarmid, M.P. and Thomson, D. (eds) (1977) *Bards and Makars*. Glasgow: University of Glasgow Press.

Alexander, M. and McGonigal, J. (eds) (1995)*Sons of Ezra: British Poets and Ezra Pound*. Amsterdam: Rodopi.

Alison, J. (ed.) (1976) *Poetry of Northeast Scotland*. London and Edinburgh: Heinemann.

Álvarez, R. and Carmen-África Vidal, M. (eds) (1996) *Translation, Power, Subversion*. Clevedon: Multilingual Matters.

Annand, J.K. (1978) *Songs from Carmina Burana*. Loanhead: Macdonald.

Arber, E. (ed.) (1869) *English Reprints Vol. VIII*. London.

Barbour, J. (1960) *The Bruce: A Selection*, A.M. Kinghorn (ed.). Edinburgh: Saltire Society.

Bassnett, S. (1996) The meek or the mighty: Reappraising the role of the translator. In Álvarez and Carmen-África Vidal (eds), pp. 10–24.

Bassnett, S. (ed.) (1997) *Translating Literature*. Cambridge: Brewer/The English Association.

Bawcutt, P. (1976) *Gavin Douglas*. Edinburgh: Edinburgh University Press.

Bjørn, C., Grant, A. and Stringer, K.J. (eds) (1994) *Nations, Nationalism and Patriotism in the European Past*. Copenhagen: Academic Press.

Blackhall, Sheena (1996) *Wittgenstein's Web*. Dyce, Aberdeen: GKB.

Bowman, M. and Findlay, B. (1994) Québécois into Scots: Translating Michel Tremblay. *Scottish Language* 13, 61–81.

Broun, D. (1994) The origin of Scotish identity. In Bjørn, Grant and Skinner (eds), pp. 35–55.

Brown, I.G. (1987) Modern Rome and ancient Caledonia: The Union and the politics of Scottish culture. In Hook (ed.) pp. 33–50.

Buchanan, R. (1866) *Ballad Stories of the Affections*. London: Routledge.

Burnley, J.D. (1989) Late medieval English translation: Types and reflections. In Ellis (ed.), pp. 37–54.

Buthlay, K. (ed.) (1987) *A Drunk Man Looks at the Thistle*, by Hugh MacDiarmid. Edinburgh: Scottish Academic Press.

Carbonell, O. (1996) The exotic space of cultural translation. In Álvarez and

Carmen-África Vidal (eds), pp. 79–98.
Carpenter, S. (1988) Early Scottish drama. In Jack (ed.), pp. 199–212.
Chambers, R.W. and Batho, E.C. (eds) (1938) *The Chronicles of Scotland, Compiled by Hector Boece, Translated into Scots by John Bellenden.* Edinburgh: Scottish Text Society/William Blackwood.
Cohen, J.M. (ed.) (1955) *Rabelais: Gargantua and Pantagruel.* Harmondsworth: Penguin.
Coldwell, D. (ed.) (1957–64) *Virgil's Aeneid, Translated into Scottish Verse by Gavin Douglas Vols 1–4.* Edinburgh: Scottish Text Society/William Blackwood.
Colley, L. (1992) *Britons: Forging the Nation 1707–1837.* New Haven and London: Yale University Press.
Corbett, J. (1996) COMET and *The House Among the Stars.* In *The Glasgow Review* No. 4 pp. 89–103.
Corbett, J. (1997a) *Language and Scottish Literature.* Edinburgh: Edinburgh University Press.
Corbett, J. (1997b) Writtin in the langage of Scottis natioun: Literary translation into Scots. In Bassnett (ed.), pp. 95–118.
Craig, C. (ed.) (1987) *The History of Scottish Literature, Vol IV: Twentieth Century.* Aberdeen: Aberdeen University Press.
Craigie, W.A. (ed.) (1901) *Livy's History of Rome: The First Five Books, Translated into Scots by John Bellenden.* Edinburgh: Scottish Text Society/William Blackwood.
Craik, R.J. (1993) *Sir Thomas Urquhart of Cromarty (1611–1660), Adventurer, Polymath, and Translator of Rabelais.* Lampeter: Mellen Research University Press.
Crawford, R. (1992) *Devolving English Literature.* Oxford: Oxford University Press.
Crawford, R. (1995) Pound and a young poet. In Alexander and McGonigal, (eds), pp. 169–179.
Crawford, R. and Herbert, W.N. (1990) *Sharawaggi.* Edinburgh.
Croft Dickinson, W., Donaldson, G. and Milne, I.A. (eds) (1952, 1953, 1954) *A Sourcebook of Scottish History Vols 1–3.* London: Thomas Nelson.
Cronin, M. (1996) *Translating Ireland.* Cork: Cork University Press.
Donnachie, I. and Whately, C. (eds) (1992) *The Manufacture of Scottish History.* Edinburgh: Polygon.
Duncan, A.A.M. (1971) The making of Scotland. In Menzies, G. (ed.) *Who Are the Scots.* London: British Broadcasting Corporation.
Dunlop, B. (n.d.) *Klytemnestra's Bairns.* Edinburgh: Diehard Press.
Ellis, R. (ed.) (1989) *The Medieval Translator.* Cambridge: D.S. Brewer.
Evan-Zohar, I. (1978) *Papers in Historical Poetics.* Tel Aviv: Institute for Poetics and Semiotics.
Evan-Zohar, I. (1990) Polysystem studies. *Poetics Today,* 11: 1.
Farrow, K.D. (1994) The historiographical evolution of the Macbeth narrative. *Scottish Literary Journal* 21, 5–23.
Farrow, K.D. (n.d.) *The Scots Iliad, Buik Ane-Buik Twal.* Unpublished MS.
Findlay, B. (1996a) Talking in tongues: Scottish translations 1970–1995. In Stevenson and Wallace (eds), pp. 186–97.
Findlay, B. (1996b) Translating into dialect. In David Johnston (ed.) *Stages in Translation* (pp. 199–217). Bath: Absolute Press.
Findlay, B. (ed.) (forthcoming) *Frae Fremmit Leids: The Use of Scots in Translation.* Aberdeen: Scottish Cultural Press.
Findlay, B. and Bowman, M., trans (1992) *The House Among the Stars,* by Michel Tremblay. Unpublished MS available on the World Wide Web at the

URL http://www.arts.gla.ac.uk/www/english/comet/comet.html.
Findlay, B. and Bowman, M. (1994) Québécois into Scots: Translating Michel Tremblay. In *Scottish Language* 13, 61–81.
Fitzgerald, R., trans. (1984) *The Aeneid, Virgil.* New York: Vintage Books.
France, P. and Glen, D. (eds) (1989) *European Poetry in Scotland: An Anthology of Translations.* Edinburgh: Edinburgh University Press.
Freeman, F.W. (1987) Robert Fergusson: Pastoral and politics at mid century. In Hook (ed.), pp. 141–56.
Gaskill, H. (ed.) (1996) *The Poems of Ossian,* by James Macpherson. Edinburgh: Edinburgh University Press.
Gentzler, E. (1996) Translation, counter-culture, and *The Fifties* in the USA. In Álvarez and Carmen-África Vidal (eds), pp. 116–37.
Gillespie, S. (1993) Horace's *Ode* 3.29: Dryden's 'Masterpiece in English'. In Martindale, C. and Hopkins, D. (eds) *Horace Made New* (pp. 148–58). Cambridge: Cambridge University Press.
Glauser, B. (1974) *The Scottish-English Linguistic Border.* Berne: Francke.
Goldstein, R.J. (1993) *The Matter of Scotland: Historical Narrative in Medieval Scotland.* Lincoln; London: University of Nebraska Press.
Grant, A. (1994) Aspects of National Consciousness in Medieval Scotland. In Bjørn, Grant and Stringer (eds), pp. 68–95.
Gray, Alasdair (1984) Logopandocy. In *Unlikely Stories, Mostly.* Harmondsworth: Penguin.
Gray, Alexander (1928) *Songs from Heine.* Edinburgh: Porpoise Press.
Gray, Alexander (1932) *Arrows: A Book of German Ballads and Folk Songs Attempted in Scots.* Edinburgh: Grant and Murray.
Gray, Alexander (1949) *Sir Halewyn: Examples in European Balladry and Folk Song.* Edinburgh: Oliver and Boyd.
Gray, Alexander (1954) *Four-and-Forty: A Selection of Danish Ballads Presented in Scots.* Edinburgh: Edinburgh University Press.
Gray, Alexander (1958) *Historical Ballads of Denmark.* Edinburgh: Edinburgh University Press.
Gray, Alexander (1966) *A Timorous Civility: A Scots Miscellany.* Glasgow: Collins.
Harvie, C. (1988) Industry, religion and the state of Scotland. In Gifford, D. (ed.) *The History of Scottish Literature, Vol 3* (pp. 23–42). Aberdeen: Aberdeen University Press.
Hatim, B. and Mason, I. (1990) *Discourse and the Translator.* London and New York: Longman.
Herbert, W.N. (1995) Pound and MacDiarmid. In Alexander and McGonigal, (eds), pp. 137–51.
Hermans, T. (ed.) (1985) *The Manipulation of Literature.* London and Sydney: Croom Helm.
Hobsbawm, E.J. (1990) *Nations and Nationalism since 1780.* Cambridge: Cambridge University Press.
Hood, S. (ed.) (1988) *Mistero Buffo* by Dario Fo, trans. Ed Emery; reprinted in *Dario Fo, Plays: One* (1992). London: Methuen.
Hook, A. (ed.) (1987) *The History of Scottish Literature, Volume 2: 1660–1800.* Aberdeen: Aberdeen University Press.
Hook, A. (1987) Scotland and romanticism: The international scene. In Hook (ed.), pp. 307–22.
Hubbard, T. (1987) Reintegrated Scots: The Post-MacDiarmid Makars. In Craig, C. (ed.), pp. 179–94.

Hubbard, T. (ed.) (1991) *The New Makars: The Mercat Anthology of Contemporary Poetry in Scots*. Edinburgh: Mercat Press.
Hutchinson, D. (1977) *The Modern Scottish Theatre*. Glasgow: Molendinar Press.
Hyde, G.M. (1992) Mayakovsky in English translation. In *Translation and Literature, No. 1*, pp. 84-93.
Jack, R.D.S. (1968) William Drummond of Hawthornden: The major Scottish sources. *Studies in Scottish Literature* 6, 36–46.
Jack, R.D.S. (1972)*The Italian Influence on Scottish Literature*. Edinburgh: Edinburgh University Press.
Jack, R.D.S. (ed.) (1978) *A Choice of Scottish Verse, 1560–1660*. London: Hodder & Stoughton.
Jack, R.D.S. (1986) *Scottish Literature's Debt to Italy*. Edinburgh: Edinburgh University Press/Italian Institute, Edinburgh.
Jack, R.D.S. (ed.) (1988) *The History of Scottish Literature, Volume 1: Origins to 1660*. Aberdeen: Aberdeen University Press.
Jack, R.D.S. (1989) The French connection: Scottish and French literature in the Renaissance. *Scotia*, Vol. XIII, pp. 1–16.
Jack, R.D.S. (1997) Critical introduction: Where stands Scottish literature now. In Jack, R.D.S. and Rozendaal, P.A.T. (eds) *The Mercat Anthology of Early Scottish Literature 1375–1707* (pp. vii–xxxix). Edinburgh: Mercat Press.
Jack, R.D.S. and Lyall, R.J. (eds) (1983) *The Jewel by Sir Thomas Urquhart*. Edinburgh: Scottish Academic Press.
Jamieson, R.A. and Macdonald, M. (1995) An Ossianic miscellany. In the *Edinburgh Review* 93, 91–124.
Jones, C. (1995) *A Language Suppressed: The Pronunciation of the Scots Language in the 18th Century*. Edinburgh: John Donald.
Kastner, L.E. (ed.) (1913) *The Poetical Works of William Drummond of Hawthornden*. Edinburgh: William Blackwood and Sons.
Kerrigan, C. (1987) MacDiarmid's early poetry. In Craig, C. (ed.) pp. 75–86.
Kinghorn, A.M. (ed) (1960) *The Bruce: A Selection*. Edinburgh: Saltire Society.
Kinghorn, A.M. and Law, A. (eds) (1970) *The Words of Allan Ramsay, Vol. IV*. Edinburgh and London: Blackwood/Scottish Text Society.
Kinghorn, A.M. and Law, A. (eds) (1974) *Poems by Allan Ramsay and Robert Fergusson*. Edinburgh and London: Scottish Academic Press.
Kinghorn, A.M. and Law, A. (1987) Allan Ramsay and literary life in the first half of the eighteenth century. In Hook (ed.), pp. 65–78.
Kratzmann, G. (1980) *Anglo-Scottish Literary Relations 1430–1550*. Cambridge: Cambridge University Press.
Kratzmann, G. (1988) Sixteenth century secular poetry. In Jack (ed.), pp. 105–124.
Law, T.G. (ed.) (1901–5) *The New Testament in Scots* by Murdoch Nisbet. Scottish Text Society, 1st Ser. 46, 49 & 52. Edinburgh: William Blackwood and Sons.
Lefevere, A. (1992) *Translation, Rewriting, and the Manipulation of Literary Fame*. London: Routledge.
Lefevere, A. (ed.) (1992) *Translation/History/Culture: A Sourcebook*. London: Routledge.
Lenman, B. (1981) *Integration, Englightenment and Industrialization: Scotland 1746–1832*. London: Edward Arnold.
Leonard, Tom (1984) *Intimate Voices 1965–1983*. Newcastle: Galloping Dog.
Leonard, Tom (ed.) (1990) *Radical Renfrew: Poetry from the French Revolution to the First World War*. Edinburgh: Polygon.

Lochhead, L. (1985) *Tartuffe: A Translation into Scots from the Original by Molière.* Glasgow and Edinburgh: Third Eye Centre/Polygon.

Lorimer, R.L.C. (1992) *Macbeth: Shakespeare's Macbeth Translated into Scots.* Edinburgh: Canongate.

Lorimer, W.L. (1983) *The New Testament in Scots.* Edinburgh: Southside.

Lupack, A. (ed.) (1994) *Lancelot of the Laik and Sir Tristrem.* Kalamazoo: Medieval Institute Publications/Western Michigan University.

Lyall, R.J. (1976) Politics and poetry in fifteenth and sixteenth century Scotland. *Scottish Literary Journal* 3(2), 5-29.

Lyall, R.J. (1988) Vernacular prose before the Reformation. In Jack (ed.) pp. 125–40.

Lyall, R.J. (1989) Books and book owners in fifteenth century Scotland. In Griffiths J. and Pearsall, D. (eds) *Book Production and Publishing in Britain* (pp. 239–256). Cambridge: Cambridge University Press.

Lyall, R.J. (1993) Montgomerie and Marot. A sixteenth century translator at work. *Etudes Ecossaises* 2, 79–94.

Lyall, R.J. and Riddy, F. (eds) (1981) *Proceedings of the Third International Conference on Scottish Language and Literature (Medieval and Renaissance).* Universities of Stirling and Glasgow.

Lynch, M. (1994) National identity in Ireland and Scotland, 1500–1640. In Bjørn, Grant and Stringer (eds), pp. 109–36.

Macafee, C. (1983) *Focus On: Glasgow.* Amsterdam: John Benjamins.

Macafee, C. (1986) Dialect vocabulary as a source of stylistic effects in Scottish literature. *Language and Style* 19(4), 324–37.

Macafee, C. (1994) *Traditional Dialect in the Modern World: A Glasgow Case-Study.* Frankfurt am Main: Peter Lang.

Macaulay, R.K.S. (1991) *Locating Dialect in Discourse.* Oxford: Oxford University Press.

Macaulay, R.K.S. (1997) *Standards and Variation in Urban Speech.* Amsterdam: John Benjamins.

MacCallum, N. and Purves, D. (eds) (1995) *Mak it New: An Anthology of Twenty-one Years of Writing in 'Lallans'.* Edinburgh: Mercat Press.

MacDonald, R.H. (1971) *The Library of Drummond of Hawthornden.* Edinburgh: Edinburgh University Press.

MacDonald, R.H. (ed.) (1976) *William Drummond of Hawthornden: Poems and Prose.* Edinburgh and London: Scottish Academic Press.

MacGillivray, A. (1997) Interview with Donny O'Rourke. In *Laverorck* No. 3, Association for Scottish Literary Studies, pp. 5–13.

Mackie, A.D. (1995) Frae Ither Leids. In MacCallum and Purves (eds), pp. 99–101.

Maclaine, A. (ed.) (1996) *The Christis Kirk Tradition.* Glasgow: Association for Scottish Literary Studies.

Maclean, Sorley (1985) *Spring Tide and Neap Tide: Selected Poems 1932–72.* Edinburgh: Canongate.

Mapstone, S. (1998) Shakespeare and Scottish kingship: A case history. In Mapstone and Wood (eds), pp. 158–94.

Mapstone, S. and Wood, J. (eds) (1998) *The Rose and the Thistle: Essays on the Culture of Late Medieval and Renaissance Scotland.* East Linton: Tuckwell Press.

Martin, B. and Oliver, J.W. (eds) (1945) *The Works of Allan Ramsay, Vol. I.* Edinburgh and London: Scottish Text Society/Blackwood.

McCarey, P. (1990) Edwin Morgan the translator. In Crawford, R. and Whyte, H. (eds) *About Edwin Morgan* (pp. 90–104). Edinburgh: Edinburgh University Press.
McClure, J.D. (1981) Scottis, Inglis, Suddroun: Language labels and language attitudes. In Lyall and Riddy (eds), pp. 52–69.
McClure, J.D. (1988) Douglas Young and Sorley Maclean. In Derick S. Thomson (ed.) *Gaelic and Scots in Harmony* (pp. 136–48). Glasgow: Glasgow University, Dept of Celtic.
McClure, J.D. (1990) 'O Phoenix Ecossois': James VI as Poet. In Gardner-Medwin, A. and Williams, J.H. (eds) *A Day Estivall*. Aberdeen: Aberdeen University Press.
McClure, J.D. (1991) Is translation naturalisation? Some test cases from Scots. In Simon and Sinner (eds), pp. 193–213.
McClure, J.D. (1995) *Scots and its Literature*. Amsterdam: John Benjamins.
McCulloch, M.P. (1998) 'I'd sing my sang in spite o aa . . .': The significance of 'song' in the early Scots-language poetry of Alexander Scott. Unpublished paper, delivered to the ASLS Conference, Perth, 16 May.
McDiarmid, M.P. (1988) The metrical chronicles and non-alliterative romances. In Jack (ed.), pp. 27–38.
McDonald, E. (1991) *The Gangan Fuit*. Edinburgh: Chapman.
McIntyre, A. (ed.) (1976) *Hugh MacDiarmid: Contemporary Scottish Studies*. Edinburgh: Scottish Educational Journal.
McKean, C. (1985) *Stirling and the Trossachs*. Edinburgh: RIAS/Scottish Academic Press.
Meikle, H.W. (ed.) (1936) *The Works of William Fowler, Vol II*. Scottish Text Society, 3rd Ser. Edinburgh: William Blackwood and Sons.
Meurmin-Solin, A. (1993) *Variation and Change in Early Scottish Prose*. Helsinki: Suomalainen Tiedeakatemia.
Milton, C. (1987) Modern poetry in Scots before MacDiarmid. In Craig, (ed.) pp. 11–36.
Mitchell, A.F. (ed.) (1888) *The Richt Vay to the Kingdome of Heuine*, by John Gau. Scottish Text Society, 1st Ser. 12. Edinburgh: William Blackwood and Sons.
Moore, D. (1997) James MacPherson and Adam Ferguson: An Enlightenment encounter. *Scottish Literary Journal* 24(2), 5–23.
Morgan, E. (1977) Gavin Douglas and William Drummond as translators. In Aitken, McDiarmid and Thomson (eds), pp. 194–200.
Morgan, Edwin (1992) *Edmond Rostand's Cyrano de Bergerac*. Manchester: Carcanet.
Morgan, Edwin (1996) *Collected Translations*. Manchester: Carcanet.
Murison, D. (1977) *The Guid Scots Tongue*. Edinburgh: Blackwood.
Murison, D. and Young, C. (eds) (n.d.) *A Clear Voice: Douglas Young, Poet and Polymath*. Edinburgh: Macdonald.
Neill, W. (1992) *Tales frae the Odyssey o Homer, Owreset inil Scots*. Edinburgh: Saltire Society.
O'Rourke, D. and Price, R. (1996) *Eftirs, Afters*. Glasgow: Au Quai.
Ogilvie, R.M. (1980) *Roman Literature and Society*. Harmondsworth: Penguin.
Omberg, M. (1976) *Scandinavian Themes in English Poetry, 1760–1800*. Uppsala: University of Uppsala.
Ouston, H. (1987) Cultural life from the Restoration to the Union. In Hook, (ed.), pp. 11–31.

Paterson, L. (1996) Language and identity on the stage. In Stevenson and Wallace (eds), pp. 75–83.
Peacock, N.A. (1993) *Molière in Scotland: 1945–1990.* Glasgow: University of Glasgow French and German Publications.
Philp, G. and MacDonald, I. (eds) (1994) *Twa Leids/Dà Chànan.* Scotsoun/ Albfhuaim.
Pittock, M. (1995) Forging North Britain in the age of Macpherson. In the *Edinburgh Review* 93, 125–39.
Praz, M. (1928) *Machiavelli and the Elizabethans.* London.
Purves, D. (1992) *The Tragedie o Macbeth.* Edinburgh: Rob Roy Press.
Purves, D. (1997) MacDiarmid's use of Scots: Synthetic or natural? In *Scottish Language* 16, 82–7.
Ritchie, R.L.G. (ed.) (1925) *The Buik of Alexander.* Edinburgh: Scottish Text Society/William Blackwood.
Robb, D. (ed.) (1994) *The Collected Poems of Alexander Scott.* Edinburgh: Mercat Press.
Robertson, J.L. (1925) *Horace in Homespun, and other Scots Poems.* Edinburgh and London: William Blackwood & Sons.
Royan, N. (1998) The relationship between the *Scotorum Historia* of Hector Boece and John Bellenden's *Chronicles of Scotland.* In Mapstone and Wood, (eds), pp. 136–57.
Said, E. (1978) *Orientalism.* London and New York: Routledge & Kegan Paul.
Schäffner, C. and Kelly-Holmes, H. (1995) *Cultural Functions of Translation.* Clevedon: Multilingual Matters.
Scott, P. (1983) The Lorimer New Testament. Reprinted in Scott, P. (1991), pp. 141–143.
Scott, P.H. (1991) *Towards Independence: Essays on Scotland.* Edinburgh: Polygon.
Scott, Tom (1993) *The Collected Shorter Poems of Tom Scott.* Edinburgh: Agenda/ Chapman.
Simon, J.J. and Sinner, A. (eds) (1991) *English Studies 3: Proceedings of the Third Conference on the Literature of Region and Nation, Part 1.* Luxembourg: Publications du Centre Universitaire de Luxembourg.
Smith, J. (1934) *The French Background of Middle Scots Literature.* Edinburgh: Oliver & Boyd.
Smith, J.J. (1996) *An Historical Study of English.* London: Routledge.
Smout, T.C. (1969) *A History of the Scottish People 1560–1830.* London: Collins.
Soutar, W. (1988) *Poems of William Soutar: A New Selection,* ed. W.R. Aitken. Edinburgh: Scottish Academic Press.
Spiller, M. (1988) Poetry after the Union, 1603–1660. In Jack (ed.), pp. 140–162.
Steiner, G. (1992) *After Babel,* 2nd edn. Oxford: Oxford University Press.
Stevenson, J.H. (ed.) (1901) *Gilbert of the Haye's Prose Manuscript, Vol I: The Buke of the Law of Armys or Buke of Bataillis.* Edinburgh: Scottish Text Society/ William Blackwood.
Stevenson, R. (1996) Snakes and Ladders, Snakes and Owls: Charting Scottish Theatre. In Stevenson and Wallace (eds), pp. 1–22.
Stevenson, R. and Wallace, G. (eds) (1996) *Scottish Theatre Since the Seventies.* Edinburgh: Edinburgh University Press.
Stuart, Jamie (1997) *A Glasgow Bible.* Edinburgh: St Andrew Press.
Syndergaard, L. (1995) *English Translations of the Scandinavian Ballads: An Analytical Guide and Bibliography.* Kalamazoo: Medieval Institute Publications.

Trevelyan, R. (ed.) (1965) *Italian Short Stories I/Racconti Italiani I.* Harmondsworth: Penguin.

Tulloch, G. (1989) *A History of the Scots Bible.* Aberdeen: Aberdeen University Press.

Turquet, G.M., trans. (1939) *The Defence and Illustration of the French Language by Joachim Du Bellay.* London: J.M. Dent.

Tytler, A. (1790) *Essay on the Principles of Translation* (2nd edn). Edinburgh: William Creech.

Venuti, L. (1995a) *The Translator's Invisibility: A History of Translation.* London: Routledge.

Venuti, L. (1995b) Translation and the formation of cultural identities. In Schäffner and Kelly-Holmes, pp. 9–25.

Walker, W. (1887) *The Bards of Bon-Accord 1375–1860.* Aberdeen: Edmond & Spark.

Weber, H. and Jamieson, R. (1814) *Illustrations of Northern Antiquities.* Edinburgh: Ballantyne.

West, D. (trans) (1997) *Horace: The Complete Odes and Epodes.* Oxford: Oxford University Press.

Wood, Barry (1987) Scots, poets and the city. In Craig, C. (ed.), pp. 337–48.

Wormald, J. (1981) *Court, Kirk and Community: Scotland 1470–1625.* London: Edward Arnold.

Wormald, J. (ed.) (1991) *Scotland Revisited.* London: Collins & Brown.

Wright, D.F. (1988) *The Bible in Scottish Life and Literature.* Edinburgh: St Andrew Press.

Young, D. (1946) *'Plastic Scots' and the Scottish Literary Tradition.* Glasgow: William McLellan.

Young, D. (1958) *The Puddocks, by Aristophanes* (2nd edn). Tayport: Makarsbield.

Index